IN THE COMPANY OF GREATNESS
(Personal Encounters with Passed Sports Icons)

By

Andy Purvis
Sports Enthusiast

PRESS

Mike,

Great Stories of
Great men for the
Greatest man I know.
Thank you for everything
you have done for me and my
family. We love you.

Love
Mike.

Books also written by Andy Purvis

Upon Further Review
By Andy Purvis
Copyright © 2009 Andy Purvis
On Cover William Gordon Purvis, c. 1939

Love, Laughter & Cornbread
By Andy Purvis
Copyright © 2001 Andy Purvis
On Cover Edith Moore House, c. 1932

Buy Me Some Peanuts...
By Andy Purvis
Baseball enthusiast/philosopher
Copyright © 1999 Andy Purvis

Until Next Wednesday
We'll See You at the Park
By Andy Purvis
Baseball enthusiast/philosopher
Copyright © 1998 Andy Purvis

Dedication

This book is dedicated to my two stepsons, Bill and Harry James. They have been and remain two shining lights on my journey through life. They have both grown into fine young men, wonderful husbands and fathers. I'm so proud to have played a small part in their success. I do hope they realize how much they are loved. They are both included in my Hall of Fame.

Preface

The book you are about to read contains stories about some of the most famous athletes, coaches, writers, and owners from my childhood, who have now become shadows of my past. I hope that these thoughts, words, and stories will bring them back to life in your imagination, as they have in mine. Our imagination is the most powerful tool we own, and to be able to read the words and then close your eyes and see them in your mind creates wonderful visions and memories. If you didn't get a chance to see these people, or hear about them, then you missed out on some of the greatest athletes and game-time events. These are their stories. They are all here, from Mantle to McKay, Payton to Patterson, "Wilt" to Willie Shoemaker, Unitas to Upshaw, "Teddy Ballgame," "Slingin' Sammy," and the "Yankee Clipper." Most of them I met in person and some I did not; nevertheless they are all very much a part of my sports memories. I truly love telling their stories, and in many ways I know these people better than I know some of my own family. The ancient maxim, "Never get to know your heroes," does not apply to these folks. The time line spans back fifteen years, from 1995 though 2009. Some of them were thought of as "more famous"

than others, but all were considered one of the best in their own time. They each had a passion for their game and a purpose that separated them from the average player. You could say they all rose above their circumstances. So sit back and relax, pull up a chair, and let me tell you a story about my brush with greatness, tales of how these folks lived and died while becoming the best of the best with dedication, sacrifice, talent, and desire. It's quite a list.

Andy Purvis

Table of Contents

Short Arm

Everyone that follows baseball has heard of a no-hitter, a triple play, or a walk-off home run. Shut-outs, perfect games, and inside-the-park-home runs are also considered feats of skill, but a "perfect season?" How rare is a 13-0 record for a pitcher during an entire regular season? I can't find another. The year was 1937 and this twenty-one-year-old, right-handed, fire-balling sensation would daze and confuse even the best hitters with his no-wind-up pitching motion. "I just jerked it at them," he would later say, "and it fooled a lot of hitters." Part of the aura of this guy was his size. He was small, stood 5 feet 9 inches tall, and only cocked his arm back as far as his ear before delivering his best pitch, the fastball. Put that 95-mile-per-hour fastball with a decent change-of-speed pitch and a curve with a little wrinkle in it, and we are talking about the pitcher who holds the strike-out record for the Negro National League, the Puerto Rican League, and the East-West All-Star game.

He is also the only one so far, the only member of the Baseball Hall of Fame to wear the cap of a team from another country on his induction plaque. The symbol on his cap is a large white "A," which stood for the "Aguadilla Sharks," a Puerto Rican team for which he had once played.

He played six winters of baseball in Puerto Rico while pitching for four different teams in the Negro Leagues. Two more winters of pitching in Cuba, two years with the Mexico City Reds, and a year in Venezuela would ensure that all of Latin America would recognize the name, Leon Day.

Born on October 30, 1916, in Alexandria, Virginia, Leon would soon move with his family to Baltimore, Maryland. It was here that he would spend every waking minute playing baseball. In fact, Leon would eventually drop out of high school during his tenth-grade year, at age 16, to sign and play for player-manager Herbert "Rap" Dixon of the Baltimore Black Sox, a local Negro League team. His pay would be $60 a month. A year later in 1935, this flame-throwing strikeout artist would catch the attention of "Candy" Jim Taylor, the owner of the Brooklyn Eagles, and was offered a contract along with Dixon, to jump to this better team. The Eagles boasted such other stars as Ted "Double Duty" Radcliffe and Ed Stone. Taylor would then sell his team in 1936, to Abe and Effa Manley, owners of the Newark Dodgers. These two teams would be consolidated to become known as the Newark Eagles from New Jersey. Roy Campanella once wrote that the Eagles' infield was the greatest he had ever seen. The infield featured Lenny Pearson at first, Dick Seay at second, Willie Wells at shortstop, and Ray Dandridge at third. "And Leon Day — it's a shame he was born when he was. He played every position on the field except catch, and played them all magnificently," said owner Abe Manley. "Those boys, my heart just aches for them that they were born too soon to play in the Major Leagues." For the next 20 years, Day received very little money, not quite enough to eat, would ride and sing in a bus all night, and play a game the next day. "You had to love it to go through it," he exclaimed.

"Day had smoke!" said "Cool Papa" Bell. Like many of his predecessors, Day was often accused of cutting the baseball while pitching. "I ain't never threw a cut ball in my life," Day said, "I'm just blinding you." Buck O'Neil would nod when hearing this story: "Hard as that man threw; he didn't need to cut the ball." There is no doubt that Day threw hard and fast, but he did not resemble the tall, gangling six-footers of his day. "He looked like he was too small to be a batboy," laughed first baseman George Giles. "Little bitty guy, but oh, could he throw hard!" "Day was a short-arm," said Roy Campanella of the Baltimore Elite Giants. "He used very little motion, but he was very quick, had good control, plus a breaking pitch and a change of speed." Leon Day, not Satchel Paige, holds the record for strikeouts, with 18 against the afore-mentioned Giants. Was Campanella playing that day? "He was three of them," Day chuckled. Quincy Trouppe used to shake his head when remembering his at-bats against Day in Puerto Rico; "I used to go up there with that timber and bring it back two straight times against Day, with all my owners sitting on the bench." "Day also had the best right-handed move to first base," said Dick Seay.

Day would be drafted by the United States Army in the middle of the 1943 season. He would be shipped off to England with the 818th Amphibian Battalion and land on the beaches of Normandy, six days after D-Day. After the war was over, Day's unit would play baseball against General Patton's Third Army team in Nuremberg, Germany. That stadium is where the 1932 Olympics were held and also the site of many speeches by Adolph Hitler. Day thought there were "over 100,000 people that day. It

17

was full! It was a big place, you know." Leon Day would be the starting pitcher and walk off the mound when it was over, a 2-1 winner on a four-hitter. When Day returned to the States in 1946, he was over 30 years old and sensed that he had missed his chance to sign with a big league club. Scouts were leery of his age and his so-called questionable arm. He would sign again with Newark and throw a no-hitter against Philadelphia on opening day. No-hitters were a rare thing in the hard-hitting Negro Leagues. So much for the arm! He would spend the summers of 1947 and 1948 playing ball in Mexico. "I made more money in Mexico than I ever made here in the States," he said. By 1950, Negro League baseball was falling apart with the best young players jumping to the Major Leagues, so Leon headed for Canada. In 1951, Leon Day would finally get his chance in the white leagues. He would pitch for Toronto, in the International League, at the age of 35. Although the results were okay, Day had lost a lot of "smoke" off his fastball. It was time to do something else. Leon would work as a security guard, a mail carrier, and a bartender, before retiring for good.

Day was always quiet and unassuming. When sitting in a room of veterans, he would simply nod and smile while listening to their stories of the old days. Bragging was not his way, and he rarely offered his opinion unless he was asked. Leon Day was the exact opposite of Satchel Paige when it came to storytelling, but he did win all three of their meetings on the pitcher's mound, against the great "Satch." He would average nearly ten strikeouts per game and Day's winning percentage of .708 was higher than any pitcher currently in the Hall of Fame. "I would say he was the most complete ballplayer I've ever seen. I've never seen a better baseball player all-around," exclaimed Monte Irvin.

Day finally retired to the quiet life of pinochle and watching baseball in Baltimore, Maryland. Folks around the game would whisper, "It will be a great day for Cooperstown if Leon Day ever gets elected." I agreed.

I wrote to Leon Day in 1990. He answered my letter and even sent me an autograph. I wanted him as a guest my radio show in Corpus Christi, Texas. We played phone tag, but I was never able to secure him for an interview. Leon Day could have pitched for anybody.

Unfortunately, just six days after learning that he had indeed been elected to the Major League Baseball Hall of Fame, Leon Day died of a sudden heart attack at the age of 78. It was March 13, 1995. It was a sad "Day" for all of baseball, but at least he knew...

Faster Than Electricity

This year marks the twenty-fifth anniversary of Mickey Mantle's Hall-of-Fame induction. After viewing ESPN's segment on Sports Century's Fifty Greatest Athletes, I had forgotten how happy Mantle had made me as a kid and how sad, as an adult. He was chosen as the thirty-seventh of the fifty greatest, but there's no doubt in my mind that without the many knee injuries and his inability to say "no" to life's excesses, he would have been in the top ten and perhaps the greatest baseball player of all time. You see, sometimes the greatest mystery in life is who we truly are , but I can't imagine Mantle doing anything else; and for kids born during World War II and after, he was baseball. He was cat-quick, faster than electricity, had power from both sides of the plate, looked just like Sir Lancelot, and had a Southern drawl that sounded like he spoke with marbles in his mouth.

I also remember being upset with my parents when baseball magazines ran ads that said, "Has Mickey Mantle hit a home run on your birthday?" I was born the 24th of December, so I had no chance. I could not believe my parents would do that to me.

I only saw Mickey Mantle play in person one time, the summer of 1964 in New York City. It was the year of the Worlds Fair and I was twelve and so excited I could hardly sit still or hold a thought in my head. I sat in the upper deck, first base side. I had never seen so many people in one place or a park as big as Yankee Stadium. The big Stadium in the Bronx just rose right up, straight out of the ground. The grass was Irish green and seemed to go on forever. The clay was brown and smooth, the bases as white as a hospital gown. There were statues, which I thought were tombstones in dead centerfield. I was afraid to ask who was buried there. The game went into extra innings and this twelve year old went to sleep from pure exhaustion. To this day I have no idea who won. I later met Mickey Mantle in person. I was thirty-nine, and Mantle was fifty-nine. It was 1990 and Mickey had already been worn down by life. His legs still hurt and his hair was turning gray, but he still had that gleam in his eye. We spoke, took a picture, shook hands and he signed some autographs for me. Five years later, he would be dead. He was never my role model but he was one of my heroes.

Mickey Charles Mantle was created on October 20, 1931. Actor Billy Crystal once said, "If you had an opportunity to make a baseball player from scratch, using any parts from any player, you would just point to Mantle and say, Hey, just give me that guy." At 5'11" tall and 200 pounds, he looked like a baseball player. Spavinaw, Oklahoma is a small town located on the way from Tulsa, Oklahoma to Joplin, Missouri, in the northeast corner of the Sooner state. It was also the birthplace of Mickey Mantle. His father, Mutt Mantle, would name him after the Detroit Hall-of-Fame catcher Mickey Cochrane. Little did Mutt know that Cochrane's real first name was Gordon? Mickey always spoke about his father with reverence. No boy ever loved a father as much as Mick. At the age of four, the Mantle family moved to nearby Commerce, Oklahoma. It was here that Mantle became an all-around athlete. He played basketball, football and, of course, baseball. Mickey was once asked if he received an allowance when he was a kid. His answer was "Yes, I was allowed to go outside and play." It was a football injury received while playing at Commerce High School that would require a trip to the hospital in Tulsa, Oklahoma and a new drug called penicillin to save his athletic career. Amputation of his leg from a deadly disease known as osteomyelitis had been avoided, but he would suffer the effects of that disease for the rest of his life. No scout would give him a second look.

As a boy he was always creating games for him and his friends to play. Only problem was, he always won. He loved cherry pie, and he slept with his socks on, turned inside out. Mutt would teach young Mickey to be a switch-hitter and some family members say that there are still dents in the wall of a shed where Mickey practiced his hitting. Mickey played shortstop in the Minor Leagues after signing a contract for $1,100 dollars, but was switched to right field when he arrived with the Yankees, in 1951. Seems that centerfield was taken by some guy named DiMaggio. Mantle would become known as "The Commerce Comet," a tremendous switch-hitter with power, and always considered him self a better right-handed hitter even though most of his home runs were hit from the left side. "One of these days he'll hit the ball so hard, it'll burst, and all he'll get for his efforts will be a single," exclaimed skipper Casey Stengel. He would astound fans with a tremendous blast in Washington's old park, Griffith Stadium, on April 17, 1953. This ball would sail over the left field wall and travel an estimated 565 feet. Mickey would crush another ball over the right field wall in Detroit's old Tiger Stadium for an estimated 643 feet on September 10, 1960. These mammoth home runs would give rise to the new term "tape measure home runs". Yankee pal, Phil Rizzuto was quoted as saying, "I never saw anybody hit the ball so hard. When he swings the bat, you just have to stop and watch." Mantle led the league 27 times in various batting titles, four times in home runs, runs scored six times, four times in walks, and won three slugging titles. Mantle also won the Most Valuable Player awards in 1956, 1957, and again in 1962. He is still the only switch-hitter to win the Triple Crown. Ralph Houk once said, "I played with DiMaggio before I played and managed Mickey. Nobody, but nobody could hit a ball as hard and as far from both sides of the plate as Mickey could. He was just awesome." Mantle loved to tell the story of how he sat next to Ted Williams at an All-Star game. Of course Williams wanted to talk hitting and asked Mickey many questions about how he held his hands. Which hand was his dominant hand, did his top hand guide or pull the bat through the strike zone. What did he look for when the ball left the pitchers hand and on and on and so forth. Mantle laughed and said Williams had him so confused and thinking so much about hitting that he went hitless in his next 30 at-bats. Mantle said after that, he refused to speak to Ted Williams about hitting, nevertheless the fans now called him, "The Mick."

But even with all that power, Mantle's real talent lay in his blinding speed. "He ran like deer," said Yogi Berra. He could go back on a fly ball like an outfielder and come in on a line drive like an infielder. "Man he was fast," agreed Johnny Blanchard, as he nodded while listening to Yogi. Mantle, when batting left-handed, was timed at 3.1

seconds, while running from home-plate to first base, (the fastest time of any player in history). Scouts now called him a five-tool player. Mantle could hit for power, hit for average, run like the wind, catch, and throw from anywhere. "We never thought we could lose as long as Mickey was playing," said teammate Tom Tresh. Whitey Ford said it this way, "That's what Mickey was all about – winning. Nobody cared more about winning, and nobody took losing harder." Casey Stengel would smile from ear to ear every time someone mentioned Mantle's name. Mickey once said about Stengel, "Casey became almost like a father to me. He always called me 'my boy.' He would say 'That's my boy there.'" This sixteen-time All-Star would not only grace the cover of every sports magazine, but also publications like *Time* and *Life* magazines. Mantle could run with the speed of Ty Cobb, hit left-handed like Babe Ruth and right-handed like Jimmie Foxx.

In 1951, Mickey was originally given the # 6 to wear on his pinstriped uniform but later switched and made the # 7 famous. You see, all the Yankee greats had worn their numbers in succession. Ruth wore # 3, Gehrig wore # 4, and DiMaggio had worn # 5. It was only fitting that the next great Yankee player would wear # 6. But the pressure was too great for this country kid from Commerce, Oklahoma. Mickey's batting average slumped and eventually he would be sent down to Kansas City, a farm club, to work on his hitting. Mickey phoned his dad and told him he didn't think he could play in the Majors. Mutt decided to pay his downhearted kid a visit. Mickey expected sympathy from his dad but was told to pack his things, he would be going back home to work in the mines. From that day forward, Mickey Mantle would hit and hit and continue to hit, like nobody's business. When he returned to the Yankees, he was given

7 to wear for the next 18 years. Teammate Bobby Brown had reclaimed the # 6 in Mantle's absence. As the Hall-of-Fame announcer, Mel Allen, would say, "He kept a smile on his face, his head on straight and became a leader of one of the greatest teams ever assembled." Sadly, in 1952, Mutt Mantle would die of cancer at the age of 39, just as Mickey's career was starting.

His breakout year would occur in 1956. Not only would he receive the Hickok Belt as top professional athlete of the year but he would also win the Major League Triple Crown. He led the Major Leagues, (both American and National) with 52 home runs, 130 RBI and a .353 batting average. He still remains the last player to accomplish that feat. A sportswriter once asked Mickey if he ever went up to the plate trying to hit a home run. A big grin spread across that tanned face when he said, "Every time."

He would remain the American League Triple Crown winner in 1957 and parlay those two years into a new $75,000 contact in 1961. That January 16 contract would make him the highest paid, active player of his time. Only Babe Ruth, Ted Williams, Hank Greenberg, and teammate Joe DiMaggio had earned a higher salary playing baseball, but all of them had since retired. The year 1961, would also be the same year that Mantle and teammate Roger Maris would both threaten Ruth's single season record of 60 home runs. Mantle would be slowed by injuries and finish with 54 while Maris would hit 61 and establish a new record. Controversy followed the new record since Maris had played in a season that had eight more games scheduled than when Ruth set the record in 1927. Mantle would later say about Roger Maris, "I don't know why he hasn't been elected for the Hall of Fame. To me, he's as good as there ever was. I have four boys of my own, and if I could pick somebody for those boys to grow up to be like, it would be Roger." Maris has since passed away without a call from the Hall.

There are many stories being told about Mickey and his teammates, but one of my favorite Mickey Mantle stories includes one of his best friends and teammate, Billy Martin. In fact, Mickey would name one of his sons after Billy. Anyway, these two were as different as night and day except when it came to drinking and having fun. Mickey, of course, grew up in a country setting in Oklahoma, while Billy grew up a city boy, born in Berkeley, California. Billy had never been deer hunting and Mickey decided to take Billy to a friend's ranch in South Texas. As they arrived, Mickey told Billy to stay in the car while he went to the door to let his friend know that they were there to hunt. Mickey's friend welcomed him and told him sure they could hunt but he wanted Mickey to do him a favor. The rancher had an old mule that was in his last days and he wanted him put down and did not have the heart to do the deed. That if Mickey would kill the old mule, the rancher would have the vet come out and dispose of the mule and Mickey would have his many thanks. Mickey agreed. It was here that the trouble started. On the way back to the car, Mickey decided to play a joke on Billy. Mantle wore a mad look on his face and when he got to the car, he went immediately to the trunk and opened it while muttering under his breath. Mickey took out his shotgun while Billy questioned what was going on. Mickey said, "We've come all this way and that old son-of-a-gun will not let us hunt on his land, so I'm going to shoot his mule." With that, Mickey loaded his shotgun, pointed and killed the mule. No sooner had the smoke cleared, Mickey heard gun fire from behind him and when he turned to see what was happening, Billy had his shotgun out, loaded, and was shooting the rancher's cows and chickens. Anyone who knew the feisty Billy Martin would understand this story. The reason I liked this story is because it was always Billy Martin who loved to play jokes on other people and a little bit of it must have rubbed off on Mickey. Mantle once said about his friend, "Billy was always a great one for jokes. He loved to pull a joke on somebody. He'd get a bigger kick out of that than anybody that I've ever played with and Billy wasn't afraid of anything." I wonder what it cost them to get out of that mess.

Mantle announced his retirement on March 1, 1969 and would be elected and join his teammate and buddy, Whitey Ford, into the Baseball Hall of Fame in 1974. He still holds six World Series records: Most home runs (18), RBI (40), runs (42), walks (43), extra-base hits (26), and total bases (123). He led the New York Yankees to twelve pennants and seven World Championships in eighteen years. It was well known that if Mickey Mantle and the Yankees were playing your team, no lead was safe. Mickey's career stats are 2,401 games played, 2,415 hits, 536 home runs, 1,734 walks, and he struck out 1,710 times. Mickey once said while laughing, "If you get an average of 500 at-bats a year, that's means I went over three years without getting a hit." His career batting average was .298; he stole 153 bases, and collected 1,509 RBI's while scoring 1,677 runs. About his teammate, Whitey Ford, whom Mickey called "Slick", he said, "If I could choose anybody I wanted to play for my team, the first player I'd choose would be Whitey. There's no one I'd rather have on my team than Whitey Ford. When the game was on the line he's the guy I'd want pitching."

A combination of charm, fun, and great play propelled Mantle to one the most popular players of the fifties and sixties. He almost single handedly invented the autograph craze of the seventies and eighties and commanded huge fees for his appearance. His signature, still to this day, far outsells most other players, with the exception of Babe Ruth. Not only would the Yankees retire Mickey's #7 but they also made a space for him in the famed Monument Park, behind the left center-field fence at Yankee Stadium. His plaque would read, "A great teammate. A magnificent Yankee, who left a legacy of unequaled courage."

Mantle's last days were sad as years of alcohol abuse finally caught up with him. Hard living had taken its toll on his playing baseball and his family. His failures in business ventures created more personal difficulty which led to more drinking. In 1994, he would finally enroll himself into the Betty Ford Clinic for alcohol rehab. He was heard quite often saying, "If I'd known I was gonna' live this long, I'd have taken better care of myself." After completing treatment, he would lose one of his sons, Billy, to heart trouble in 1994. Mantle stayed clean and sober and began to make amends with friends, family, and fans too, to whom he had often been hurtful while drunk. Mantle would become a born-again Christian with the help of fellow teammate Bobby Richardson and help another teammate, Bobby Mercer to raise money for the families of the victims of the Oklahoma City bombing of the Federal Building. On June 8, 1995, Mantle would enter Baylor University Medical Center in Dallas for a liver transplant. He initially recovered enough to give a press conference, where he announced that he had established the Mickey Mantle Foundation to raise awareness for organ donations. On National TV, he said to his fans, "This is a role model:

Don't be like me." During the liver operation, the doctors informed Mantle that they had found cancer in his lungs and did not think they could save him. Mickey's last at-bat in life occurred on August 13, 1995. The world of baseball had lost its symbol of intense competitive spirit and the burning desire to reach heights that most of us have never even thought about. I think skipper Casey Stengel summed it up best by saying, "The big thing about this boy is that he likes to play baseball. The knee bothers him and still he comes to me and says, 'Let me play.'" Boy could he play. I miss Mickey Mantle.

Are There Rain Delays in Heaven?

Ahh, yes that was his secret, rain delays. Full of Southern charm, he was from Alabama, bright and educated, with a voice as smooth as maple syrup and a smile as wide as the Mississippi River. He was easy to listen to and although, at times, the volume level of his voice would increase, he never screamed into the microphone like some of his peers do today. His sense of timing was natural and he was a born storyteller if there ever was one. I learned more about baseball from listening to him than I did my father. But, it was during rain delays that he was at his best. Rain delays were when he filled my mind with pictures of Cobb, Speaker, Gehrig, Dickey, Foxx, and the great Babe Ruth. Stories of yesteryear like stealing home, mammoth home runs, and game winning hits were told as if they were happening right then. Picture a ten-year-old boy in his bed on a warm summer's evening, listening to the sounds of baseball coming from the transistor radio, hidden beneath his pillow. It's 1961 and the Yankees are playing. Who they are playing makes no difference. The excitement of the game fills my mind like flittering fireflies caught in an old mason jar. Just the way he pronounced the names of players like Mantle, Maris, Kubek, Bauer and Ford were enough to stir my imagination. Mom and Dad were in the next room and I'm supposed to be asleep. Suddenly, play is stopped by bad weather. I'm being told that it has begun to rain and the players are heading to their dugouts while the grounds crew covers the infield. But, no sadness here; a rain delay was when his stories began. I fell asleep many nights listening to his stories. Baseball and radio just seem to go together like peas and carrots.

His name was Melvin Allen Israel and he was born in Birmingham, Alabama on Valentines Day, February 14, 1913. He would enroll as a freshman at the University of Alabama at the age of fifteen. Even though he was educated as a lawyer at Alabama, his childhood love for baseball continued to dominate his thoughts. He became the public address announcer and broadcaster for Alabama football and, eventually, Auburn University. Allen's first radio broadcast as a play-by-play guy occurred during the first game of the 1933 football season, against Tulane. Melvin graduated in 1937 and decided to take a vacation to New York City. That train ride would turn his entire life around and help determine the next sixty years of his life. While in New York, Melvin Israel auditioned for the CBS Radio Network and was hired for $45 a week. Game shows, big band remotes and other non-sporting events fell to him. Melvin even interrupted the *Kate Smith Show* to announce "breaking news." The German blimp known as the Hindenburg had crashed. CBS also suggested that Melvin Israel change his name to something easier to pronounce. Melvin chose his middle name "Allen" as his last name. He would legally change his name in 1943 to Mel Allen. The new Mel Allen would find himself behind the mike for the 1938 World Series, as the "color guy."

The month of June, 1939 would be special for Mel Allen. Mel would replace Garnett Marks and join Arch McDonald behind the Yankee microphones. Mel's first broadcast game for the Yankees was against the Boston Red Sox and they had a rookie on their team by the name of Ted Williams. Also, July 4, 1939 was Lou Gehrig Appreciation Day at Yankee Stadium, and Mel was the Master of Ceremonies. Lou had been forced to retire the year before, after being diagnosed with a fatal illness. Mel claimed that Lou spoke to him in the dugout after the festivities. Lou said to Mel, "Mel, I never got a chance to listen to your games before, because I was playing every day. But I want you to know they're the only thing that keeps me going." Allen waited until Lou had left and then began to cry. At the end of 1939, McDonald would leave for the Washington Senators job, and Mel Allen would become the lead announcer for the Yankees and Giants. This was made possible by the fact that only their home games were being broadcast for both teams.

In New York, there was very little baseball on the radio in 1941 as neither the Yankees nor the Giants could find a sponsor. Both broadcasts resumed in 1942 with a new sponsor, and Mel continued until he joined the United States Army during World War II. After the war, Allen returned as the Yankee announcer for both home and away games. Because of the greatness of the Yankees and their many World Series appearances, Mel's name would become synonymous with championship baseball. Allen would call a total of 22 World Series on radio and television including 24 All-Star Games. His popularity was incredible. His catch phrases like "Hello there, everybody," before game time, and "Going, going, gone!" for a home run, had become famous. Allen worked with Russ

Hodges before Russ left for the New York Giants job and also mentored Curt Gowdy, who later became the play-by-play announcer for the Red Sox.

By 1964, the New York Yankees were scheduled to play in the World Series for the fifteenth time in the last nineteen years but, Mel would not be there to call the game. He was fired, and no reason was ever given by the Yankee hierarchy. He was replaced by Phil Rizzuto for the 1964 World Series and Joe Garagiola for the 1965 regular season. There is much speculation on why his contract was not renewed, but the truth remains hidden. In 1965, Mel would join Merle Harmon on the radio for the Milwaukee Braves, and he also did some TV work for the Cleveland Indians, in 1968. Allen was asked by the new ownership of the Yankees to return in 1976. He would call play-by-play for the Yankees cable company and remain with them until 1985. In 1990, Allen was asked one last time to call play-by-play for the Yankees for WPIX. That game would make him the only seven-decade announcer to broadcast baseball.

Although baseball became Allen's forte, his popularity spilled over into college and professional football. Allen would deliver the play-by-play for 14 Rose Bowls, 2 Orange Bowls, 2 Sugar Bowls, 1952-53 Washington Redskins, 1960 New York Giants games and the very first season (1966) of the Miami Dolphins. He also broadcast Miami Hurricane football games.

In addition, Allen expanded his popularity by hosting *This Week in Baseball,* from its beginning in 1977 until his death.

I never met Mel Allen in person, but I did see him in person and I do have an autographed picture of him in my collection. I saw him in 1964 at Yankee Stadium before a game. He was presenting an award to one of the

Yankee players. I was twelve years old and with a group of newspaper boys from the Raleigh, North Carolina *News and Observer*. I had won a trip to the World's Fair and it included a Yankees game. I knew who he was but had no idea at the time it would be his last year with the Yankees. I purchased that autographed photo of him several years ago as a remembrance of a simpler time, and I wish I had saved that transistor radio.

Allen was inducted into many different sportscasters Halls-of-Fame including being one of the first two winners of Baseball Hall of Fame's Ford C. Frick Award for broadcasting, in 1978. The other announcer was Red Barber. Allen was also inducted into the Radio Hall of Fame in 1988.

Mel Allen, the Voice of the New York Yankees, left us on June 16, 1996. He was 83 and passed from natural causes. I wonder if there are any rain delays in Heaven. If not, I'm sure he will find a place to sit and tell his stories to others. Millions of fans knew his name, his face and, oh yes, that voice. The Yanks would dedicate a plaque for Mel Allen in Monument Park at Yankee Stadium on July 25, 1998. It read, "A Yankee institution, a national treasure."

"How about that?"

There's a Drive...

He never played, or managed. Never even put on a professional uniform, but boy, was this guy born into the game of baseball. He became and remains one of the many great personalities of the game. He stood for everything that was fun about the game of baseball; excitement, yelling, shamelessly rooting for the home team, and sheer joy for the game would spew from every fiber of his being. He also owned one of the absolute worst singing voices in the world but as only he could, he turned that into one of his most unique trademarks. Anyone who ever heard him sing, "Take Me Out to the Ball Game" would automatically join in, because they could surely sing better than him. He "murdered" the English language while painting wonderful pictures of the game on your radio. He was the sort of fellow who always looked as if he was about to say something really dumb and usually did. He was beloved, yet controversial. He would praise and criticize players with equal zest. He was a baseball man, and his love of the game would provide him with everything he would ever hold dear in his life. Even his son, Skip, would follow in his footsteps. He would spend most of fifty-three years with the St. Louis Cardinals, Chicago White Sox and

Chicago Cubs, talking about the game he loved. His voice would be recognized on every corner of every small town, USA. He was none other than Harry Caray, professional baseball announcer. Sometimes I think the game of baseball may have been invented for guys like Harry. So close your eyes real tight, listen closely and you just might hear these words, "There's a drive...It might be...It could be... It is a home run...Holy Cow!"

He was born March 1, 1920, in St. Louis, Missouri. His given name was Harry Christopher Carabina. His father was Italian and his mother Rumanian. Unfortunately, Harry would never know either of his parents very well. His father left the family shortly after Harry's birth, and his mother remarried when he was five years old and died when Harry turned seven. His new stepfather tried to raise Harry for awhile, but he eventually ended up sending him to live with his uncle who was married to his Aunt Doxie. Harry had no brothers or sisters, but this new family had four kids. But bad times still followed Harry as his uncle soon deserted this family soon after he arrived. So Aunt Doxie raised the five children which included Harry. He grew up at 1909 LaSalle Street, located near a section known as "The Hill," in St. Louis. This section was known as a tough Italian neighborhood and also the birthplace of Yogi Berra and Joe Garagiola. Harry never talked much about his youth, because the memories were mostly unpleasant. His days as a youngster were spent hawking newspapers after school, for the evening *Post-Dispatch,* at a couple of pennies each. Maybe that's how he got his start, by yelling out headlines and stories of cops and robbers, ballplayers and movie stars, enticing people to purchase his papers. In 1930, a good day of selling newspapers would yield him forty cents. He was a fair student who received mostly

B's in school. Harry loved reading and chocolate-marshmallow sundaes, but not necessarily in that order. I guess you could say he made his own way. The worst time of the year for Harry was Christmas, because he never had what others had at that time of the year. No family, no money and no fond memories. Even as he grew older he felt that he had to be by himself at Christmas. He wanted to be alone with his thoughts, to reflect and think about how things could have been but never were. Christmas was always a sad time for Harry.

The one thing that Harry fell passionately in love with, as a young boy, was the game of baseball. He loved to play it, watch it, and read about it and most of all, to talk about it. The St. Louis Cardinals would be at the center of Harry's world for many years. He couldn't wait to get out of school each day and find out if they had won or lost. His wildest fantasy was that he would someday wear a Cardinal uniform. As a kid, he would become a member of the famous "Knot Hole Gang" and would attend the Cardinal games every chance he had, at old Sportsman's Park on Grand Avenue. As Harry got older, he turned into a pretty good little baseball player. He spent some time playing second base and shortstop in high school and even received a tuition scholarship from the University of Alabama. But Harry could not accept, because he did not have the money for room and board. During the week he took on odd jobs like bartending, waiting tables and selling newspapers. On the weekend, he played semi-pro baseball for fifteen to twenty dollars a game. Eventually, his poor eyesight would limit his ability to go any farther up the ladder of professional baseball. Married now, he would have to find a steady job in order to raise his family.

Through it all, baseball still remained his one true love. Just being at the ballpark excited him beyond his wildest imagination. The vastness of the ballpark, the smells of hotdogs, roasted peanuts and cigars, all appealed to Harry. It was at home, when he listened to the game on the radio, that he noticed a difference. The broadcast was boring and did no justice to the greatness of the game. So Harry, still making his own way, wrote a letter to Merle Jones, the man who ran KMOX, the largest radio station in St. Louis. "I told Mr. Jones why he should hire me to broadcast the St. Louis baseball games," said Harry. "I didn't know anything about broadcasting, nothing. I had never in my life seen a radio studio, or even a microphone, but I was not about to let any of that stand in my way." Then Harry made one of the smartest decisions of his life, he sent the letter to Mr. Jones' home address marked <u>PERSONAL</u>. Harry's initiative impressed Jones, and he invited him up to his office for a meeting. After a short chat, Mr. Jones told Harry he would give him a chance and wanted to hear his voice in an audition. Harry thanked him profusely, and the audition was set up at the station. Harry went home to study. Well, the audition did not go as well as Harry would have liked, and the script he was asked to read included names like Puccini, Tchaikovsky, and La Boheme. "It wasn't exactly Tinkers-to-Evers-to-Chance," whispered a dejected Harry. As Harry immediately began to plead his case to become an announcer, Jones just smiled and said, "Sort of tough, huh?" But then Jones said something else. "All I wanted to hear from you was your voice, and let me tell you something. You have an exciting timbre. You could be really exciting." Harry was feeling good now. "If you're ready to gamble, I will get you a start," Jones said. Harry would be placed in touch with Bob Holt, who was the station manager for WCLS in Joliet, Illinois. It was Holt who convinced Harry to change his last name from "Carabina" to "Caray." "It had a much quicker sound," said Holt. Starting a new job in a new town and having no paternal relatives, Harry decided, why not? Welcome to the world of sports on radio, Harry Caray. It would take Harry all of about fifteen minutes to realize that being a broadcaster was not going to be easy. Mistake after mistake occurred as he interviewed local high school and college athletes, but Harry pressed on and got better each day. After a year and a half in Joliet, he began to write letters again to bigger stations in bigger markets for a bigger job. WKZO in Kalamazoo, Michigan, offered Harry the Sports Director's job on AM 590. Little did Harry Caray know, but he was about to meet their News Director, Paul Harvey. "And now… you know the rest of the story." (Sorry, I just had to do that.) Now back to Harry. Paul and Harry would become lifelong friends. Another guy whose name you may also know worked at this same station during Harry's time. His name was Tom Snyder. In the years to come, Tom would rival Johnny Carson for the title of "King of late night TV." It was an exciting time to be in radio broadcasting.

Kalamazoo would also be the town where Harry announced his first baseball game and, of course, he was a natural. It was now 1943, and other big names like Walter Winchell and Dizzy Dean were being heard on the airwaves. He would head back to St. Louis, as the war effort was in full force and Harry was called in to complete his military physical. This time, his poor eyesight would work in his favor, and he was classified 1-AL, which meant limited service. There was one more thing happening that was very close to Harry's heart. They say timing is everything and, in 1944, baseball was tops in St. Louis, Missouri.

The Cardinals had won the World Series in 1942 and lost the 1943 Series to the New York Yankees. But in 1944, it would be an all-St. Louis World Series, as the St. Louis Browns would meet the St. Louis Cardinals for the title. It would be the only time these two teams would ever meet in a World Series. Harry wasn't even 25 years old yet, and the world of baseball announcing was opening up in front of him like a steamed oyster.

In the summer of 1944, Griesedieck Brothers Brewery, of St. Louis announced that they would broadcast all Browns and Cardinals home games on WIL radio station beginning in 1945. One way to get their station up and running was to start broadcasting minor sporting events like college basketball, ice hockey, boxing, and even wrestling. Harry was hired to handle these insignificant events. Then the search was put on to hire the best play-by-play and color guys in the business, to broadcast America's favorite sport, baseball. Gabby Street, former Cardinal Manager, was hired for the color spot; but as the winter months slipped by, no play-by-play guy had been secured. Harry's take on this was, "Why not me?" "You're too young," was always the answer from the station manager, Oscar Zahner. During the early years of baseball on the radio, most broadcasts only featured balls, strikes and the score. "You could read the paper while listening to the game," said station owner Ed Griesedieck. "With Harry, he wouldn't let you read the paper. He demanded your attention," laughed Ed. Harry was fresh and different, and his style was in direct contrast to their competition. Harry Caray was a salesman if there ever was one. Harry's whole philosophy was to broadcast the game the way a fan would broadcast. Eventually Zahner would come around and offer Harry the job. Harry Caray and Gabby Street would form one of the best broadcast teams in the Midwest. For the next 25 years (1945-1969), Harry would broadcast the St. Louis Cardinals games. He would then spend one year with the Oakland Athletics (1970), 10 years with the Chicago White Sox (1971-1981), and 16 with the Chicago Cubs (1982-1997). You could even hear Harry's voice on the popular 1959-60 television show, *Home Run Derby*. Still, Gabby Street would always be Harry's favorite partner, although he shared the booth with many other Hall-of-Fame announcers. Names like Jack Buck, Gus Mancuso, Joe Garagiola, Jimmy Piersall and Steve Stone, read like a list of Who's Who as Harry's partners. And there were even others like Lou Boudreau and Dewayne Staats. Oh, and don't forget "Dutch" Reagan. Yes that's right. Dutch was none other than Ronald Reagan, who at one time worked for WHO radio station in Des Moines, Iowa, recreating Cubs games from a ticker in the 1930's. Reagan would join Harry in the booth for some stories and play-by-play. "You could tell he had done it before," said Harry. "He was very professional." But Gabby had been Harry's first partner, like family, and that was always special to Harry. Anheuser-Busch would purchase the Cardinals in 1954, and Harry Caray would join the KMOX broadcast team. In his first 41 years on the air, Caray never missed calling a game and would eventually broadcast over 8,300 games during his career.

Harry's star shown even brighter, after joining the Chicago Cubs broadcast team in 1982. WGN, a television cable super station, is owned by The Chicago Tribune Company, which also owns the Cubs, and broadcasts the majority of their games to all corners of the U.S. Caray did not necessarily have a face for television, but his popularity with the Chicago fans and jovial spirit was enough to carry the broadcast. During his years with the Cubbies, he would be proclaimed "The Mayor of Rush Street," a famous bar-hopping neighborhood outside of Wrigley Field. He would open each broadcast with, "Hello again, everybody, it's a bee—yooo—tiful day for baseball," and of course he hoped to close each game with another one of his signature calls, "Cubs win! Cubs win!" During close games or when the Cubs were behind, he would be heard screaming, "Let's get some runs," just like any other fan. Once...in Montreal, while trying to be funny, he said, "They (Expos fans) discovered 'boo' is pronounced the same in French as it is in English." Harry could be a funny guy. Another favorite line of Harry's fans was, "Aw, how could he (Jorge Orta) lose the ball in the sun; he's from Mexico. The sun shines there all the time." One of my personal favorites occurred during a critical at-bat when one of the Cubs popped up for a sure out. Harry screamed, "He popped him up; four million a year, and he pops him up." Only Harry could get away with that. Another story finds Harry meeting Oakland A's, Charles O. Finley for the first time. Harry asked Finley what the O stood for. "Owner," said Finley and he did not smile. He would be impersonated by many comics in his later years and even find his humor displayed in skits on *Saturday Night Live*, played by Will Ferrell.

There are literally hundreds more stories that could be told about Harry. You don't spend 53 years on the radio and travel all over the country and not have stories to tell. But this one, I found unique and intriguing. Harry tells this story himself to *The Sporting News*, July 2, 1966 and it goes as follows. "I'm in Memphis one winter, early 1960's, to do a basketball game, the St. Louis Hawks, on TV [broadcasting] back to St. Louis," Caray recalled. "I'm in my hotel room the afternoon of the game. The phone rings." 'Harry,' the voice says. 'Been listening to you for years; how are the Cardinals gonna be this season?' 'I think we're gonna be OK,' Caray replies. 'We've got a good ball club. Uh, who is this?' 'Elvis,' the voice says. 'Elvis who?' Caray asked. 'Elvis Presley,' the man answers. 'C'mon, don't give me that,' Caray roars. 'You're not Elvis Presley.' 'You're a sporting man,' the fellow goes on. 'If you don't think it's me, be down in front of the hotel in 10 minutes.' " Ten minutes passed, and a big Cadillac pulled up with Elvis in it. "Well, he took me to his mansion," Caray recalled. "We talked baseball, music, what have you. Then he dropped me off at the arena so I could do the basketball game, and picked me up 15 minutes after the game. We went back to his house and wound up eating ribs and drinking Budweiser and 'shooting the bull' until the wee hours. I'll never forget that phone call," said Harry. Neither will Elvis. Harry has met or interviewed nearly every player who has played in the last 50 years. He's met some other folks too, like Frank Costello, the gangster, and Toots Shore, the famous night club owner.

In 1987, Harry's skills would begin to diminish. He would recover remarkably from a stroke, but would not consider retiring. When criticized for his mispronunciations, Harry said, "I've only been doing this for nearly 50 years; with a little experience, I might get better." Harry has called three World Series, one All-Star Game and was named Baseball Broadcaster of the Year seven times. In 1989, the Baseball Hall of Fame presented Harry Caray with the Ford C. Frick Award for his contributions to baseball and broadcasting. He also received his own star on the St. Louis Walk of Fame. In 1990, Harry was also inducted into the Radio Hall of Fame. Sadly, on February 14, Valentines Day 1997, Harry collapsed at a nightclub in Rancho Mirage, California, after having dinner with his wife "Dutchie." He lay in a coma for four days and died of a heart attack, shortly after being removed from life-support on February 18, 1997. His funeral was one of the largest in Chicago's history. He was survived by his wife and one son, Skip, who works for the Atlanta Braves. The Cubs had just hired Harry's grandson, Chip, to join Harry in the booth for the upcoming season, but that union would never take place. The Cubs dedicated the 1998 season to Harry and a small patch showing Harry's face with those huge glasses would be worn on the sleeves of their uniforms. The Cubs went a step farther and erected a statue of Harry holding his microphone and leaning out the window of his booth. It stands near Wrigley Field for all to see. It is only fitting that since Harry's death, for every home game, the Chicago Cubs have had a different guest for the singing of "Take Me Out to the Ball Game," during the seventh-inning stretch.

Harry Caray will be missed for a lot of reasons, but very few understand the real reason why. It's because he knew that it's not the city you fall in love with. It's not the team. It's not the players or their personalities that keep you coming back. It's the game. The game goes on forever. Baseball was the object of his affections. I will always remember Harry saying, "You just can't beat fun at the old ballpark."

His Last Five Dollars

The year was 1937, in Oakland, California. He and his wife, Valerie were dead broke, down to their last five dollars. It had taken all they had to make the trip from Texas and pay the entry fee. But luck, with a little skill, was on his side, and the gods of golf smiled down on him that weekend. Although he only placed second in the tournament, the prize money came to $380.00 cash. He has always said that it was enough incentive to keep him after his game. The old saying is that if you want to do something you have never done; then do something that everyone else does not want to do— *practice.* So, practice he did. "It made me feel like a hundred-dollar bill in a two-dollar wallet," he said. He was not a natural, rarely spoke on the golf course, and constantly worked on his game to get better. So, over and over and over again, he practiced, and played without the use of a glove. He claimed it helped him with the feel of the club when striking the ball. He could not wait to get up in the morning to practice. It was at practice that he learned to fine-tune his swing. He claims to have never had a lesson, but learned by watching others play. He watched the way they swung their clubs and the way they would strike their golf ball. He was once asked why he practiced so much and worked so hard. His answer, "I was trying to make a living." He had already failed several times to make the tour, but he loved the game of golf and continued to persevere. He may have invented practice as we know it today. I think every great athlete has a bit of a mean streak, and we sometimes confuse that with being competitive. He was competitive and turned pro for the first time in 1929, as a 17-year-old kid. With little more than pocket change, he chased that little white ball all over the country. He did not win his first PGA tour event until 1940, a full eleven years after turning pro. For those of us who like golf, it was worth the wait.

William Ben Hogan was born in Dublin, Texas, on August 13, 1912, to Chester and Clara Hogan. Chester had been a blacksmith and, sadly, he committed suicide when Ben was only nine years old. Clara moved the family to Fort Worth, where Ben attended school; but he never graduated. He preferred to caddy and deliver newspapers. There is a story that he would sleep in a bunker on the golf course at night near the 18th green so he could be the first caddie in line the next morning. In 1927, Hogan met a fellow caddie who later became a tour rival, at Glen Garden Country Club, and his name was Byron Nelson. These two would become life-long friends. In 1935, Hogan married long time acquaintance, Valerie Fox.

Several times in the thirties, Hogan played in major golf tournaments, without success. By 1939, all his hard work would start to pay off. He had switched from a right-handed to a left-handed swing and made a change to his grip. Using a special wrist movement he invented, which was known as "cupping under," he was able to straighten out his drives and produce what has been called the "Hogan Fade." This corrected his duck-hook and allowed him to hit majestic drives with such distance that fellow players and fans began to take notice. From 1939 to 1941, Hogan would finish in the money in 56 consecutive tournaments, winning over $10,656 in 1940 alone. He would be the leader on the money board again, in 1941 and 1942. World War II called him in 1943, and he joined the United States Air Force.

Hogan would return with a vengeance in 1945. By 1946, after initially suffering putting woes, he lost a chance at his first Masters win. He would still be the leading money winner that year. Two years later, in 1948, Hogan would become the first golfer to win three Major Championships in the same year.

Hogan's resolve would be tested on February 2, 1949. He and his wife, Valerie, were driving back to their home in Fort Worth, Texas, when they were hit head-on by a Greyhound bus. To protect his wife, Hogan threw himself to the right across her body and saved her life and his from the steering column, which would have surely killed him on impact. The doctors predicted he would never walk again. Sixteen months after the accident, Hogan not only had taught himself to walk again but also to play the game he loved, golf. He would be named Player of the Year for the 1950 season. He would also win six Major Championships after his car accident. Eventually, he found it hard to walk the golf course during events. Famed sportswriter Grantland Rice once wrote, "His legs simply where not strong enough to carry his heart any longer." His final PGA title came at the 1959 Colonial Open.

In five decades, Hogan had won 64 events, nine Major Championships; four U.S. Open Titles, the career Grand Slam, and was the winner of three professional Grand Slam events in a single season. His reputation for perfection and practice continues to be the talk of today's players. He would receive the nickname, "The Hawk," for his fierce determination which usually ended in wearing down his opponents. He was a taskmaster, hard on himself and aloof at times. Some would say he was as odd as a forty-cent piece. At five-feet and seven inches tall, he was belittled and pushed aside at the start. "I had to learn how to beat the people I was playing," said Hogan. He was later quoted as saying, "I play golf with friends sometimes, but there are never friendly games." There is no doubt that Ben Hogan was the best golfer of his era, and he is still considered one of the greatest of all time.

Hogan became a recluse in his later years and was rarely seen in public. In 1995, he underwent emergency surgery for colon cancer. He survived but was never the same. His wife remained by his side as Ben was later diagnosed with Alzheimer's disease. He suffered a massive stroke and died on July 25, 1997, at the age of 84. Someone once said, the only thing we get to decide in life is what to do with the time we are given. I'm sure Ben was still working on his swing.

Eighty-Six Percent

His real name was Don, but no one ever called him that except his mom and Donna, his twin sister. That's right; he is the only Hall-of-Fame baseball player to have a twin. Do you have any clue who I'm talking about? I didn't think so. Okay, Don was the only rookie elected to the 1948 All-Star game. Does that ring a bell? Man, you need to brush up on your baseball history. Maybe another hint will help. Don was not recognized as a Hall-of-Fame ballplayer until 1995, 28 years after he became eligible. Wow, I thought you knew some baseball. Okay, one last hint: He was known as one of the "Whiz Kids" of 1950. Now you've got it. That's right; I'm talking about Don Richard "Whitey" Ashburn. Perhaps the most consistent lead-off hitter in Major League history. Richie, Whitey or "Putt-Putt" as he was sometimes called, was born on a farm in Tilden, Nebraska on March 19, 1927. The town of Tilden had been named for the famous lawman of the old west, Bill Tilden. Richie would be small for his age, very fair skinned, fast as lightning, look like your newspaper boy and develop a heart the size of all outdoors.

Richie was signed as an amateur free agent in 1945, by the Philadelphia Phillies. He would join the big club in 1948 and debut in his first game on April 20, wearing the No. 1. In the early days of baseball, hitters wore the number that corresponded to where they batted in the lineup. Richie would bat first and record a .333 batting average and win Rookie-of-the-Year honors that same year. Ashburn was one of those rare players who threw with his right hand but batted left-handed. Richie was the ultimate singles hitter and would bat over .300 nine times in his 15 year career. He was what the old-timers called a spray hitter and in fact 86 percent of his hits would be singles. An example of this would occur on May 20, 1951, when he singled eight times in ten at-bats during a doubleheader against the Pirates, or on June 3, 1956, when he got five hits, all singles, in six at-bats against the Cardinals. He also led the National League four times in walks. Richie Ashburn knew how to get on base. He would lead the league in on-base percentage four times and finish his fifteen years with a .396 career average.

Richie won two batting titles, three hitting titles and led the league in runs scored, four times. He also held the crown for most triples hit twice and was elected to the All-Star game five times. His incredible speed and defensive skills would also allow Ashburn to tie a Major League record by leading all outfielders in put-outs nine times from centerfield. As my dad would say, "He could run faster than a chicken can pick up corn." If you have ever seen a chicken pick up corn, off the ground while eating, then you know what I'm talking about. In fact, Ashburn's first home run, hit on May 29, 1948, was a lead-off inside-the-park home run against the New York Giants.

During Richie's early playing days, the Phillies played in Shibe Park. This park opened in 1909 with huge dimensions, a testament to why the game was played base-to-base or "small ball" as it is called today. The fences were 340' from home plate in right field, 378' in left field and the centerfield fence a whopping 515' away. With distances like these, it's easy to see why Richie chose to bang out singles, one after the other. It was here, in Shibe Park that the young Phillies, known as the "Whiz Kids," would take on the powerful Yankees in the 1950 World Series. Philadelphia would be dismissed in four straight games after facing Raschi, Reynolds, Ferrick, and Ford. In 1953, Shibe Park would change its name to Connie Mack Stadium in honor of the long-time owner of the Philadelphia Athletics.

My favorite Richie Ashburn story occurs on August 17, 1957. Besides being a great singles hitter, Ashburn was also known for fouling off pitches until he got a good pitch to hit. On this day he would hit a spectator, Alice Roth, twice in the same at-bat. The first foul ball breaks her nose, and the second one hits her while she is being removed from the stands on a stretcher. Now that's what I call bat control.

A trade after the 1959 season would find Richie with the Chicago Cubs, where he would spend two years in the friendly confines of Wrigley Field before being traded again to the expansion Mets.

Shortly after his retirement in 1962, Ashburn would join the Phillies commentary team alongside legendary broadcaster Harry Kalas. It was here, in the booth, that he became a beloved institution of all Philadelphia fans. He liked his new job because it kept him close to the game he loved, baseball. "You're not involved with the constant pressure to win up here in the booth," he said in 1988. "As a result you get a different perspective. You can take the time to enjoy the baseball."

Finally after waiting 28 years, Richie Ashburn and his 2,574 hits would be elected to the Baseball Hall of Fame. On July 30, 1995 he would accept his plaque along with Mike Schmidt, Leon Day, Vic Willis, and the largest crowd in the history of the Hall-of-Fame inductions.

I met Richie Ashburn later that same year as he signed my Perez-Steele Postcards. He was kind as usual and didn't seem to know how to handle all the additional attention he was being given. I don't think Ashburn ever thought about the Hall of Fame during his career. He was just doing what he loved most, playing baseball.

One of the best lead-off hitters "ever," Ashburn struck out for good on September 9, 1997, of an apparent heart attack. He was 70 years old and had suffered for many years from diabetes. One of the true gentlemen of baseball has left us. So long, Richie!

Heavily Armed

It was January, 1989, Super Bowl week back in the States, when I approached my tee shot. Although I was not a good golfer by any means, I considered this spot of ground a little piece of heaven. Not only was I about to play a round of golf in beautiful Hawaii, but my partner was a man I had watched and followed during my early years of growing up. He was 53 years of age, bald, wore black-rimmed glasses and was missing his two front teeth. On his face and forehead, he wore the scars of fifteen seasons of smash-mouth football. His hands were huge and appeared rough and broken from the hand-to-hand combat in the trenches. He walked proudly but gently, as if every step hurt. His head seemed as big as Goliath, while his shoulders were broad enough to serve breakfast on. He just looked like a middle-linebacker should look. It had been said by his peers that he was ferocious and that he indeed enjoyed hitting other people, on his team or yours. He could snap a ball carrier in half like a dry bag of spaghetti. This large, happy-go-lucky guy changed when he stepped on the football field. His demeanor became as dark as the inside of a football. His arms, from the elbows down, were hardened by rolls of white trainer's tape and his legs were strong like a fence post. There was even a story floating around about his being able to remove the lug nuts from the wheel of a car with his teeth. I was sure the story was not true, or at least I hoped it wasn't; I still had seventeen holes left to play with this guy. After my tee shot, my partner addressed his ball. As I properly stood quietly behind him, I closed my eyes for a second and whispered under my breath, "I'm playing golf with # 66, Ray Nitschke of the Green Bay Packers." Nitschke, Johnny Unitas and Dick Butkus had been my favorites to watch early on. There was one thing they all three had in common—toughness. At 6' 3", 225 pounds, Ray Nitschke entered every game heavily armed, a grown man among mere boys.

On December 29, 1936, Raymond Ernest "Ray" Nitschke was chiseled from stone, in a tough neighborhood known as Elmwood Park, Illinois. By the age of 13, Ray had lost both his mother and father and would be reared by an older brother. Ray used sports to vent his pent-up anger while playing quarterback for Proviso East High School. Not only did they win the league title, but Ray was also selected to the Illinois High School All-State team. By 1954, Ray had turned down a contract to play professional baseball with the St. Louis Browns and instead signed a scholarship to play college football with the University of Illinois. He would find a home at fullback and linebacker, positions where his brute strength and speed benefited the team the most. Even though Ray scored four touchdowns against Iowa State, he was considered by NFL scouts to be a born linebacker.

On December 2, 1957, the 1958 NFL Draft got underway. Green Bay chose three players that would become the heart of future Packer teams. Fullback Jim

Taylor of LSU was chosen in the second round with the fifteenth pick, linebacker Ray Nitschke was chosen in the third round with the thirty-sixth pick, and right guard Jerry Kramer of Idaho was chosen in the fourth round with the thirty-ninth pick. At the age of twenty, Nitschke was now a professional football player. Although Ray started eight games as a rookie, the Packers would finish their 1958 season with one win, one tie and the worst record in the league; but help was on the way.

Thirty days after the 1958 season ended, one of the best NFL coaches "ever," arrived in Green Bay; his name was Vince Lombardi. In a short three years (1960), Lombardi would lead the Packers to a title game against the Philadelphia Eagles. With Lombardi at the helm and talented players like Bart Starr, Paul Hornung, Forest Gregg, Jim Ringo, Willie Wood, Willie Davis, Max McGee, Henry Jordan, Herb Adderley and Ray Nitschke, the Green Bay Packers would win five NFL titles and the first two Super Bowls in the 1960's.

Lew Carpenter, a friend of mine and a teammate of Ray's, loves telling stories about the glory days of the Lombardi Packers. Lew played on the 1961 and 1962 NFL Championship teams with the Packers and proudly wears the 1961 Championship ring and 1962 Championship watch. "Ray had two personalities," said Lew. "Off the field, he could be kind, gentle and gracious, but on the football field he was frightening." Lew claimed that Ray's wife held a calming influence over him at home. Lew also told the story about a metal observation tower that fell on Nitschke one day during practice. As players gathered around, Lombardi came running over and yells, "What happened here?" When told that the tower had fallen on Nitschke, Lombardi said, "He'll be fine. Get back to work!" Lew went on to say that the fallen tower had driven a metal spike into Nitschke's helmet, but didn't injure him. "That helmet with the hole in it," said Lew, "is on display at the Packers Hall of Fame in Green Bay." Nitschke went on to earn MVP honors in the 1962 NFL Championship Game and was awarded a brand new 1963 Chevrolet Corvette.

Nitschke retired in 1972, at the age of 36. He had earned first or second team All-NFL honors seven times in eight years, from 1962-1969. He was a complete player with twenty-five interceptions for 385 return yards and two touchdowns. He is the only linebacker to be named to the NFL's 50th and 75th Anniversary Teams. Ray became a member of the NFL Hall of Fame in 1978 and had his #66 retired by the Packers in 1983.

Ray Nitschke continued to live in Green Bay and you could find his address and number in the phone book. He appeared on TV, in a couple of movies, and was ranked #18 on the 1999 *Sporting News* list of the 100 Greatest Football Players of all time. There was also a funny line mentioned in the ABC movie, Brian's Song. Actor James Caan played Chicago Bear running back and cancer victim, Brian Piccolo. In the movie, when the Doctor asked Piccolo if he was allergic to anything, Piccolo responded, "Just Nitschke."

On March 8, 1998, one of my childhood heroes left the big playing field for the last time. Ray had been visiting family and friends in Venice, Florida, and suffered a heart attack. He was 61.

Every year, the day before the Hall of Fame inductions, there is a luncheon for all the members and new inductees. Ray Nitschke always attended and made it a point to speak to the new fellows about the honor and the responsibility that was being bestowed on them. This luncheon is now named after him.

As for our golf game, sure he won; he didn't know how to lose. We had a blast and I will carry those memories forever. Rest well, Ray, and save me a tee time.

Best of the Best

There will never be another like him, not now nor in the future. He just saw things differently than the rest of us and possessed the ability to write in a way that helped us understand the difference. He spent 30 years hanging around the sports department of the *Los Angeles Times*. While there, he won the Sportswriter of the Year Award fourteen times, including twelve in a row. The award should have been named after him. He won a Pulitzer Prize for commentary and was inducted into the Sportswriters' Wing of the Baseball Hall of Fame. You may not have liked him personally, but you loved his work. He was the king of the sportswriters, best of the best, Moses with eyeglasses. He was clever, funny, and loved meshing sports with historical events or places to give them credibility. Every sportswriter ever read has probably stolen his material at one time or another. Plagiarism can be considered a form of praise, but it wasn't just his writing; it was the attitude and style in which he wrote. He was once asked if he was upset by his words being used without his permission; his answer, "Go ahead, I'm done with them." Someone once claimed he ruined a whole generation of sportswriters, because everyone wanted to write like him and none of then could ever come close.

The thing you might find interesting about Jim Murray's writing is that you can read and reread his work over and over and it never gets old. His writing is timeless and always relevant. People who weren't even sports fans read Jim's articles. When I want to laugh, think or become inspired to write, I pick up one of his books with a collection of his writings, and in minutes I'm taken back into the world of sports through the eyes of Murray. Jim Murray told us about the person, what made them different, what made them tick. He very rarely wrote about scores, stats, or results.

James Patrick Murray was born December 29, 1919, in Hartford, Connecticut. He discovered his gift of gab and writing while attending Trinity College located in Hartford. He loved being the campus correspondent for the *Hartford Times* while attending college. He would become the Police Beat Reporter for the New Haven Register in 1943 and eventually moved to the Los Angeles Examiner as a rewrite man in 1944. By 1948, Murray wrote for "Time" magazine and became the West Coast editor for *Sports illustrated*. Finally, he landed at his home for the next 37 years, as sports columnist for the *Los Angeles Times*. Along the way he played golf with Arnold Palmer, poker with John Wayne, and schmoozed with Frank Sinatra. He was every bit the star. Eye surgery set him back, along with some heart problems. After heart surgery, Murray once wrote, "Where the hell are the Rams? They were in Anaheim when I went under anesthesia." Jim Murray was elected to the Baseball Hall of Fame in 1987, for his contributions in writing.

Jim Murray's one-liners were considered masterpieces. His writing style was hard-hitting and informative. If Murray didn't write about you, you were nobody. It was like Don Drysdale throwing at Frank Robinson; he only threw at you if you were any good. One sentence from Murray could paint you a paragraph. Below are a few examples:

1) "Willie Mays' glove is where triples go to die."
2) "John Wooden was so square, he was divisible by four."
3) "Buddy Ryan is Patton without the tanks."
4) "Ricky Henderson has a strike zone the size of Hitler's heart."
5) "Dizzy Dean died the other day at the age of 11 or 12. The little boy in all of us died with him."
6) When he first attended the Indy 500, he began his article by writing "Gentleman, start your coffins."
7) "All things considered, it's better to have Earl Campbell."
8) "When you think everything is hopeless, just remember Yogi Berra."
9) "The wrong Ram quarterback is the one that's in there."
10) "Branch Rickey could spot talent from the window of a moving train."

Also added below are just a few of my favorite excerpts from some of the many thousands of daily sports articles written by Murray. I would suggest that anyone who ever wants to write for a living, pick up one of Murray's collections of writings. You will not be sorry. Enjoy!

"I always thought if you could cut Rocky Marciano's hand off at the wrist and weigh it, it would weigh twice as much as an ordinary fist. It was not that Rocky meant to cripple people; he just meant to win the fight. He had a club for a left and an ax for a right; he sawed people in half."

"Well, God is getting an earful today. I hope he understands the infield-fly rule, the hit and run, how to pitch to Hornsby with men on, when to platoon, and when it would be good for you to bunt. They finally slipped a called third strike past Casey Stengel. The game is over."

"Willie Shoemaker rode a horse the way DiMaggio caught a fly ball or Sinatra sang a ballad, with the effortless ease and grace of a guy who was born to do what he was doing."

"All Reggie Jackson can do is hit, and all Rembrandt could do was paint. All Secretariat could do was run."

"Ben Hogan was barely 5-foot-7, couldn't have weighed 125. His butt was so nonexistent his hip pockets ran together."

On the size of pro football player Merlin Olsen: "He went swimming in Loch Ness, and the monster got out."

"Ben Crenshaw takes a crack at the ball the way Dempsey would hit a chin or Larry Csonka, a line. Not since another Ben—Hogan—has anyone 5'9" driven a ball so far. But sometimes the ball curves foul; and when it does, you need two men and a dog to find it."

"The first thing anyone notices about Bob Lanier is his feet. He's got the biggest feet of any creature that wears shoes. If you saw his footprints in the snow, you'd run like hell."

"John McEnroe hasn't shaved yet. In fact, he hasn't even gotten a haircut. He's the kind of kid who asked a cocktail waitress if she's has milkshakes. He's got these big blue eyes which glow even in the light, like a big cat's in a tree. The sensation of losing to him is a little like getting run-over by a baby carriage."

"He looked like something out of the Bible, an Old Testament prophet with fierce, burning eyes, a rabbinical beard, long black locks, a John the Baptist in cleats. There was a smoldering violence about him. If he came in a box, you'd put him in water before opening. He was a New York City kid, destined for the electric chair. The betting was if Lyle Alzado were playing football by the time he was age 28, it would be for Sing Sing."

"Roger Staubach was as square as a piece of fudge. He made Pat Boone look kinky. When he was named MVP in a Super Bowl, the sponsoring *Sport* magazine offered him a souped-up sports roadster. Roger frowned and asked if he could have a station wagon instead. In an era when quarterbacks were supposed to buy drinks for their offensive line, or pick up tabs for the hotel party, Staubach could hardly do this. He was at early Mass at the time."

"The first time you see linebacker Jack Lambert, you're tempted to ask what he did with the fangs. Is that really tomato juice he's drinking or something he bit out of the neck of Earl Campbell? Was his coffin comfortable last night and what time does he turn into a wolf? The pro from Pittsburgh, Transylvania, he's Boris Karloff in cleats. Lambert didn't come out of college; he escaped from the laboratory."

"He's the most improbable-looking captain you'll ever see. He looks like he's playing hooky. Not too long ago, if you saw him on the street you would have bought him a balloon and told him not to cry, that you'd find his folks for him. The joke was, Watson had two lumps in his throat, one put there by Adam and the other by the last three holes of a golf course. Not anymore. If Tom Watson shows up it's a championship, if he doesn't it's just a tournament."

"The voice, when he spoke, was an indistinct rumble like the sound of a distant avalanche, or a thunderstorm 10 miles away. The blue eyes squinted as if they were trying to see who missed the block downfield in one corner of the game film. The pants were characteristically baggy. The real "Bear" Bryant, as they will tell you down in Mobile, wouldn't need a boat to go to Cuba, could have saved the Titanic and not only that, he can beat Auburn. He's like the guy who is always turning up four aces and apologizing because there aren't five. 'I don't suppose these are any good,' he'll sigh."

"He had skin so fair you could almost see through it. He looks as if he's standing in a load of corn shucks. He needs to run to jump over an egg. He was 'Down Home,' moonlight on the Wabash, and he said 'we wuz' and 'you wuz.' All he needed was a pitchfork. You don't get basketball players out of French Lick, Indiana. You get them from playgrounds, the projects, the sidewalks of New York or Chicago. You get apple pickers out of French Lick. You can find it on the map under G-4. Go to Young's Creek and turn right. Either way, it's for sure Larry Bird's jersey will one day hang from the Boston Garden rafters. You'll have no trouble recognizing it. It'll be the one with hay on it."

"He has the face of a man who knows there is no longer any use in screaming. His mouth is turned down, his nose wrinkled in disgust, and his eyes register sheer terror. God knows what evil terrors lurk in his mind. I have seen guys look happier throwing up. So what is Don Coryell starring at, his own coffin? No, he is starring at nothing worse than the San Diego Chargers."

Last but not least, he wrote this article about my favorite sport. I always smile when I read it. "Baseball is Babe Ruth pointing, Ty Cobb sliding. It's Whitey Ford loading one up for Campanella with the Series on the line. It's Lou Gehrig standing in Yankee Stadium for the last time, trying not to cry as he tells the world how lucky he was to be a Yankee. Baseball is Musial crouched at the plate, Clemente turning slightly to throw to home plate as he settles under a high one, or Pete Rose stealing third, face first. Baseball is why didn't he bunt? Or why didn't he start Drysdale? Or why didn't he walk 'im? Or why didn't they pinch hit for 'im? Baseball is Alston, you're a bum! It's Dizzy, Rube, Sibby, Dummy, Ping, Three-Fingers and Van Lingle Mungo. We are all *Boys of Summer* when it comes to baseball."

What we all should learn from Murray is that it's the people involved and the events that are more important than the score. Keeping score is mostly for gamblers. We remember who won, but most of us don't remember the score; but the feat itself, we remember the moments. I remember Tiger slipping on the "Green Jacket" for the first time at Augusta, but I don't remember what he shot. I remember Buster Douglas knocking out Mike Tyson, but I don't remember what round. I remember Reggie Jackson's three home runs against three different Dodger pitchers in a World Series game, but I don't remember the names of all three pitchers. I remember 49er's receiver Dwight Clark's catch to beat the Cowboys in a playoff game, but I don't remember the year. It's the moments that count.

It will be a sad day when sports forget that it has a heart-beat. They are not machinery; athletes have blood running through their veins, not oil. That's the essence of sports, real people placed in circumstances that require them to excel beyond their own physical or mental boundaries.

They go faster, jump higher, hit harder, and respond more quickly than we or they believed was possible. Hours of preparation and coaching simply placed them in a position to extend their abilities and, from that effort, we all experience extraordinary feats of skill and moments that will stay with us forever. Jim Murray, master of the metaphor, understood that, and wrote about it, and that's why he was considered the best. If there were a photo taken of the best ever sportswriters, Murray may be the only one in the picture. He was special.

On August 16, 1998, Murray laid down his pen for the last time here on earth. At the age of 78, he died at his home, of cardiac arrest. I'm sure he now writes for the Daily News in Heaven.

Daylight and Shadows

In most old-timers' opinions, he was the last of the great single-wing tailbacks to play the game. As a tailback, he would do a little bit of everything from running back, wide receiver, quarterback, defensive back, to returning kicks. He also kicked extra points, field goals and punted. There was nothing he could not do. He did so many different things on a football field that he never really stood out at any one position, but when added together, he became irreplaceable. He also had the uncanny ability to come up with some sort of spectacular play every time he stepped onto the field. Many years ago, a wonderful sportswriter named W.C. Heinz wrote a bestseller entitled "Run to Daylight." It was about Vince Lombardi's Green Bay Packer teams of the early sixties. There is no doubt that Heinz got the title for his book from the great football coach, who instructed his running backs to "run to daylight." You just had to see this guy to believe what he could do. No one ever questioned his leadership. He would simply kneel down in the huddle and say, "Okay, here's what we are going to do," and everyone would bust their tail for him. Shortly after he was born, someone asked his father if he wanted his son to grow up to be president. "No. He's going to be an All-American football player," said the father. And he was—three times during his college career. He lettered in five sports in high school and once said in an interview, "Other than golf, I never really tried a sport that, inside of 30 minutes, I couldn't play pretty good." He was a natural-born athlete and his first love was football. The crowds that came to see him play in college were so big that the stadium could not hold them all, so they moved the team's home games to the Cotton Bowl, which held 47,000 fans. Eventually, the City of Dallas had to add more seats to the Cotton Bowl to accommodate the 75,000 fans who wanted to see this guy play. Any idea who I'm writing about? Well, there's a sign hanging on the wall at the entrance of that stadium that says, "The Cotton Bowl: The House That Doak Built."

Ewell Doak Walker, Jr. was born New Year's Day in 1927. His father, Ewell Sr., was a teacher and coach at North Dallas High School. As a young man, Doak would sneak into the closet where the football equipment was kept and imagine him self running and scoring touchdowns. Soon after, Doak was in the starting line-up for the football team at Highland Park and one of his teammates was Bobby Layne. In high school, Doak choose uniform # 37 which was worn by his favorite SMU college player, Harry Shuford. He would make that number famous in college and the NFL. After high school, Doak and Bobby split up, with Layne attending the University of Texas and Doak enrolling at Southern Methodist University. They would reunite after college when both joined the Detroit Lions.

While at SMU, Doak would average 4.2 yards per carry, 16.7 yards per catch, and completed more than 50% of his passes. He averaged 15 yards on punt returns and 29.1 yards per kick-off return. In three years, he had totaled 3,862 yards of total offense and scored 303 points. These numbers earned him a spot on the Associated Press All-American Team in 1947, 1948, and 1949. He was also elected to the All-Southwest Conference team, four times, and received the 1947 Maxwell Award given to the player of the year in college football. He would follow this award with the prestigious Heisman Trophy, in 1948. Doak Walker was the first junior to win this award. He was also featured throughout his career on 47 different magazine covers including *Look, Collier's* and *Life,* in 1948. Last but not least, Doak was chosen as the 1948 and 1949 MVP in two Cotton Bowls. I guess his Dad knew what he was taking about.

In 1949, Doak would be chosen with the third pick by the Detroit Lions, in the first round of the NFL draft. At 5'11" and 173 pounds, most NFL scouts had shied away from Walker. Most were afraid that the size and speed of the NFL players would be too much for Doak to endure. How wrong they were. He would earn the title of 1950 Rookie of The Year and, teamed with his high school buddy, Bobby Layne, would lead the Lions to two NFL Championships in 1952 and 1953. He also led the NFL in scoring three of the six years he played and was an All-Pro selection five times. In addition, he played in five Pro Bowls. In six years as a pro, he ran for 1,520 yards, averaging 4.9 yards per carry and scored 13 touchdowns. He caught 152 passes, for 2,359 yards and 21 touchdowns. He averaged 39.1 yards on punts, 15.8 yards on punt returns, and 25.5 yards on kick-off returns. There is no doubt that what he did best was score. He retired in 1955 with the third most points scored in NFL history. They are as follows: 534 points scored on 34 touchdowns, 183 extra points and 49 field goals. The Detroit Lions honored Doak by retiring his # 37.

Doak Walker was inducted into the College Football hall of Fame in 1959, the Texas Sports Hall of Fame in 1973, and the Professional Football Hall of Fame in 1986. He was inducted for the body of his work and his impact on the game when he played. It was the correct thing to do. His old pal and teammate Bobby Layne introduced Walker at the NFL Hall of Fame ceremonies. "Now that I have helped get Doak in the Hall of Fame," said Layne, "I can finally retire." There would be one more honor for Doak Walker. In 1989, SMU and the Dr. Pepper Company joined together to form the Doak Walker Award, given annually to college football's best running back. This is the only major college football award that requires the winner to be in good academic standing and be on schedule to graduate on time. Some of the past winners include, "Bam" Morris (Texas Tech), Byron Hanspard (Texas Tech), Ricky Williams (Texas), LaDainian Tomlinson (TCU), and Cedric Benson (Texas).

Walker retired from football in 1955 and received a job working for an electrical company that paid him the same salary that he made playing for the Lions. "I wanted to get out while I still have all my teeth and both my knees," said Walker. He was transferred to Colorado where he would live out his days. He carried with him his college sweetheart, Norma Peterson whom he had married in 1950. They raised four children together but later divorced, in 1965. Doak later met and married former Olympian, "Skeeter" Werner, a ski instructor, in 1969. Not long after the move, Walker started his own company, known as Walker Chemicals. But there were shadows on the horizon in Doak Walker's life. On January 30, 1998, Walker was seriously injured in a skiing accident which left him para-lyzed throughout most of his body. He was robbed of the use of his arms and legs, the very things that made him great on the football field. He could only speak in short phrases, but those eyes were bright and would come alive at the site of hundreds of pieces of fan mail or well-wishes from friends. On September 27, 1998, Doak Walker, at age 71, slipped into the space between daylight and shadows. May he never be caught from behind!

Award-winning *Sports Illustrated* writer Rick Reilly may have said it best in an article written before Walker's death. "He's Doak Walker, and he was as golden as golden gets. He had perfectly even, white teeth and a jaw as square as a deck of cards and a mop of brown hair that made girls bite their necklaces. He was so shifty you couldn't have tackled him in a phone booth, yet so humble that he wrote the Associated Press a thank-you note for naming him an All-American," said Reilly. Doak Walker may have been the very definition of a "Hero."

Red-Hot Temper, Blazing Fastball

S ome would later say he was Drysdale before there was a Don Drysdale. His temper was legendary and his fastball, out of control. Anger would seep into his pitches and his left-handed curve ball appeared to develop a mind of its own. Most hitters preferred the word "wicked" when describing his hook, and there is no doubt that the overhand curve would become his trademark pitch. He was born with a slingshot left arm, an uneven temperament and an evil stare; and he was as wild as a long-eared West Texas hare. Called a sorehead by most of the players, he was an immature kid and it seemed that every bad inning was followed by him firing his glove into the dugout, in anger. Heck, sometimes he would charge the opponents' bench while yelling as loudly as possible. Other players knew that his temper was his biggest weakness, and they all tried to take advantage of him. It would take time, experience and a little-known catcher named Paul Richards to set him on the path to pitching greatness.

Harold Newhouser was born May 20, 1921, in Detroit, Michigan. He was the second son of Theodore and Emilie Newhouser and dreamed of playing sports for a living. This hard-working, blue-collar family would find some success in this growing city. With a population of over one million, Detroit was the fourth largest city in the U.S. in the 1920's, and the home of Charles Lindberg, bootleg liquor, and the Ford Motor Company. Detroit also had a pretty fair Major League baseball team known as the Tigers. With stars like Ty Cobb, Sam Crawford, Harry Heilmann, and manager Hughie Jennings, the Tigers would make appearances in the World Series three times: 1907, 1908, and 1909. It was an exciting time in Detroit for baseball. Hal's older brother, Richard, would sign a professional baseball contract, and play several seasons with the Tigers and Red Sox, as an infielder, until his career ended when he was hit in the head by a pitched ball. Surprisingly, young Hal did not play baseball until he was 13 or 14 years old. Football and ice hockey had been his games until he found out he could throw a baseball as fast as all the other boys in the neighborhood. From that point on, days on end of playing baseball would give Hal an outlet for his pent-up emotions, while discovering that he threw pretty darn well. Someone once said, "Dreams are what makes life tolerable." This kid's dream really did come true. From sandlot ball, to block teams, to the City All-Stars, and finally the Class-E level, this sudden success on the pitcher's mound assured the young lefthander that he was going to be a professional ballplayer. After he pitched his first game at age 15, he said, "I knew then because I could throw pretty hard. As long as I got the ball over – I was a little bit wild – but when I got the ball over, why, I knew then 'that' was gonna be my category."

In 1939, Hal would sign his first professional baseball contract as an amateur free agent, with his hometown team, the Detroit Tigers. His age was 18. That year was also a banner year for some other newcomers in Major

League Baseball. Along with Hal Newhouser, other great players like Ted Williams, Mickey Vernon, Early Wynn, Dizzy Trout, and Johnny Hopp, all made their debut. Hal would pitch his first game on September 29 of that same year. He would be plagued with control problems his first two years, and would in fact walk more batters than he struck out, while winning only 18 games and losing 20. To make matters worse, on April 27, 1940, a rookie short-stop with Cleveland named Lou Boudreau, would hit the first and second home runs of his career, off pitcher Hal Newhouser. This infuriated Hal. He would become an intense competitor but in the process, alienated his team-mates with his temper tantrums. It only got worse when he started "showing up" his fellow players when an error was made. "I have seen Hal turn a withering glare toward Charlie Gehringer and upbraid him for making a critical error when Hal was pitching," said catcher Billy Sullivan. "That was like blaspheming God." Lamar Newsome, with the Red Sox, said Newhouser had everything a big league pitcher could have, "except control of himself." As a result, his fellow teammates gave him no support. "I thought Newhouser was a hell of a pitcher. I know he was one of the toughest for me to hit," said Hall-of-Fame catcher, Bill Dickey. Ted Williams once said of Newhouser, "He was wild at first, and a fiery guy. You would hit one off him and it was like you had taken his blood. He'd give you that rotten stare. He didn't think anybody was supposed to hit Newhouser." Hal indeed had a red-hot temper and a blazing fastball.

Things would change dramatically for Hal in 1943 when a little-known player-manager from the Atlanta Crackers (Southern Association) by the name of Paul Richards, was signed to catch for the Tigers. Richards couldn't hit a lick but, man, could he catch. Richards would concentrate his efforts on straightening out Newhouser's head along with his fastball. Hal had a nice fluid delivery; he just didn't know where it was going when it left his hand. Right away, Richards spotted two things wrong with Hal's delivery: a floppy wrist and his release point. When Hal held his wrist firm and released the ball the same way every time, his control improved dramatically. Then Richards went a step further and helped Hal develop a change-up. The important thing with a change-up is that it must look exactly like his fastball when released. Richards would drill him over and over on the change-up. It was this change-of-pace pitch that would make his fastball even harder to hit. Before long, young Hal had three effective pitches: a fastball over 90 mph, a curve that appeared to fall off the table, and an undetectable change of pace. Roy Partee, the Red Sox catcher, went a step further when he called Newhouser's change-of-pace "tantalizing." Now with his pitching straightened out, Richards would go to work on Hal's head. Richards knew that Hal was a shy and pleasant young fellow, and that his anger was directly mostly at himself. Richards convinced Hal that his anger only made his teammates behind him, tense and prone to make mistakes. The secret was to take it easy, relax, to realize that they wanted to win as badly as he did. When Hal appeared to lose his temper on the mound, Richards would stall around behind home plate and give Hal time to regain his composure. Writers, players, and fans began to take notice of this new "Prince Hal;" he was on his way to the top.

Newhouser would post a 29-9 record in 1944. Not only did he lead the league in wins but also in strikeouts, with 187. He would record 25 complete games, six shutouts, all while posting a 2.22 ERA, and end the season being named the MVP. His performance in 1945 would be even better while leading the Tigers to the World Series Championship against the Chicago Cubs. He would win two games in that series, including the deciding seventh. Prince Hal won 25 games and lost 9, while lowering his ERA to a stunning 1.81, and recorded 212 strikeouts. These numbers would reward him with the pitcher's Triple Crown for 1945 and another MVP Award. Bobo Newsom would say of Hal, "Every time he walks to the mound, you know you'll get a good-pitched game." But because these numbers were produced during wartime baseball, most writers felt he could not repeat similar results in 1946, when the war was over and many of the so-called "real major leaguers" returned from Europe. Hal proved himself again and again by winning 26 games in 1946, 17 in 1947, 21 in 1948, and 18 in 1949. Only the performance by slugger Ted Williams kept Hal from receiving his third MVP Award in a row, in 1946.

Because of Hal's past performance, two things occurred in 1947 for Hal that would shape his future: Millionaire Jorge Pasqual offered Hal $500,000 to jump to the Mexican Leagues, which Hal used to bargain for a new contract and stay with Detroit; and a little known trade was offered by the Yankees. New York offered Joe DiMaggio to Detroit for Hal Newhouser. Detroit refused. As announcer Mel Allen would say, "How about that?"

The year 1950 would bring arm trouble to Newhouser, and his time on the mound would be greatly reduced. On September 25, 1952, Newhouser would claim his 200th victory. It would be his last as a Detroit Tiger. Although he continued to pitch well, he could not recapture his magic on the hill. On July 27, 1953, Hal would be released from the Tigers. Prince Hal signed with the Cleveland Indians in early 1954 and helped them get to the World Series. Hal would now become the teammate of his biggest nemesis throughout his career, Bob Feller. Feller, the dominant right-hander of his era, had dueled many times against Newhouser. Hal would pitch very well, mostly out of the bullpen, and recorded 7 wins and 7 saves, with 2 losses for the Indians. It would be in Cleveland that Hal would close out his career as a professional baseball player. The year was 1955.

During his seventeen-year career, Hal played in seven All-Star games while posting a 207-150 win-loss record, and recorded a lifetime .306 ERA. He is still the only pitcher ever to win two consecutive MVP Awards. On March 17, 1992, after waiting years to be recognized, Hal Newhouser, was elected by the Veterans Committee along with umpire Bill McGowan, to the Baseball Hall of Fame. On August 2 that same year, they would be joined by the baseball writers' choices, Rollie Fingers and Tom Seaver. You see, dreams really do come true.

After retirement, Hal worked as a scout for the Houston Astros, Baltimore Orioles, and the Detroit Tigers. While with the Astros, Hal was credited with discovering short-stop Derek Jeter. But Houston passed on Jeter and chose catcher, Phil Nevin instead. Hal and I became fast friends during the summer of 1995. We had met on an Astros caravan tour. I was introduced to Hal by another scout, Joe Matina. It was hard to believe that this mild mannered guy could be so fiery with a baseball in his hand. Maybe I had met Prince Hal and not the pitcher.

Hal also signed Milt Pappas out of high school, for the Orioles. Pappas would go on to win 209 games in his career. On July 27, 1997, the Tigers retired Hal's uniform #16. He would join other Tiger greats like Hank Greenburg, Al Kaline, Willie Horton, and Charlie Gehringer. A little over a year later, "Prince Hal" left the pitcher's mound for the last time, but this time there was no anger. On November 10, 1998 in Bloomfield Hills, Michigan, he would be laid to rest. He was 77 years of age.

I've Got Everything

Yep, that describes Joe DiMaggio to a "T". He was "something," made every catch look so easy, as if he were gliding instead of running. No diving, sliding or slamming into outfield walls for this guy. He caught everything chest high, with two hands, and both feet on the ground. That was the magic of Joe DiMaggio, nothing looked hard. Everything he did on and off the ball field was like money in the bank. Yes, Joe had it all, including fame, money, endorsements, Marilyn Monroe, and a job in centerfield with the New York Yankees. Joe's instructions to Yogi before Berra played his first game in right field for the Yankees went like this, "If I don't hear you (call for the ball), I've got everything," said Joe. He was as close to a perfect ballplayer as any one could get. "He never did anything wrong," exclaimed Yogi. "And I never saw him walk during a game." He knew how good he was and, after his retirement, he demanded that before each of the 47 Old-Timers Day games he attended, that he be introduced by public address announcer as "The greatest living Yankee player, Joe DiMaggio." "The Yankee Clipper," would never consider taking a backseat to Mickey Mantle, Phil Rizzuto, Whitey Ford or Yogi Berra, all Hall-of-Fame players who could have easily qualified during some of those years. Yeah, he had everything.

There is no question that "Joltin' Joe" began to cement his name in the history books on May 15, 1941. That day, Joe DiMaggio managed only one hit in four at-bats in a 13-1 loss to the Chicago White Sox. What would follow is considered by most baseball historians to be one of the most famous records in baseball history. In fact, most sportswriters believe it's the purest record in the game. Joe would begin to hit, then continue to hit, and hit, and hit, for the next 55 games in a row, setting a new record for getting a hit in consecutive games. It was reported that he rubbed his bats with olive oil and his teammates swore that he never broke a bat, he simply wore them out. This 56-game hitting streak finally ended on July 17, 1941, in Cleveland, against the Indians. Indians third baseman, Ken Keltner made two splendid backhanded stops on hard-hit ground balls and threw DiMaggio out each time. There is a little known story that DiMaggio and pal Lefty Gomez were in a cab, on their way to the ballpark in Cleveland for the game that day when the cab driver told Joe he thought his hitting streak would end tonight. Gomez became enraged and blasted the cab driver. The cab drivers prophecy came true. Since that afternoon, this record has never been challenged. During the streak, DiMaggio had been the subject of every newspaper, radio broadcast and newsreel in America. DiMaggio and the streak completely captured the imagination of the public. In fact, Yankee Hall-of-Fame first baseman Lou Gehrig, known as "The Iron Horse," for his tireless work ethic, passed away on June 2, 1941; and no one seemed to notice. It had been DiMaggio who hit in front of Gehrig in the Yankee lineup. That summer, the question most asked by baseball fans everywhere was,

"Did he get one?" (A hit) Joe, during the streak, actually hit better on the road (.434) than he did at home (.383) and would win the American League MVP Award that year, even though Ted Williams of the Boston Red Sox would hit .406 for the season. The writers of those days had seen .400 recorded a few years earlier, but no one had come close to hitting in 56 consecutive games. Neither feat has been duplicated since. Even today if you say 56 or .406 to any real fan, they will instantly say, 1941. It's like a base-ball code.

Joe DiMaggio had spent his life trying to live up to how great we all wanted him to be, but he was extremely jealous that Ted hit .400 and he didn't. Williams, one of the game's very best hitters, would follow DiMaggio's results daily. Between batters, Ted would listen to a tran-sistor radio through a hole in the wall of Fenway's famed "Green Monster." He would then tell his teammate and Joe's younger brother Dominic, if Joe had gotten a hit. Dominic was Ted's best friend on the ball club beside Johnny Pesky and Bobby Doerr. It was quite a year and one of diversion as America moved unknowingly towards World War II.

There is an interesting picture taken during the 1936 World Series between the New York Giants and New York Yankees. In this picture, four players including DiMaggio are lined up facing away from the camera. The numbers on the back of their jerseys standing side by side say 1-9-3-6 in reference to the year of the Series. The four pictured are Joe Moore (NYG), Joe DiMaggio (NYY), George Selkirk (NYY), and Travis Jackson (NYG). That's right; DiMaggio wore # 9 during his rookie season before making the # 5 famous. Imagine that, Ted Williams and Joe DiMaggio could have worn the same number throughout their careers. Of the four, only DiMaggio is looking back at the camera. I was later able to get him to sign the photo for me. The other interesting observation is that George Selkirk was wearing # 3 for the Yankees which everybody knows had been worn by the great Babe Ruth. Well, Ruth was no longer with the Yankees in 1936. He had joined the Boston Braves in 1935, and his Yankee number had not yet been retired. DiMaggio was given the # 9 in his first season because Yankee great, Frankie Crosetti was wearing the # 5. In 1937, Crosetti agreed to change his jersey to # 1 and retired at the end of the following year. Now you know the rest of the story. By the way, Joe's brother Dominic of the Red Sox wore # 7 just like Mickey Mantle of the Yankees.

He was born Giuseppe Paolo DiMaggio, Jr. on November 25, 1914, in Martinez, California. Joe was a high school dropout who fell in love with the game of baseball. He would develop into what scouts called a five-tool player. Both his brothers Vince and Dominic would play professional baseball. He was a 3-time MVP winner and a 13-time All Star. In fact, he is still the only player to be selected to the All-Star team in every year that he played. Joe was also the first baseball player to break the $100,000 mark in earnings for a single-season. He served in the United States Army Air Force, rising to the rank of sergeant. He was a 9-time World Series Champion and was inducted into the Baseball Hall of Fame in 1955. He was married twice, once to Dorothy Arnold (1937) and once to Marilyn Monroe (1954). There is no doubt that the great DiMaggio was a loner. Trapped by his fame, he roomed by himself on the road and spent his free time out of sight. He admitted that he went to the ballpark four or five hour's early on game day just to have some time to himself. He retired on December 11, 1951, after several years of playing, with injuries. He was only 36 years of age. When asked why, he said, "I no longer have it." For the rest of his life, he would be immortalized in music, television, commercials, film, and literature. As singer Paul Simon wrote, "Where have you gone Joe DiMaggio, a nation turns it's lonely eyes to you."

The autograph and memorabilia craze took hold nationwide during the early eighties, as millions of fans who were kids in the forties and fifties finally grew up. Baseball card shows sprang up all over the country and athletes were given extraordinary opportunities to make lots of money selling their signature. Joe DiMaggio took full advantage of this craze and charged outrageous prices for his "John Hancock." He also limited what he would autograph and refused to sign anything that had been already signed by another player. I know this for a fact as I tried to get him to sign his brother Dom DiMaggio's book, entitle <u>Real Grass, Real Heroes.</u> Dom had already signed and Joe refused. I remember uttering under my breath as I left his table, "It's your brother's book, you dummy."

The last time I saw Joe DiMaggio in person was in Dallas, Texas, at the 1995 All-Star game. The baseball world buzzed with the news that the "Yankee Clipper" would make a rare appearance at "The Ballpark in Arlington," before the game and Mickey Mantle was making what no one knew at the time would be his final appearance in public. A few days before the game, Mantle went on local TV and pleaded for kids not to follow in his footsteps. "I'm not a role model, don't be like me," said Mantle. He had received a liver transplant, as his was damaged by years of alcohol abuse; and he asked baseball fans everywhere to consider being an organ donor. He would later die in August at a local Dallas hospital.

There have been literately hundreds of thousands of words written about Joe DiMaggio, so anything I have written here could be redundant. I will say, that all my older baseball friends including ex-major league scouts who actually saw DiMaggio play, all say the same thing. Williams, yeah he could hit, Mantle he had power and yes Mays could do it all but... If you haven't seen Joe DiMaggio play, then you haven't seen the real thing. Nevertheless, Joe DiMaggio's 56-game hit streak lives on. That record is often compared to Johnny Unitas' throwing at least one touchdown in 47 consecutive games or Martina Navratilova's winning 74 straight matches in tennis. DiMaggio's record may never be broken.

So, did Joe DiMaggio really have everything he wanted out of life? I don't think so. He confessed to being born shy and after his retirement from the Yankees, he often talked about how intense he had been as a ballplayer and later a businessman. That's why he never managed; he was always tight as a knot inside. He reminded me of a duck in the water. On top of the water the duck looked calm, cool and collected but underneath the water, he was always paddling like hell. I think DiMaggio lived and died a lonely man, suffocated by his fame, fortune, arrogance, and the loss of the only woman he ever really loved, Marilyn Monroe

Joe DiMaggio finished his baseball career with a .325 average, hit 361 home runs, and recorded 1,537 RBI's. His slugging percentage of .579 remains one of the highest in baseball history. Remarkably, he only struck out 369 times, in his career. Following lung cancer surgery in October of 1998, Joe would fall ill again in December and never recover. On March 8, 1999, he would die at the age of 84. He is buried in Hollywood, Florida. Even though he was immortalized most of his life, I still don't think we knew or understood the real Joe DiMaggio.

Pals

V in Scully, longtime Brooklyn Dodgers' announcer, would begin the game's line-up like this: "Starting at shortstop, # 1, 'Pee Wee' Reese." Another of the "Boys of Summer" has gone on to join his teammates in heaven. Harold Henry Reese was born July 23, 1918 in Ekron, Kentucky, a stone's throw south of Louisville, Kentucky. This son of a railroad detective would grow to be five feet nine inches tall and weigh 140 pounds. Scully would later say, "Reese was # 1 on your scorecard and number one in our hearts." He would later become known as the "Little Colonel," but first he received the nickname Pee Wee, at age 12, where he spent most of his time knuckling down over a circle of marbles. Pee Wee won the city championship and went on to place second to the National Champion. Kids in the thirties and forties called their marbles many names like "mibs," "ducks," "peewees," and "steelies." Whether you were playing for keeps or playing for fair, marbles was a serious game, and many kids were experts in collecting the other guys' marbles.

Pee Wee joined the Louisville Colonels Club of the American Association of Baseball in 1938 as a shortstop and spent two years there. This club was bought by the

Boston Red Sox to gain the rights of this slick fielding short-stop; but their current shortstop Joe Cronin was not ready to retire, so Reese's contract was sold to Branch Rickey of the Dodgers, for $40,000. He arrived in Brooklyn in 1940. His Dodger days were initially cut short when he was hurt during his first season with a broken foot and also got hit in the head by a pitch. Reese became a regular in 1941 and helped Brooklyn win its first pennant in 21 years. As with most players, World War II took him away for three years (1943-45). He returned to Brooklyn in 1946 to become a complete player who, despite limited power, helped make the offense go. He also became the anchor on defense, of a team that won seven National League pennants in twelve seasons. This ten-time All-Star was given another title by the team, "The Captain." From then on, it would be Pee Wee Reese, not the manager, who brought out the line-up card to the umpires at the start of their games.

Reese's teammates poured praise on the shortstop. Duke Snider said, "He was the greatest Dodger of them all." He was so much more than a player. He was the voice in the clubhouse and the team's conscience on the field. Pee Wee Reese was everybody's "pal." After catcher Roy Campanella's accident, it was Pee Wee who chose to roll Roy's wheelchair out onto the field in front of 90,000 fans on "Campanella Night," at the Los Angeles Coliseum. This is the same guy who sat quietly by pitcher Ralph Branca, who cried in the clubhouse after he had given up the winning home run to Bobby Thomson of the Giants, during the final game of the 1951 National League pennant race. He was "the salt of the earth," as my dad would say. Pee Wee stood the tallest in 1947, when teammate Jackie Robinson was catching hell from the Cincinnati Reds bench and their fans. Pee Wee simply walked over to Jackie and placed his hand on Robinson's shoulder. As he spoke to Jackie, the crowd began to settle down; and some say the face of baseball changed forever. This show of sportsmanship by a white southerner to a black teammate helped pave the way for many great-players of color. There is a bronze statue of Reese and Robinson that stands in KeySpan Park in Brooklyn, New York. It depicts this gesture of the teammates. It was unveiled on November 1, 2005.

Reese was elected to the Baseball Hall of Fame in 1984. Besides being a superb fielder and a great base runner, Reese had accumulated over 2,100 hits, scored 1,338 runs (best of any Dodger), and finished eight times in the top ten for MVP candidate. In his career, Reese also recorded 885 RBI's, 126 home runs, and 252 stolen bases during a time in the game when shortstops were known for their fielding. He would also become a World Champion in 1955, when the Brooklyn Dodgers beat the New York Yankees. Interestingly, Reese and Yankee catcher Elston Howard hold the record for playing in the most World Series for the losing team (six each).

Reese married Dorothy "Dottie" Walton on March 29, 1942. She and their two children survived Pee Wee. Reese moved with the team to Los Angeles, California in 1957 and played until 1958, when he was then replaced by Charlie Neal, another black ballplayer. He would stay with the now Los Angeles Dodgers during the 1959 season as a coach, and he earned his second World Series ring. After retirement, Reese joined with Hall of Fame pitcher Dizzy Dean on CBS Television (1960-65) and then Curt Gowdy on NBC (1966-68) to call play-by-play. After his retirement from television, you could find him working at Hillerich & Bradsby, makers of Louisville Slugger bats.

I was lucky enough to meet Pee Wee on an autograph tour. I had purchased a Brooklyn Dodger uniform with Reese's number from Mitchell and Ness. Reese signed his name in blue sharpie just under the spot where his heart would be. How appropriate, this little guy had a lot of heart.

It's with much sadness that I inform you that on August 14, 1999, Pee Wee Reese , at age 81, will now take his place in the Dodger line-up in heaven, along with Gil Hodges, Carl Furillo, Roy Campanella, Jackie Robinson and the rest of "Dem Bums," and I bet he's still wearing # 1. Reese had battled lung cancer since 1997. Teammate Carl Erskine once said about Pee Wee, "He never shouted, and he played every day. He didn't have to say anything, he just showed everyone." You know, it's tough when you lose your pals.

Swing, Batter; Batter, Swing

Three-year old Taylor called him "Granddad," and his friends called him Jimmy. He was a farm boy who grew up chasing rabbits and working hard on his family's spread. Sure, he went fishing, camping and even hunted a bit, as did every kid from the country. But Jimmy had another passion, baseball. God had blessed Jimmy with a slingshot right arm and the grit to let it go. He was what scouts called a "high school phenom." He posted a twenty-six and two record with five no-hitters, for a small school in Hertford, North Carolina, while local folks sat in the stands and hollered, "Swing, batter; batter, swing." Not only was Jimmy attracting attention locally, but his success placed him on the fast track straight to the Major Leagues. At nineteen years of age, he left the "Tar Heel" state for the first time and joined the Kansas City Athletics for $75,000. That, my friends, was all the money in the world to a country boy in the sixties. With no stop in the Minors, Jimmy went to "The hill" for the first time on May 13, 1965. He also pitched well enough for the A's to be elected to his first All-Star team, in 1966. The team moved to Oakland, California, from Kansas City, Missouri, early in 1968, and again Jimmy shined in the spotlight as he pitched a perfect game against the Minnesota Twins, on May 8, 1968. At age twenty-two he had faced Killebrew, Carew, Tovar, Oliva, and Allison, with the charm of an axe murderer, a fastball that hated wood, and pinpoint control, to record the seventh perfect game in modern baseball history. There have only been a total of seventeen perfect games pitched.

Jimmy put together his first winning season in Oakland, while posting an 18-14 record, in 1970. It only got better from there. Jimmy won twenty or more games in five consecutive seasons, from 1971 to 1975. His best season occurred in 1974, when he won his only Cy Young Award, after a 25-12, 2.49 ERA season with the A's. This eight-time All-Star led the American League in at least one major pitching category, eight times.

With all his success on the field, Jimmy will also be remembered for a bookkeeping blunder by the Athletics. When part of Jimmy's salary was paid late to a third party for a tax-free annuity fund, he cried foul and claimed breach of contract and won free agency. This so called "free agency" had not yet become part of baseball's basic agreement, and top salaries of the day rarely reached 300,000 a year. Jimmy was able to parlay his pitching success into a $3.75 million contract with the New York Yankees, spread over a five-year period. Not only had Jimmy become the cornerstone of baseball's big-money era, but he rejuvenated the Yankees and taught them how to win. In 1975, he also became the highest-paid pitcher in the Major Leagues. The New York Yankees won three straight pennants with Jimmy, from 1976 to 1978.

Jimmy retired from the Yankees in 1979, at the age of thirty-three. Jimmy had always kidded that, "My brothers taught me to throw strikes, and thanks to that, I gave up

379 home runs in the big leagues." His once strong right arm was now weak from over-use and he began to suffer from the effects of diabetes. Jimmy had gotten paid "big time" for throwing lots of fastballs; but in doing so; cut his career short by several years. So Jimmy packed up and went home to North Carolina to be with his family, his dogs and his memories. I bet he did some fishing too.

He was diagnosed in November of 1998 with ALS, better known as Lou Gehrig's disease. Determined to fight for his life he started a foundation to raise money for a cure and to show that people with ALS were not bound to wheelchairs. There is no cure for ALS and soon this dreaded disease left him without the use of his arms and hands. On August 8, Jimmy took a bad fall down some stairs. He spent several days in the hospital unconscious, but recovered well enough to go home. On September 9, 1999 Jimmy was finally called "out" in the game of life. Jimmy never questioned what had happened to him and said that he "trusted in the good Lord." Yankee owner George Steinbrenner said, "This one took me hard." Jimmy was only fifty-three years of age.

Many things have been written about the A's owner, Charlie O. Finley and, yes, he was the one to give Jimmy his nickname, "Catfish." Finley thought that every ballplayer should have a nickname, to provide color and a way for the fans to identify with the players. Finley also paid his players to grow mustaches, and he provided those green and gold uniforms to attract attention. So when this country boy with a great smile, covered by a thick mustache, talked to reporters with that smooth Carolina accent, they realized that "Catfish" was the perfect nickname; and to Finley's credit, the nickname would end up on James Augustus "Catfish" Hunter's Hall-of-Fame Plaque in

1987. Interestingly enough, Jim Catfish Hunter's Plaque pictures him with no insignia on his cap. He had spoken highly of both the Oakland A's and the New York Yankees. His appreciation for owners Charlie O. Finley and George Steinbrenner made it impossible to choose between the two teams. He joined the Cubs' favorite, Billy Williams, in Cooperstown. Oakland also retired Jimmy's uniform # 27.

Jimmy was born on April 8, 1946, in Hertford, North Carolina, the youngest of eight children. During his senior year in high school, Jim lost one of his toes in a hunting accident. This very well could have jeopardized his baseball career, but the Kansas City A's would roll the dice. Jimmy did not let them down. Jimmy won 224 games while losing only 166. He posted a 3.26 earned-run average and recorded 2,012 strikeouts in his 15- year career. Jimmy was a five-time World Series Champion, three times with the A's and twice with the Yanks. Jimmy hit six home runs in his career while holding Hank Aaron, Orlando Cepeda, Harmon Killebrew, Mickey Mantle, Brooks Robinson, Frank Robinson and Carl Yastrzemski to a .211 collective batting average. One of my favorite quotes from Jimmy was about his teammate Reggie Jackson and it went like this, "He (Reggie) would give you the shirt off his back. Then he'd call a press conference to announce it." That sure sounds like Reggie to me. Jimmy would be remembered in song and movies long after his death. Bob Dylan, Joe Cocker, Kinky Friedman and Bobby Hollowell all wrote songs about him, while in the motion picture, *The Bad News Bears,* the coach asked one of his players, "Who do you think you are, Catfish Hunter?" The kid responded, "Who's he?" Hertford, North Carolina holds an annual softball event every year in Jimmy's memory. The tournament has collected over $100,000 since 1999, with all proceeds going to ALS research.

You may wonder why I called him Jimmy throughout this piece, until the end. You see, I'm from North Carolina, and he was always just Jimmy to us. If you happen to travel the backwoods baseball fields of North Carolina, you can still hear the fans holler, "Swing, batter; batter, swing!" They all loved Jimmy, period.

No Place to Hide

Hard fouls, that's what they thought it took to stop him from beating them. His body took the most brutal pounding of any basketball player ever. Constant double and triple-teaming by opposing teams wore on him. "Half the fouls against him were hard fouls," exclaimed Boston Celtic center, Tommy Heinsohn. "Take him down" or "Don't let him shoot" could be heard from the opposing coach in every huddle. Free-throw shooting was his only weakness, and opposing teams were ruthless at exploiting this area of his game. Every time he touched the ball he would be hacked, pushed, or pulled on, in an all-out effort to send him to the free-throw line. "Intentional fouls" against him became part of every opposing team's game plan. Unfortunately, time and time again, this tactic proved effective against him. He was one of the worst free-throw shooters in the NBA history, with a career percentage of only .511, meaning he missed almost half. But interestingly enough, only his demeanor kept him from retaliating. Why, because, he preferred to play though the fouls. He feared his own strength; he feared what could happen if he lost his "cool."

Wilton Norman "Wilt" Chamberlain was a giant among men. In real life, he was a "Goliath" without the nasty attitude. At 7'1" tall and 275 pounds when he came into the league, he could do or say whatever he wanted; but he did not. The facts are that he was taller and stronger than any player he ever lined up against, but still, he was a nice guy; and most would agree he was one of the top three best basketball players in the history of the game. He was not an enforcer and in fact only fouled out of two games during his college career. He knew how to control his body and his emotions and rarely got into altercations. Yet, even with all the punishment he endured, he stills holds nearly 100 NBA records. Yes, you heard right, nearly one hundred NBA records. In fact, his name appears so often in the record book that you could use it as the answer to any question concerning an NBA scoring record, and most of the time, you would be right. That's the reason why they fouled him so hard and often, simply because he was basketball's most unstoppable force. Announcers created words for his offensive skills like "slam dunk," "finger rolls," and "fade-away jump shots." His pure physical strength forced them to create rule changes to try and harness his awesome power. Widening the lane, three second rule, offensive goaltending, and alternating possessions instead of the jump ball, were some of the new rules implemented to level the playing field for his opponents. So how did he respond to all the physical force used against him? He got bigger and stronger until his playing weight approached 300 pounds. When Hall-of-Fame guard, Oscar Robertson, was once asked by the *Philadelphia Daily News* if Chamberlain were the best ever? His response was, "The record books don't lie."

"Wilt the Stilt" (a name he hated) was born August 21, 1936, in West Philadelphia, Pennsylvania. Wilt was born the sixth of nine brothers and sisters. The Chamberlain family was reared in a four-bedroom house located in a middle-class neighborhood, by two parents who loved each other very much. They were both generous and hard-working folks who were married for 46 years before Wilt's dad died in 1968. As a youngster, Wilt washed windows, shoveled snow and delivered newspapers to provide himself with spending money. He had a huge appetite for information and would bet on almost anything from a football game to the population of Chicago. Interestingly enough, he always wanted to be a lawyer. By the age of twelve, he had grown to 6' 3", had finally stopped sucking his thumb, and had also discovered a new way to make money. Wilt would pull a wagon down to the produce section of town known as Second Street and fill the wagon with watermelons, cantaloupes and tomatoes. Then he would go door to door in his neighborhood trying to sell his produce, shouting, "Watermelon Man." "Turned a good profit," laughed Wilt. It's funny, here was a guy who would have a slew of nicknames as he grew older, yet he chose, as a kid, to call himself, "the Watermelon Man." When he was young, his family and most of his close friends called him "Dip," "Dippy," or "Dipper." Then for obvious reasons, Dipper evolved into the nickname he liked most, "The Big Dipper," because of the way he had to dip his head when he entered through a doorway. While growing up, the "Big Dipper" also participated in the Police Athletic League in the city and competed against other future great players, such as Tom Gola and Guy Rodgers. It was during his childhood that Wilt started wearing rubber bands around his wrist. Seems that his socks were always falling down and he used the rubber bands to hold them up. It eventually became a superstition for Wilt.

He drew national attention while playing basketball and participating in track and field events at Overbrook High School. He once scored 90 points in one basketball game, while leading his team to the City Championships, in 1954 and 1955. "I could have scored more," said Wilt, "but the other team tried to freeze the ball." He would also average 38.2 points per game in his high school career and be named to the 1955 All-American Team. During high school, he grew to 6'11" tall and was very agile for his age. In fact, Wilt was so much taller than everyone else that his coaches actually had the team practice *missing* free throws, so he could get the rebound and score! It was in high school that Wilt began to realize that his height would become the overwhelming dominant factor in his life. He had a need to prove he was good and smart, not just big. Banging his head on doorways, clothes that didn't fit, and sleeping with his feet hanging off the bed were just some of the things he began to deal with on a daily basis. His senior year, Wilt would be recruited by more than 200 colleges and universities, 77 major universities, and 125 small colleges. Wilt narrowed his choices to four schools: Michigan, Indiana, Dayton and Kansas. You can't imagine all the recruiting violations that occurred in the fifties. While on one trip to visit the University of Kansas, Missouri coach Wilber Stalcup intercepted Wilt at the airport and said, "Boy, how'd you like to be the first Negro to play at the University of Missouri?" Wilt answered, "I think I'd rather be the second one." Remember this was 1955. He would also be drafted right out of high school by Eddie Gottlieb, the owner of the Philadelphia Warriors, but choose to head to Kansas instead. There would be no place to hide for the "Big Dipper."

His track and field exploits would find him high jumping, running in the 440-yard and 880-yard races, and dominating the shot-put event. Because of his height, he owned a nine-foot stride which gave him tremendous speed. At the end of the 1955 season, he would leave Overbrook to play basketball for the University of Kansas. He had led his high school team to a 58-3 record and scored 2,252 points in his career. In 1955, NCAA rules prohibited freshmen from playing on the varsity club in college, so Wilt would make his presence known during the annual freshman vs. varsity game. "We whipped 'em, 81-71. I had 40 or 42 points, about 30 rebounds, about 15 blocks. I knew I had to show them either I could do it or I couldn't," roared Wilt. In the winter of 1956, Chamberlain would get his first start for the Jayhawks' varsity squad and set a new Kansas record by scoring 52 points against Northwestern University. During the spring, he would continue to show his athletic dominance by winning the high-jump and shot-put competition at the Big Eight Track and Field Championships. In 1957, Wilt would lead the 24-2 Kansas Jayhawks' basketball team to the finals of the NCAA Championships. Their opponent would be the 31-0 Tar Heels from the University of North Carolina, led by Hall-of-Fame coach, Frank McGuire. Coach McGuire claims he told his team before game time, "We are playing Wilt, not Kansas—just stop him and don't worry about those other guys on the team—they're not all that good."

Final score: UNC 54...Kansas 53, in triple overtime. He had scored 23 of Kansas' points in the loss. Wilt remained bitterer about that loss than any other single game in his entire career. It was this very game that started all the

"Wilt's a loser" garbage that was written about him for the rest of his career. Chamberlain was named the tournament's Most Outstanding Player. In 1958, Wilt would set another Kansas mark by pulling down 36 rebounds against Iowa. In two years, Wilt had been elected a Unanimous First Team All-American (1957-1958), *The Sporting News* First Team All-American (1958), All Big-Seven Team (1957-1958), won two conference championships (1957-1958), scored 1,433 points (29.9 average),and grabbed 877 rebounds (18.3 average). "Unstoppable" was an understatement. "Loser" was simply not true.

He would forego his senior year at Kansas to make some real money. When asked why he had chosen Kansas to play basketball, the answer was simply, "Dr. Forrest C. Allen." "Phog" Allen, as he was known, had been the head coach at Kansas since 1920, and was a legend in college basketball. By 1955, he had won almost 600 games, 22 conference championships, and one national title. "The spending money and car I received on the side wasn't bad either," exclaimed Wilt. Chamberlain estimated that he received between $20,000 to $25,000 dollars while he was at Kansas; and three years later, the university would serve two years of probation for breaking NCAA rules. Something else Wilt would experience in the Midwest was that discrimination and segregation were as rampant here as they were in the South. Wilt made sure coach Allen knew that he expected to eat, sleep and ride with the team and, if not, he would leave Kansas. Teams like Rice, Southern Methodist, Louisiana State, and Texas Christian were quickly removed from the schedule. Unfortunately, Coach Allen was removed also. At the age of 70, Allen was asked to retire and was replaced by Dick Harp. With Coach Allen retired and lots of heat being placed on Wilt and the program by the NCAA, he decided to move away from college basketball. Hello, "Sweet Georgia Brown."

Wilt joined the Harlem Globetrotters on July 12, 1958 in Milan, Italy. Trotter favorite, "Goose" Tatum lived in Kansas City during the off season and had befriended Wilt while he was in college. With some prodding from Goose, Wilt, at the age of 21 was now ready to play some serious basketball. The Globetrotters paid him 65,000 dollars and took Wilt on a worldwide tour of Europe. They played in every kind of arena available. Bullfight rings, wheat fields, tennis courts, and empty swimming pools were just some of the make-do courts where they would perform. Trotter stars like "Curly" Neal, Marques Haynes, "Sweetwater" Clifton, "Showboat" Hall and "Meadowlark" Lemon would show him how the world of basketball and showmanship merged together. Owner Abe Saperstein was considered the P. T. Barnum of basketball at that time and it was his idea to start Wilt at point guard. Since 1927, the Harlem Globetrotters had entertained literally millions of people all around the world and Wilt was now a part of their history. "I played with the Harlem Globetrotters and we won 445 games in a row," he said smiling, "and they were all on the road." He would play a little over one year with the Globetrotters.

Next stop, the Philadelphia Warriors. In 1958, the newspapers reported that Wilt signed for $35,000, which would make him the highest paid player in the league at that time, but it was really closer to $100,000. His NBA debut occurred on September 9, 1959, against the St. Louis Hawks in an exhibition game. Wilt, wearing No. 13, scored 28 points, and the Warriors won 106-102. Philadelphia's home opener was played against the Detroit Pistons, and again Wilt shined while scoring 36 points and pulling down

34 rebounds in a win, 120-112. In his first game against the Boston Celtics, opposing center Bill Russell blocked one of Wilts shots during the Celtics' win. That's all the Boston media would talk about for days, even though Wilts shot had been blocked several times before by others, in the past. In Wilt's second game against Boston, Wilt would destroy Russell by outscoring him 45-15, out rebounding him 35-13, and pushed the Warriors past the Celtics, 123-113. So, "the rivalry" would be born and, in a lot of ways, is still been talked about today. Chamberlain versus Russell, who do you think was best? Wilt would go on to have a terrific rookie season, even though he would miss a few games and a few teeth, compliments of one of the dirtiest players in the game, Hawks' center Clyde Lovellette. It seems that Wilt's mouth, along with his two front teeth, got in the way of Clyde's elbow. Wilt would be forced to wear a mask for protection. Chamberlain ended his first year with a 37.6 scoring average, while hauling in 26.9 rebounds per game. As a rookie, he would lead his last place team to the playoffs. He would win the 1960 NBA Rookie-of-the-Year Award and the Most-Valuable-Player Award. It was the first time anyone had ever won both awards in the same year. Wes Unseld would be the only other player to accomplish that feat. Wilt was also selected the starting center for the All-Star game and ended up winning that game's MVP Award, too. The Warriors moved to San Francisco to begin the 1963 season, and it would be Wilt's last year with that organization. Wilt traded? Unbelievable! He would find himself back home in Philadelphia with the 76ers for the start of the 1964 season. He would be traded again to the Los Angeles Lakers before the 1968 season and then finish his career there in 1973.

His career basketball accomplishments are literally too many to list here. It would take pages to recap. So let's just—highlight a few of his most unbelievable achievements. He is the only NBA player to score 4,000 points in a season. He averaged 50.4 points per game during the 1961-62 seasons while playing 48.5 minutes per game, two incredible records. He is still tops in rebounds for a career, with 23,924, and is now fourth in scoring, with a total of 31,419 points. During the 14 seasons he played, Wilt led the NBA in scoring for 7 years and rebounding for 11 years. He was the first NBA player to make more than half his shots (50.5%) in a season. During the 1967-68 seasons he became the only center to lead the NBA in assists. He set the NBA single-game records for most points (100), most consecutive field goals (18), and most rebounds (55). Wilt scored over 50+ points in a record 118 games and still holds the record for highest field-goal percentage in a season, at .727. Also, his No. 13 jersey is retired by five different basketball teams: University of Kansas, Harlem Globetrotters, Philadelphia 76ers, Golden State Warriors, and Los Angeles Lakers. The "Big Dipper" would win two NBA Championships during his career, first with the Philadelphia 76ers in 1967, and then in 1972, with the Los Angeles Lakers. Last but not least, Wilt never fouled out of a professional basketball game, but, he was ejected three times.

In regards to Wilt's height, *Los Angeles Times* columnist Jim Murray once wrote, "Even in the summer, Wilt has snow on top. If he ever gets tired of basketball, he could rent himself out as a community antenna. To rush him to the hospital, you'd need a hook and ladder." You see, Wilt's legs were disproportionately long for the rest of his body. His pants leg required a 41-inch seam, and it did appear that he was walking on stilts. I met Wilt in Houston in the early nineties at an autograph show. I had him sign a book for me and noticed that his hands were as big as shovels. His voice was incredibly deep, as if he were talking in a canyon. He was wearing long pants which, from an appearance standpoint, exaggerated the length of his legs. He also walked gingerly from the many knee surgeries performed during his playing days. I have to say, his leg length was not as noticeable when he wore his uniform shorts and those knee-high socks. There was also a reason Wilt wore those long socks and knee pads. Every summer, Wilt's family would travel to Virginia to see relatives and Wilt would suffer from a tremendous number of mosquito bites, which left permanent scars on his legs. The socks were used to cover up the scars and protect them. Standing in line watching and listening to him, I can't imagine what it would have been like to face this guy on the court.

On October 12, 1999, the "Big Dipper" left this world as he had entered, quietly and in his sleep. Wilt was found dead in his bed at home, in Los Angeles, California, which he had named "Ursa Major," after the constellation containing the stars that form the "Big Dipper," his trademark in the world of basketball. He had suffered for several years from heart problems and was under the care of several cardiologists and physicians. His death was officially ruled a heart attack. Wilt was inducted into the Basketball Hall of Fame in 1978 and also elected in 1996 as one of the 50 Greatest Players in NBA History. He was a life-long bachelor and fathered no known children. Wilt was a DJ in college, an actor, celebrity, and businessman after basketball. He flirted with coaching basketball, becoming a professional boxer, was offered a contract to play pro football with the Kansas City Chiefs and also played professional volleyball in the late seventies. He enjoyed auto-racing, water skiing and once met Nikita Khrushchev. He owned three Great Danes, many fast cars, including a Rolls Royce and a few harness horses for racing. In his short 63 years, no other player in the NBA had made such an impact. Throughout his career, Wilt was fond of saying that "Nobody roots for Goliath." There is no doubt fans will continue to talk about him for years to come.

King of the One-Night Stands

He was tall and lanky with a "funny bone" the size of Mars. He was so skinny that when he stuck out his tongue and turned sideways he would resemble a zipper. Some say he was so thin that he had to run around in the shower to get wet. Do you get the picture? When watching him you would swear he was double-jointed in every part of his body. His very long neck, arms and legs appeared rubbery and capable of being placed at any angle. It was once said, that his body looked like it had been assembled by someone who had trouble reading the instructions. That face may have been the most outrageous part of his body and, in fact, he had enough nose to mind everybody's business. With a nose that big and pointed, some swore that if he ever fell face-forward in the dirt, it would take two weeks to dig him out. Even with his knees "shot" and his back a mess, he never missed a show until 1993, always coached for the home team, and constantly worried about not being able to make the fans laugh. He once said, "My biggest fear was hearing someone say, you know that guy used to be funny." In more than fifty years' time, he traveled over seven million miles and performed over 4,500 one night stands in every small town that had a ballpark in the USA, Canada and Mexico. From Albuquerque, New Mexico to Durham, North Carolina; from Appleton, Wisconsin to Sumter, South Carolina; from Tucson, Arizona, to Chattanooga, Tennessee; from Toledo, Ohio to Salt lake City, Utah and from Midland, Texas to New Britain, Connecticut; he showed up at ballparks time and time again to do what he did best, make people laugh. I guess you could consider him a stand-up comic, but the big difference was that his show was always the same, never changed. If you saw his show at the ballpark with your dad at the age of 11, you would see the same show with your son when you were 30. He didn't perform an act, he *was* the act. His specialty was children, and he drew kids to the ballpark like horseflies are drawn to spare ribs. His show always started at the beginning of the third inning whether the crowd was made up of only four people, like on July 20, 1969 in Great Falls, Montana, (as the rest of the world watched Neil Armstrong walk on the moon) or if the crowd was over 70,000 as in Cleveland, Ohio during the Indians' 1948 championship season. He was indeed the king of the one night stands.

Max Patkin spent 51 of his 79 years making folks laugh. He was born on January 10, 1920, in Philadelphia, Pennsylvania. His love for the game of baseball led him to the pitcher's mound for a minor league team known as the Wisconsin Rapids. An arm injury curtailed his career, and Max joined the Navy during WWII. During the war he would end up stationed in Honolulu, Hawaii, pitching in a pick-up game against other major and minor leaguers. One of those other players hit a Patkin fastball 500 feet into the warm Hawaiian air. His name was Joe DiMaggio and, as Joe began to circle the bases, Max began to run behind him, mimicking DiMaggio's famous home run trot.

The crowd roared and a star was born. Even the staunch-faced DiMaggio laughed. Max continued to develop his clown act throughout the war. By 1947, after the end of the war, Max caught the attention of "the P. T. Barnum of Major League Baseball," Cleveland Indians owner Bill Veeck. Veeck hired two of what he called his team's "clown coaches." Jackie Price was one and Max Patkin the other. These two created outrageous comedy acts with the intention to not only entertain the fans at the game, but to draw additional fans to view the game. Patkin's act would have him take over the home team's first-base coaching job in the third inning, and the third-base coaching job in the fourth inning. He would show the home town team's catcher how to catch in the fifth inning, before returning to first base; and finally in the sixth inning, Max would grab a bat to show the home town's team how to hit. Eventually Patkin would be thrown out of the game and the gig was over. "It was a corny act," said Patkin, "but the fans liked it." Price, on the other hand, would take his act a bit further by shagging fungo's in a jeep, while riding around in the outfield and then unzip his fly and catch an 80 mph fastball in his pants.

At the end of the 1949 season, Veeck sold the Indians, and Max took his act on the road to minor league ballparks everywhere. He had been convinced by Veeck, DiMaggio and others that his slap-stick routine would be a hit with fans while keeping him close to the game he loved. Max would from that day forward be known as "the Clown Prince of Baseball." If you have seen Max Patkin work or watched his scene in the movie "Bull Durham," what I'm about to describe will be familiar. First is the way he looked (described above) and second is the way he dressed. It was a huge baggy pin-striped uniform that was worn, from repeated use. Even though he had three uniforms, they all looked like they should have been thrown away many years earlier. A large question mark decorated the back of the uniform where the number would be and his cap was tri-colored and seemed to only fit his head when it was on crooked. As for his hi-jinx, he could take a mouth full of water and create a huge geyser spout from his mouth, sometimes as many as five or six times. This geyser would be spit straight up into the air as if "Old Smokey" had erupted. While making the most God-awful facial expressions, Max would constantly slap his chest and pants like someone trying to find their car keys. He would give wacky signs to the hitters while flapping his arms like wings and making noises, while his favorite song "Rock Around the Clock" blared throughout the park. Max called "time out" a lot, argued with umpires, and often ran to the wrong base. Patkin thought nothing of hitting with two bats and was often thrown at by opposing pitchers, all a part of the act. He seemed to have the most fun with catchers. Patkin loved to crawl between their legs when running to home plate or push them over while they tried to catch a pitched ball. Of course, stealing the catcher's glove was also a big hit with the fans. The trick was to know when to pull these hi-jinx and when not to. In a 10-0 ball game, Max could be an absolute riot, but then his act would be toned down during a no-hitter or a very close game.

I had the privilege of seeing Max Patkin in real life, twice, not counting the movie "Bull Durham." The first time was in Corpus Christi, Texas at a minor league game and the second time was in Houston, Texas at a card signing show. I had him sign his book for me and asked him about the movie. I had heard that his part had been changed and some of his work had been cut out of the movie. What I had heard was correct. In the original script of "Bull Durham," Patkin had asked Annie Savoy (played by Susan Sarandon) that after his death, he was to be cremated and she was to spread his ashes behind home plate and even place some in the rosin bag, so he would always stay in the game. Annie promised and Patkin later died in the original movie when he was hit by a train while driving beside the players' bus and clowning around. As promised, Annie does spread his ashes behind home plate and places a pinch in the rosin bag hoping that Max's love for the game would rub off on new pitcher Nuke LaLoosh. It was here that Patkin smiled and said to me, "They cut the scene out. People walked out of the sneak previews and said, 'Why did you have to kill the clown.'" Think about that. It could only happen to Max Patkin, getting killed on screen, playing himself.

Life on the road has its drawbacks and Patkin ran the gamut. His love for the game and acting cost him his marriage and sometimes his sanity. Max suffered a nervous breakdown in a dugout in Mexico City during the 1965 season. Luckily the game was rained out and with the help of a friend and lots of Valium, Patkin was able to perform the next night. Max was arrested in Valley Forge, Pennsylvania, while doing his show in a hospital gown. Seems the audience and management thought he was a mental patient from a hospital close by. It was never easy for Max until he stepped onto that field. Hours of sitting in hotel rooms waiting for game time would stir him up and make him feel insecure, always wondering if he could still be funny. His blood pressure would go off the charts; he suffered from insomnia, and a heart murmur.

Finally in 1994, his brother Eddie died, and Max's grief turned into full blown melancholia. He would visit the hospital many times the next few years. Xanax, Ritalin and group therapy became his way to cope and most of his close friends seemed to think it helped. His last show, 1993, was performed in Glen Falls, New York, but even he didn't know it at the time. Patkin's plight would reach the media and a story by the National Enquirer spurred the writing of over 5,000 letters to the "Clown Price of Baseball." These letters came from every state in America and 20 other countries. He even received letters from guys in prison. Max spent hundreds of dollars on postage sending them back an autographed baseball card of him self. It was important that he be remembered. (Wow, who could forget?)

Max Patkin, the "Clown Prince of Baseball," performed his last act from his hospital bed at Paoli Memorial Hospital in Pennsylvania. His doctors claimed he was handing out autographed baseball cards of himself the day before he died, unexpectedly, of an aneurysm. The date Patkin died was October 30, 1999, at the age of 79. Max has probably stood for the National Anthem more than any other man alive. Max Patkin had met and caroused with players who now seem more mythical then mortal. Tris Speaker, Ty Cobb, Babe Ruth, Satchel Paige, Josh Gibson, and of course Bill Veeck, were some of the many thousands of players Max had befriended. In fact, the great Jim Thorpe gave him the glove he used in his act. He suffered most of his life from chronic depression and stage fright, but most fans could never tell. He loved the attention, the ballplayers, and wanted badly to be remembered. Max always swore that pitcher Steve Carlton rubbed his nose for good luck one time and then won six straight games. Big Frank Howard received a kiss from Max one time and hit a home run his next at-bat. He *will* be remembered, as one of his uniforms now hangs in the Baseball Hall of Fame. The most interesting thing of all is that the very act he performed over and over again, in ballparks all over North America, was strictly forbidden in the rule book; yet the act still went on. Even now, it's hard to say "Max Patkin" without smiling; and for anyone who ever saw him, they— like me— will never forget. He didn't *used to be* funny, he was funny.

Easy

He made it all look so easy. The way his whole body seemed to glide and slide as he moved forward. His ability to feel the action behind him was unprecedented. He was able to read what was about to happen in front of him before it actually happened. It was as if he could see the whole field at once and even predict the future. He claimed that he never saw the guy closest to him, but always focused on the next guy instead. He knew that one little juke and he would be past that closest guy. His powerful legs cut like a buzz saw and seemed to be able to churn in any direction, as they moved under his body in unison. His balance was incredible as he only planted the balls and toes of his feet on the turf, while keeping his heals elevated. His body was able to absorb blows that would stop others in their tracks. He just never stopped running, always trying to gain ground. If he could not run away from you with his speed, he ran over you with his power; and if neither of those worked, he dived over the top of you with agility. He simply refused to be stopped. He arrived to work in a nasty mood, played with a bad attitude, and never finished a play by running out of bounds. He could also throw devastating blocks that left blitzing linebackers in a pile at the line of scrimmage. His waist was small, solid, invincible, and provided very little to grab hold of. His arms worked opposite each other as one was used as a weapon, strong and straight, to keep you away, while the other was flexed and coiled around the football as if the ball were attached to his body. His hands were worn and twisted on the outside from the constant pounding, but remained soft and intelligent when it came to carrying and catching the pigskin. The eyes were wide open, bright and burning with excitement. His head was owl-like and worked as if it were on a swivel. He was a running back in the National Football League, and maybe one of the best. The goal line was his objective, the end zone his prize, and glory was the result. Maybe it was easy for him, "Easy like Sunday morning."

He was born Walter Jerry Payton on July 25, 1954 in Columbia, Mississippi. Walter's parents, Peter and Alyne, saw that their kids would be reared in a hard-working, blue-collar atmosphere where local church and the Boy Scouts took their place of importance in Walter's life. He also sang in the church choir, long jumped for the track and field team, lettered in basketball, and was an avid member of the school band, where he played the drums. In fact, Walter did not even play football until his junior year at Jefferson High School, but boy, did he play then. The story goes that Walter lost a bet to another band member and the penalty was that he had to try out for the high school football team. That was some penalty, huh? Football fans everywhere now sit and wonder what they would have missed if he had continued to play the drums in the band instead of running for touchdowns. He quickly became one of the team's featured players as a running back and in fact gained 65 yards on his first carry in a high school game. His senior year almost became a disaster, when his school integrated with an all-white high school. He was forced to attend Columbia High School and, even with all the racial tension, led his team to an 8-2 record and earned a spot on the Mississippi All-State football team. He had no idea that this game was about to take him to the very pinnacle of success in the world of football.

At 5' 10" tall and 203 pounds in high school, Payton was overlooked by most colleges as too small or lacking experience. Eddie, Walter's older brother, had attended and played football for the Tigers at Jackson State University, so Walter would follow in his footsteps. As a member of the Tigers, Walter amassed 3,500 yards of offense while averaging 6.1 yards per carry, during his career. He also broke the NCAA scoring record by rushing for 65 touchdowns during his time at Jackson State. Payton finished fourth in the Heisman Trophy voting and many believed that if he had attended a better-known university, he may have won the award. Payton always said his real reward was the Bachelor's degree in Communications that he earned in 1975, from Jackson State, at the age of 20. During his time at Jackson State, Walter played along side many future NFL players, including Robert Brazile, Jackie Slater, and Jerome Barkum.

January 28, 1975 would be a day that Walter would remember for the rest of his life. He was drafted in the first round by the Chicago Bears, as the fourth overall pick. The Bears had endured several losing seasons after their star running back, Gayle Sayers, had retired. Chicago offered Walter a 126,000 dollar signing bonus as an incentive to join the Bears. It was the highest signing bonus ever offered to a college player at that time. In his first game with the Bears, Walter was held to zero yards gained on eight running attempts, not the start everyone was looking for, especially Payton. He would finish the season strong by rushing for 134 yards on 20 carries, against the New Orleans Saints. Payton's first-year combined totals were seven touchdowns scored and 679 yards gained. It would be a different story in 1976 and one that would place his name among the best. Walter rushed for over 1,000 yards and scored 13 touchdowns that year. He earned the Associated Press and Pro Football Writers of America's Most Valuable Player awards. He was also selected to the Pro Bowl, where he earned the Pro Bowl MVP award. Walter also married Connie Norwood that same year, July 7, and the couple would go on to have two children, Brittney and Jarrett Payton. It was some season for "Sweetness," a nickname he received that year but, it got even better for Walter Payton in 1977. Sixteen touchdowns and over 1,800 rushing yards would send him to the top of the list as the leading scorer of the year. Along the way, Walter would also earn "kudos" for playing quarterback and emergency punter for the Bears.

Despite the Bears' new running attack, they still could not sustain consecutive winning seasons. In 1983, Chicago management brought in Mike Ditka to replace Neill Armstrong, as head coach. Ditka, a legendary tough guy, would also bring with him defensive coach, Buddy Ryan. For the next two seasons, these two coaches would begin to mold a championship team in Chicago that displayed a balanced offensive attack with the famed 46 defense. Payton would continue to rush for over 1,400 yards in each of these seasons while the team finished 8-8 and 10-6, respectively. Ditka would intrigue the league with his use of a defensive tackle as a blocking back named William "The Refrigerator" Perry. Time and time again, Walter and this unlikely blocker would pound their way into the end zone. Payton would also break the career rushing record of Jim Brown in 1984.

It all came together for the Bears in 1985. Payton helped Chicago establish the league's second best offense, while rushing for over 1,500 yards and leading the team to a 15-1 record and a trip to the Super Bowl. The Chicago Bears defeated the New England Patriots 46-10 in Super Bowl XX. Coach Ditka would later state that he regretted the fact that he didn't give Walter enough chances to score a touchdown in the Super Bowl. The Bears won the NFC Central Division again in 1986, but lost to the Washington Redskins on the way to Super Bowl XXI. Payton was also elected to the College Football Hall of Fame in 1986. Walter would amass another 1,333 yards for the Bears that year and then announce his retirement after completing the 1987 season. Walter set many team records while completing 13 years in the NFL. He rushed for 16,726 yards and scored 110 touchdowns. The Chicago Bears would retire his #34 jersey in 1993 and he was also inducted into the NFL Hall of Fame at Canton, Ohio on July 31 of that same year.

In 1988, Payton joined the board of directors of the Chicago Bears. Owner Michael McCaskey felt that Walter was a very smart and able man and would bring special insight to the board from a player's perspective. In the early 1990s, Payton would also be appointed to the NFL commissioner's board. In 1995, Walter and a few of his friends and investors tried to bring a NFL expansion team to St. Louis, Missouri; but the NFL decided to create teams in Charlotte, North Carolina and Jacksonville, Florida. Two other ventures intrigued Payton and he became involved in CART racing as an investor and participant and also opened a restaurant and pub known as "Walter Payton's Roundhouse." This restaurant would also function as a museum for Walter's sports memorabilia.

Life was good for Walter for the most part until early 1988. After losing weight and experiencing severe indigestion, Payton consulted a doctor's advice at the Mayo Clinic in Rochester, Minnesota. In October of 1998, doctors discovered he had a progressive disease known as primary sclerosing cholangitis (PSC), a very active disease of the liver. He was told that without a liver transplant his condition was terminal. I will never forget seeing Walter Payton on TV with his son Jarrett as an advocate for organ transplants. He was offered the opportunity to move up on the waiting list because of his celebrity but refused. He would wait his turn. His last public appearance occurred in April of 1999 where he threw out the first pitch at Wrigley Field for the Chicago Cubs. The man everyone called "Sweetness" died on November 1, 1999 in Barrington, Illinois at the age of 45. Many dignitaries, political figures, friends, fans, and family attended the funeral. A public memorial was held at Chicago's Soldier Field and was televised on November 6. In his remembrance, the Bears wore Walter's #34 on their jerseys. In the coming days, more and more prominent personalities continued to express their thoughts about Payton in public. Longtime football coach Mike Ditka dubbed Payton as "The very best football player I've ever seen, period, at any position." President Bill Clinton praised Payton for his ability to endure illness with, "the same grit and determination that he showed every week on the football field." NFL commissioner Paul Tagliabue labeled Payton as, "one of the greatest players in the history of the sport." Needless to say, it was a sad day for professional football, and the

American public. Walter Payton was an exceptional athlete, a role model and a fine man. There have been little boys, high schools and numerous awards named for Walter Payton since his death. Anyone who ever saw him run with a football needs only to close their eyes to re-live the greatness of Walter Payton. Living and dying never looked so easy.

Huckleberry

Mark Twain had no idea when he penned his story about Huckleberry Finn that he was actually writing about Hall-of-Fame pitcher Bob Lemon. What a compliment!

Born at the beginning of the Roaring 20's," when the rapidly changing world of baseball was filled with ruffians and tough guys, Lemon stood out from the rest. His nickname (Lem) spoke to his demeanor, quiet, funny, and easygoing. He was one of the likeable guys in the game. Lem signed with the Indians at the age of seventeen for $100 a month and bounced around the Minors for five years.

He finally made the Cleveland roster in 1941 as a third baseman and outfielder. He developed a fine throwing arm, but before his Major League career could really get started, World War II called and Lem joined the Navy. It was here that Lem learned to pitch while competing in service games held in the Pacific.

Returning from the war intact, in 1946, Lem was quickly placed in center field where Cleveland needed help. Throughout the 1946 season his batting average dipped below .200 and skipper Lou Boudreau began to look for another position for Lemon.

The results of Boudreau's effort would take Lem to the loneliest place on the diamond, the pitchers mound. It would be 1948 before Lemon became a full time starter. That year would establish him as a premier twirler with a 20-14 record, ten shutouts, and a no-hitter on June 30th against the Tigers. This effort gave Cleveland their first American League pennant in 28 years. Lem would then be rewarded with two starts in the 1948 World Series against the Boston Braves. He would win both starts and help Cleveland become World Champions in six games.

Lemon had a great natural sinker along with a good overhand curve and slider. Ted Williams often called Lemon one of the three toughest pitchers he faced, along with Spud Chandler and Hal Newhouser. This right-hander would also become a flawless fielder and a fine hitting pitcher, posting 37 home runs in a fifteen-year career.

His 1953 Major League record of participating in fifteen double plays as a pitcher still stands. Bob was also "the man" away from the game, a good-natured character who could throw a complete game shutout during the day and tell the best stories in the bar that night.

That's right, this Huckleberry loved his cocktails. He was famous for saying, "I never passed a bar I didn't like." Lem would go on to win 20 games a season seven times, a Cleveland Indian record, and post a 207-128 record in the Major Leagues. Three times he would lead the American League in wins and complete games on five occasions.

In 1954, Lemon was a member of one of the greatest starting rotations in history, including Bob Feller, Early Wynn, Mike Garcia, and Art Houtteman. This group went on to lose the 1954 World Series to Willie Mays and the New York Giants.

Lemon retired as a player in 1958, and worked for a number of years as a scout and pitching coach before becoming the manager for Kansas City. For the next eight years, he would continue to manage the Royals, White Sox, and Yankees posting a 430-403 (.516) record. As the Yankee skipper, Lem managed New York to a pair of World Series appearances. The Yankees met the Dodgers in both Series, winning in 1978 and losing in 1981.

Bob Lemon was inducted into the Baseball Hall of Fame in 1976. With his induction, Bob Lemon would become the only Hall of Fame player in the 20th century to start his career as a hitter and end it as a pitcher. The Cleveland Indians retired his No. 21 in 1998 and he also remained on the Yankee payroll as a scout and consultant to owner George Steinbrenner until his death. On January 11, 2000, the real Huckleberry Finn passed away.

When Mark Twain wrote, "I can live two months on a good compliment," he had no idea that Bob Lemon would receive enough compliments to live for 79 years. This Lemon had turned out to be a great buy.

"Do You Believe in Miracles?"

Once I heard the great baseball scout Red Murff say that the hardest task in baseball is to catch a line drive in centerfield, to rob the batter of a hit. The center fielder is standing some three hundred or more feet from home plate and has to have the vision of a hawk to even see the ball being pitched, much less follow the ball off the bat when hit. His first step must be correct and true. The speed of a greyhound and the quickness of a rabbit are needed to follow a straight line to intercept the ball before it hits the ground or wall. If his first step is in the wrong direction, he will more than likely fail at his attempt to make the catch for an out. Depending on which side the batter hits from and how hard the ball is hit, the flight of the ball will bend or curve like a banana. Let's not forget Mother Nature, who provides intense sunlight some days, along with what the outfielders call the "high sky" during others. "I lost it in the sun," has been used by some of the best outfielders. The center fielder is also the captain of the outfield and calls for every ball he can reach. He normally has the strongest and most accurate arm. The strength of a team has always been determined up the middle. It's no coincidence that great teams start with a fine catcher, first class pitching, and a Hall-of-Fame center fielder.

There have been many great center fielders in World Series play. Willie Mays, Mickey Mantle, and Joe DiMaggio had all the tools of a classic center fielder. Duke Snider, Tris Speaker, Fred Lynn, Paul Blair, and Terry Moore could also play the number eight position with excellence.

Outfielders like those mentioned above have been responsible for several extraordinary catches made during World Series play. Some of them are listed here as follows:

Outfielder Josh Devore of the New York Giants made a super running catch in the bottom of the ninth inning with two runners on base and two outs. This catch saved Game Three of the 1912 World Series against the Boston Red Sox. The date was October 10 and the winning pitcher, Giants' future Hall-of-Famer, Rube Marquard.

The 1925 World Series between the Pittsburgh Pirates and Washington Senators lasted all seven games. This Series is remembered for one of the most controversial "outs" in World Series play. On October 10, Game Three, with the Senators leading 4-3 in the bottom of the eighth, Earl Smith, the catcher for Pittsburgh, hit a long drive to the centerfield bleachers. Sam Rice, attempting to catch it, fell over the bleacher railing and disappeared. He then reappeared with the ball and received the "out" call from the umpire. Rice went to his grave never telling anyone if he caught the ball on the fly. Sam was also later inducted into the Hall of Fame.

On October 5, 1931, in Game Three of the World Series, St. Louis Cardinals center fielder Pepper Martin caught a diving line drive off the bat of second baseman Max Bishop of the Philadelphia A's. Martin's catch preserved the win for veteran spitballer Burleigh Grimes of the Cardinals.

Also on October 5, 1947, New York Yankee Joe DiMaggio sent a long 415-foot drive to left field, toward the bullpen in Yankee Stadium. This sixth inning World Series shot was caught above the wall by outfielder Al Gionfriddo of the Brooklyn Dodgers with two outs and two aboard. Dodger announcer Red Barber exclaimed, "Oh Doctor," as DiMaggio kicked the dirt in front of second base in anger. It would be remembered as one of the few times that the "Clipper" displayed emotion on the field.

The scene was Game One of the World Series in New York. The Pologrounds was packed with anticipation and fans on September 29, 1954. With the score tied 2-2 in the eighth inning and two Indians on base, Vic Wertz sent a screaming blast 440 feet into dead centerfield. New York Giant center fielder Willie Mays waited with his hands on his knees. At the crack of Wertz's bat, Mays was off on a run toward the wall, like "Affirmed" at the Kentucky Derby. It was as if Mays had radar. His back now facing home plate, he glanced only once over his left shoulder. You could easily read the # 24 on his back as he finally stuck out his gloved left hand to catch the ball on the fly. Not only was this a sensational catch, but it gets better. Mays takes only one step after the catch and then spins around on the other foot, while unleashing a frozen rope throw back to the infield, to hold the runners on base. Mays' remarkable catch and throw preserved the tie. The Giants not only won Game One in the tenth inning on a pinch-hit home run by Dusty Rhodes, but continued on to sweep the Cleveland Indians for the championship. You could safely say that Mays' catch took the wind out of Wertz's and the Cleveland Indians' sails.

It took the Brooklyn Dodgers seven games and many years to finally beat the Yankees in a World Series match-up. The year was 1955 and the date, October 4. Brooklyn led 2-0 in the sixth inning with the Series tied three games each. Sandy Amoros had just replaced Jim Gilliam in left field for defensive purposes. What a great move by manager Walter Alston. With one out, Yogi Berra at the plate and Gil McDougald on base, pitcher Johnny Podres prepared to deliver the most important pitch of the game. Berra hit a hooking line drive down the third base line for what looked like a run scoring single, but Amoros saved the game with a spectacular catch and doubled up Gil McDougald after the catch. Yankee Stadium fell silent and Brooklyn went on to win their first World Series, four games to three.

Pitching took center stage during Game Five of the 1956 World Series. Mickey Mantle called his catch in Yankee Stadium on October 8, "Best catch I ever made." Fortunately for pitcher Don Larson, Mickey's catch saved the only no-hitter in World Series history. Larson would only throw ninety-seven pitches to the Dodger batters and their scorecard would read no runs, no hits, and no walks. Mantle's perfect catch saved Larson's perfect game.

Milwaukee County Stadium, October 7, Game Five of the 1957 World Series is where this next great catch takes place. Braves outfielder Wes Covington robbed New York Yankee Gil McDougald of a game-tying home run in the fourth inning. The Braves would go on to win by the score of 1-0.

A fine diving catch by Bobby Allison of Minnesota sparked the Twins to a 5-1 win over the Los Angeles Dodgers on October 7, 1965. Jim Lefebvre of Los Angeles smacked a "blue darter" to left centerfield in Game Two of the World Series, which Allison had to lay out to catch.

It's too bad that Allison's catch was overshadowed by the pitching of both staffs.

"The greatest World Series ever played," is how some folks described the Cincinnati Reds—Boston Red Sox match-up of 1975. It was night time in New England on October 21, when Game Six eased into extra innings. The Reds led the Series three games to two, when Joe Morgan of Cincinnati hit a high fly ball toward Dwight Evans of the Red Sox in the eleventh inning. The ball was hit over Evans' head, and it took a tremendous leap to snag a probable home run away from Morgan. In the twelfth inning, catcher Carlton Fisk of the Red Sox would win the game and tie the series with a lead-off home run off the left field foul pole. Cincinnati would go on to win Game Seven and the Series.

Now, having saved the best for last, some would argue that the best catches in the outfield during World Series play occurred by a mediocre center fielder of the New York Mets in 1969. In my opinion, those who agreed would be correct. The last Series of the sixties provided a stage where sure-fire stars would prepare for World Series play; players like Jim Palmer, Brooks and Frank Robinson, Tom Seaver, Jerry Koosman, Tommy Agee, and a little known thrower from Texas named Nolan Ryan.

In 1969, the Chicago Cubs had led the National League in wins for 155 straight days. The third place New York Mets were nine games out of first place on August 14. Here's where the miracle begins. At season's end, a combination of the Cubs' poor play and the Mets' winning streak left the Metropolitans on top of the National League East Division by eight games. The "Miracle Mets" would now play the heavily favored Baltimore Orioles for the 1969 World Championship. Game Three of the Series would start off with a bang for center fielder Tommy Lee Agee, who grew up near Mobile, Alabama, in a small town called Magnolia. The Mobile area has produced some of the greatest baseball players of all time. Players like Hank Aaron, Willie McCovey, Satchel Paige, Ozzie Smith, and Billy Williams all grew up near Mobile. In the bottom of the first inning, Agee would start the scoring for New York with a lead-off home run against future Hall-of-Fame pitcher Jim Palmer.

In the fourth inning, with runners on first and third, Elrod Hendricks of the Orioles sent a screamer to left centerfield, only to have Agee make a miracle running catch and preserve the 3-0 lead for New York. The top of the seventh inning would find Agee in the right centerfield, making a sliding catch off the bat of Paul Blair, with the bases loaded and two outs. These two catches were not only magnificent but kept Baltimore from scoring at least three runs. The Mets won Game Three, 5-0; and this helped New York win its first World Series title over the Baltimore Orioles.

Agee, a five-foot-eleven inch, one hundred and ninety-two pound, high school teammate of Cleon Jones, had starred at Grambling University. Tommy was signed for 60,000 dollars by Cleveland in 1961; and after a short visit to Chicago, he was traded to the New York Mets on December 15, 1967.

Agee would retire in 1973 with 130 home runs, 433 RBI's, a .255 batting average and one World Series ring. He had played the game he loved for a total of twelve years, with stops in Cleveland, Chicago, New York, Houston, and St. Louis. Tommy kicked around in the motel business and operated a lounge near Shea Stadium. He would later sell title insurance in New York City.

I had a chance to meet Tommy while he was with the Houston Astros. Agee was always accessible for interviews, autographs or just talking baseball. He was a funny guy who enjoyed the game and loved being known as a professional baseball player. I miss his laugh.

On January 22, 2001, Agee had a heart attack and died. He would leave his wife, Maxine and one daughter, Janella. His last visit to the stadium had occurred last fall during the 2000 World Series. Agee and teammates had been invited back to Shea for Game Four of the Subway Series between the Mets and the Yankees. Tommy had taken his turn throwing out the ceremonial first pitch. Tommy Agee had made the most of his fifty-eight years here with us. He had always referred to the standing ovation he received from over 53,000 fans before his at bat in the bottom of the seventh inning of Game Three, as his greatest moment in baseball. "Words can't describe how that made me feel," said Agee. I guess miracles really do happen.

Nice Punchin', Kid

It was early afternoon on May 27, 1968. Umpire Ed Runge, a fifteen year veteran, had just witnessed the greatest baseball fight he had ever seen. Runge said, "There were more punches thrown and landed than ever before." "A's" relief pitcher, Jack Aker, lay flat on his back, bleeding from several places. Aker had been decked by a hard left hand from one of the most feared sluggers and punchers in either league. Baseball fights were nothing new to the National Pastime. The great Ty Cobb and sturdy John McGraw earned reputations for being quick tempered, no-nonsense "tuffs." Both of these guys were notorious for finishing under the stands what had been started on the field of play. In fact, Cobb became so feared and hated that only three Major League players attended his funeral in July of 1961. Players like Hank Bauer, Earl Torgeson, and Clint Courtney carried a chip on their shoulder and quick fist in their pockets. Billy Martin was famous for his short fuse. Martin was quoted as saying, "I don't throw the first punch. I throw the second four punches." Shortstop Johnny Logan, like Martin, would fight at the drop of a hat and held a grudge against at least one player on every opposing team. Logan made a habit of hitting hard and often. Some of Logan's opponents swore that Johnny hit them so many times that they often thought they were surrounded.

So what do these guys have in common? Not only were they great players and good with their chins, but they were also loud and boisterous, even to the point of being obnoxious. Not this guy, he was quiet, unassuming, and never the instigator. He played hard and fought harder. He very rarely started trouble. He would never back down and no one could hit like Eddie Mathews. He would strike like a rattlesnake with no rattle. Ask Don Drysdale who was literally turned around in 1957 by a left cross before going down or Jim O'Toole who learned the real meaning of being "punched out" on July 2, 1961. This rock solid right-hander was born during the depression on the Texas side of Texarkana on October 13, 1931. Eddie now stood 6'1" and weighed 200 pounds and it was he who had laid out Jack Aker. The fiery intensity that this rough-and-tumble fellow brought to the game would not only get him out of numerous scraps with his fists, but also carry him to legendary heights with his bat.

Eddie's father moved the family to California in 1935 in search of a new start. Not only did Eddie grow up physically, but also mentally. He was smart, athletic, and considered a triple threat in high school football, but baseball was his game. He was signed at 12:01 a.m. during his high school graduation dance by scout Johnny Moore of the Boston Braves in 1949 for $6,000.00.

Brooklyn's Branch Rickey had offered $10,000.00 but Eddie and his dad had studied the teams and found out that third baseman Bob Elliott was at the end of his career in Boston. Eddie wanted to play now.

Mathews was sent to class D ball in High Point, North Carolina where he batted .363 and hit 17 home runs. It was here that my father, Gordon Purvis, found out about Eddie Mathews. You see, Eddie Mathews was my dad's favorite player. My dad had grown up in Oak City, a small town in eastern North Carolina, not more than a stone's throw from where Jim and Gaylord Perry grew up (Williamston). This was a great time to grow up in North Carolina if you were a baseball fan. Hoyt Wilhelm was born in Huntersville, Enos Slaughter in Roxboro, Rick Ferrell in Durham, Buck Leonard in Rocky Mount and Catfish Hunter in Hertford. Each and every one of these players became a Hall-of-Famer. I met my dad's hero in Houston and had him sign some things for me. He recalled his days in the Carolina's. I told him how my father used to show me how Mathews would sometimes catch a hard ground ball with the back of his glove without opening the web. Mathews explained that when there was a man on first with less than one out that he wanted to be able to turn the double play as fast as possible and not having to take the ball out of his glove would provide him that extra time to make the throw to second to complete the double play.

I came along in 1951 while Eddie continued to hit the long ball for the Double "A" Atlanta Crackers. It was here that Eddie made a name with his fist and with his bat. He was served a subpoena for violent assault and battery to a passenger agent of the Atlanta Train Station. It seems that the agent gave Eddie the wrong information about which train to take. By the end of the year, he had received a broken nose three times along with the Rookie of the Year award for the Southern League. He had hit thirty-two home runs, four or five guys, and had also met Ty Cobb.

Before arriving in Milwaukee to join the Triple "A" Brewers, Eddie had a chance to work with Billy Jurges on his fielding. Jurges taught him to stay down low, bend his knees and get his glove on the ground. Mathews learned that fielding was about rhythm. Jurges kidded that Mathews should receive the Gold Chest award because he was a knock 'em down throw 'em out player. It was Billy Jurges that showed him how to catch with the back of his glove.

Swinging the lumber was a different story. Some said he had a swing like Johnny Mize, and Paul Waner told him to just relax but don't change a thing. Ty Cobb said it best in a letter: "You have one of the most perfect swings I have ever seen."

After a short six months in the Navy during the Korean War, Eddie was discharged because his father was dying of tuberculosis. He arrived in Boston as a rookie in 1952 and promptly hit twenty-five homers to break the National League Rookie Record. He would wear number 41, given to him by clubhouse attendant Shorty Young. It would be a number we all would remember.

By 1953, the Boston Braves had moved to Milwaukee. The entire state of Wisconsin was turned upside down. There were more people at the train station to welcome them than there were at most home games while in Boston. Eddie had a fine year hitting forty-seven home runs and was named to the All-Star team. Here he faced the immortal Satchel Paige and hit into a double play.

Hank Aaron joined Eddie Mathews and the Milwaukee Braves in 1954. They would play thirteen years together and became a potent one-two punch in more ways than one. Not only did Hank hit well, but Eddie was still knock 'em out of the yard. Baseballs left the field off his bat and players left the field on stretchers. Eddie Mathews was also chosen to grace the cover of the first issue of Sports Illustrated on August 19, 1954. The picture was taken at County Stadium in Milwaukee and included New York Giants catcher Wes Westrum and umpire Augie Donatelli.

Commercials and Hollywood called for Eddie in 1955. He was asked to play Tarzan in the movies but the part never materialized. Eddie had better luck with magazine commercials. He posed for Gillette Razors, Ovaltine, and two cigarette companies, Chesterfield and Viceroy.

Long home runs and Miller High Life became Mathews' trademarks in 1956. He cleared the scoreboard at Wrigley Field and smoked a fast ball far over the left field pavilion in St. Louis. Crosley Field in Cincinnati barely held his shot that landed three rows from the top of the center field bleachers. In Milwaukee they gave you a case of beer for every home run you hit. Eddie hit lots of home runs and drank lots of Miller beer. The Braves finished one game back of Brooklyn.

The battling Braves broke through in 1957, as they not only won the National League pennant but also the World Series over the New York Yankees in seven games. Eddie started slow and was sitting on eight at-bats with zero hits before game four of the Series. A Milwaukee sports writer gave him three pennies to put in his pocket for good luck. In the bottom of the tenth inning, Eddie strolled to the plate with a Joe Adcock bat and hit the game winning home run off of Bob Grim. The Braves were back. Mathews also fielded a wonderful back hand stop of a bullet off the bat of Moose Skowron, with the bases loaded, to end Game Seven by stepping on third base for the forced out. The Braves were World Champions.

This Milwaukee team returned to World Series play again in 1958, only this time the Yankees reversed the outcome. In addition to Aaron and Mathews, names like Spahn, Crandall, Buhl, Pafko, and Burdette were becoming household names for baseball fans.

Mathews continued to shine in 1959. Forty-six home runs and one hundred and fourteen RBI's placed Mathews among the great home run hitters of his era. At twenty-seven years of age, he was sitting on three hundred career homers. Hank Aaron said, "He had hitting guts." Ask the owner of the Zodiac Lounge located in the Chase Hotel of St. Louis. Eddie left several wisecracking patrons unconscious after a loss to the Cards. A play-off loss to the Dodgers kept them from another pennant.

By 1960, Eddie Mathews had participated in several celebrated baseball fights, none of which he lost. This year would be no different. August 15, 1960, National League heavyweight champ Eddie Mathews took on contender Frank Robinson at third base in Cincinnati. Even Mathews said, "It happened so fast I don't know who swung first." Robinson slid into third where Mathews applied the tag. Words and punches were exchanged and Robinson never got up. Mathews got ejected but Robinson got stitches. Eddie remained undefeated. The title of this piece occurred at this time when Milwaukee manager, Charlie Dressen, patted Mathews on the back and said, "Nice Punchin', Kid."

The early sixties were mediocre for the Braves. They were competitive but finished out of the money. Eddie's roommate Bob Buhl was traded and replaced by Bob Uecker. "It was like living with the Marx Brothers," said Mathews. The Braves would finish in the middle of the pack until 1966.

Eddie is and will always be the only Brave to play in Boston, Milwaukee, and now Atlanta. The home of Scarlett

O'Hara welcomed the team to the south in 1966 and the Braves played better ball.

Milwaukee Sentinal sports writer, Lou Chapman, called before the 1967 season and asked Eddie how he felt about the trade? "What trade?" answered Eddie? Mathews had been traded to the Houston Astros. Mathews later admitted that after the call he broke down and cried. He had received no word from the Atlanta ownership and when they did finally release the trade information they spelled his name with two T's. Mathews played sparingly for Houston but his star shined bright on July 14, 1967. Mathews hit the 500th home run of his career off of San Francisco pitcher Juan Marichal at Candlestick Park. He later said, "I wish it would have come against the Braves."

Nineteen sixty-eight found Mathews with the Detroit Tigers and in his third World Series. He would retire after the Tigers beat the Cardinals. In fact, his last hit came against Bob Gibson during the Series. Mathews would finish with 512 homers. Four times he would hit forty or more homers and thirty or better for nine consecutive years. He was the seventh player to join the 500 home run club. Another record that may never be broken is one he owns with teammate Hank Aaron. Together they hit 863 home runs, more than Mays and McCovey or Ruth and Gehrig. Ten All-Star games and two World Championships rounded out his Hall-of-Fame career.

Mathews kicked around as a coach for awhile before Atlanta called. He would manage the Braves from 1972 through the start of 1974. Mathews would skipper his friend and past teammate, Hank Aaron, in the chase for Babe Ruth's home run record. He would be replaced later that year. Eddie was voted into the Baseball Hall-of-Fame in 1978 and was considered the best third baseman since

Pie Traynor. Only Mike Schmidt has put up good enough numbers to join those two. In his later years, Mathews despised what was happening to the game he loved. Money had turned baseball rotten. He signed autographs at card shows and scouted in Arizona and California.

On Sunday, February 18, 2001 the current undefeated Major League Champ went down fighting against pneumonia. "Eddie Mathews was my hero," said Joe Torre. "He was captain, and I always called him that. He never backed off, never was tentative." Eddie Mathews had fought the good fight for sixty-nine years; it was now time to rest. My dad loved Eddie Mathews.

Death in the Family

This gentle giant of a man hit for the cycle on July 22, 1964, versus the Cardinals in St. Louis. He also hit three home runs against the Dodgers on June 24, 1965. The first of his three clouts was delivered by Don Drysdale. He would repeat this feat three more times during his career. On June 4 and 5, 1966, he would record nine straight hits against the Astros. This mark fell one short of the National League record. On August 1, 1970, he would tie a Major League record with Lou Boudreau and Joe Adcock. He had five extra base hits in one game. Three doubles and two home runs against George Stone and the Atlanta Braves stole the headlines. The upper deck at Three Rivers Stadium would become home to some of his mighty blast. The longest measured 469 feet. This slugger also set a Major League record of eleven home runs in the month of April in 1971. He christened Shea Stadium with its first home run and hit a ball 512 feet completely out of Dodger Stadium in Los Angeles. Is there any wonder they called him "Pops?" He still holds the Pittsburgh Pirates records for most home runs (475), most RBI's (1540), and most extra base hits (953). That's hard to believe in light of the Pittsburgh Pirates history. Honus Wagner, Lloyd and Paul

Waner, Roberto Clemente, Bill Mazeroski, Kiki Cuyler, Pie Traynor, Arky Vaughn, and Ralph Kiner were all legendary Hall of Famers who wore the Black and Gold before Stargell. Pops would hit eleven grand slams and would own the record for the longest home run hit in six different parks at the same time. Waving that forty-two ounce bat, at the plate, in his windmill type fashion would cause many a pitcher to rethink his profession. Tom Seaver and Phil Niekro would give up eight home runs each to Stargell and the old timers still talk about the gold painted seat located on the fifth level of Montreal's Olympic Stadium. The seat measured 535 feet from home plate. Willie's round tripper landed in that seat on the fly. Don Sutton once said, "He didn't just hit pitchers, he took away their dignity." Stargell's 269 home runs were the most hit by any player during the decade of the seventies and he would hit twenty or more home runs fifteen times, only surpassed by Hank Aaron and Willie Mays.

Willie was born Wilver Dornel Stargell on March 6, 1940 in Earlsboro, Oklahoma. Shawnee, Oklahoma lay sixteen miles south east of Earlsboro and was the home of the great world class athlete, Jim Thorpe. Stargell would grow up in Alameda, California and become middle linebacker on his high school football team. A broken pelvis in 1958 turned him toward the game of baseball. This left-hander would top out at six foot four and one half inches and carry two hundred and thirty pounds to the plate 7,927 times in a twenty-one year career. Yes, Willie Stargell had some Seminole blood running through his veins and he was proud of that fact.

Willie came along between the great Pirates of the past and the Pirates of the future. He was signed in 1959 and was eventually called up to the show in 1962. Left field at

Forbes Field would be his home until 1970, when Three Rivers Stadium was built. This soft-spoken leader would become the symbol of class on and off the field. You could say he was Kirby Puckett before Kirby. Pops motto was "Have fun, work hard!" He would become the ambassador of the Bucs and the city of Pittsburgh. Always calm and laid back, this seven-time All-Star was also the biggest prankster in the clubhouse. "I always used my smile as a weapon," said Pops. In 115 seasons of Pirates baseball, no one had touched the people of Pittsburgh quite like Stargell. His special relationship with fellow players, managers, and legendary announcer Bob Prince, would make him a hero to all. Prince, known as The Gunner, would holler over the mike, "Let's spread some chicken on the hill with Will and send The Gunner the bill," when Stargell went to the plate with the Pirates needing instant offense. When Stargell came through with a hit, as he so often did, his All-Pro chicken restaurants would give away free chicken to all. Prince would then write Willie a check.

In 1971, the Pirates won the second of six National League East titles in the seventies. Number 8 would crank out forty-eight homers that year and carry the Bucs past Baltimore for their fourth World Series title.

Because of knee problems, first base would become home for the captain in 1974. He would hand out "Stargell Stars" to players to stick on their caps when they contributed to a victory. His love for disco music would lead to using the Sister Sledge hit, "We are Fa-ma-lee" as a rally cry for players and fans alike. A fifth World Championship would follow in 1979. Willie would become the only player to win a League MVP, a Championship Series MVP, and a World Series MVP in the same year. He would also become the oldest player to win a MVP award. He would retire in 1982 and Pittsburgh would honor him by retiring his number 8. In 1988, Pops would become the seventeenth player elected by the baseball writers in his first year of eligibility. Willie would work tirelessly away from the park to help fight sickle cell anemia and also took a turn in the press box as an announcer with Bob Prince and Steve Blass. This experiment would only last one season.

Stargell and I hooked up in Houston at the National Sports Card Convention. The list of signers at this convention included Mickey Mantle, Franco Harris, Bob Feller, Jim Taylor, Clyde Drexler, Warren Spahn, Reggie Jackson, Steve Garvey, Gaylord Perry and many, many others. I have a photo of Willie signing a program for me. He wore glasses and his hair was beginning to recede, but that smile was still there. When he walked in, the whole room changed.

Stargell moved to Wilmington, North Carolina and continued to visit in Pittsburgh. He also participated at other National Card Shows and remained a gentleman all the while. When the new PNC Park was announced to be built, fans also learned that three statues were to be placed on site. Honus Wagner, Roberto Clemente, and Willie Stargell would stand guard forever over their beloved Pirates. Stargell's twelve-foot statue of his batting-stance was to be unveiled on Monday, April 9. Willie would not get to see his statue. After sixty-one years of easing into one day at a time, Willie lay fighting for his life against a kidney disease that would not be denied. Pops would die of a stroke early that morning. Willie would leave four daughters, a son, a loving wife, and millions of fans. There has indeed been a death in the family. "Now every opening day in Pittsburgh will be Willie Stargell day," said Chuck Tanner.

It's interesting to note that a Pittsburgh native, dressed in red and white, would be the first to hit a home run at the new park. As a kid, Sean Casey of the Cincinnati Reds would watch his hero, Willie Stargell, play baseball. Even though the Pirates lost, I think Pops would have liked the idea of a kid from the Pittsburgh family doing the honors.

The Human Computer

Have you ever wondered what year would be the best year of your life? Has it already happened or is it still in your future? If you had to pick one year, what would have happened to make that year the best? Most men would pick a time like meeting your wife-to-be, or maybe the birth of your first child. Some might chose a particular birthday such as when you turned 16 and could start driving, or maybe the year you graduated from high school or college. Athletes might consider the signing of a full scholarship at some university the best of times, or maybe a professional contract worth millions of dollars would be worthy. For us older folks, it might be as simple as turning 65 years of age, celebrating 50 years of marriage, or retiring from the work force and spending the rest of your life on some beach. Younger folks may consider best the year in which they bought their first house, or paid off all their credit card debt. All of these reasons sound good and I'm sure there are many others, but I think those are just some of the best times in one's life and maybe not enough to qualify as the best *year*. I think the best year would include a combination of things happening all in one year. Here is an example of a guy who experienced quite a year.

In 1948, this slick-fielding shortstop was the most difficult ballplayer in the league to strike out, striking out only 9 times in 560 at-bats. That's only one strikeout for every 62 at-bats or once every 14 games, unheard of in today's game. His batting average was his personal best at .355 for the year, while scoring 116 runs for the Cleveland Indians. Other personal bests during the year included 199 hits, 98 walks and an on-base percentage of .453. He also hit 18 home runs, drove in 106 RBI's, and recorded a .534 slugging average. These numbers would be good enough to create a spot for him on the 1948 All-Star team, along with some of his fellow players like Bob Feller, Ken Keltner, Bob Lemon and Joe Gordon. He would lead Cleveland as a player-manager to a first-place tie with the Boston Red Sox. Then he would proceed to get 4 hits in 4 at-bats including 2 home runs in a one-game playoff at Fenway Park, to help win the American League Pennant. He would also invent a defensive move that would become known as "The Ted Williams Shift." This shift was designed to take away as many hits as possible from Williams, a left-handed hitter, by moving players from their normal positions on the left side of the diamond to the right side. This same year would also mark the entrance of the great Leroy "Satchel" Paige who would join the Cleveland Indians. This fellow would give the legendary Paige his first major league start. Paige would become only the fourth Negro League player to play in the Major Leagues, behind Jackie Robinson, Roy Campanella of the Brooklyn Dodgers, and Cleveland's very own Larry Doby. None of the other three had the reputation of Paige, or the age. In fact, Paige may have been as old as the other three put together. Heck, even "Satch" didn't know how old he was! The stats and numbers mentioned above would also propel this guy to win the American League MVP

Award and to top off the year; his Cleveland Indians team would go on to win the 1948 World Series. He is still the only person in baseball to win both an MVP Award and a World Series Championship as a player-manager. Now, that, my friends, is a fine year for any professional baseball player. But there's more; this guy had such an outstanding year in 1948 that he was also named the Male Athlete of The Year by the Associated Press. Let's all remember that the baseball season starts with spring training in February, and it ends with the World Series in October. Most Major League players would read this and consider a year like this to be a fairy-tale year; but for Lou Boudreau, 1948 was without a doubt the best year of his life.

Lawyer Louis "Lou" Boudreau was born in Harvey, Illinois, July 17, 1917. He would grow to love basketball and baseball. In 1933, he would lead the Thornton High School basketball team to the Illinois State Championship and be nicknamed the "Flying Frenchman." Lou captained both teams at the University Of Illinois until he signed an agreement to play baseball with the Cleveland Indians after graduation. When Big Ten officials found out, they ruled him ineligible to play for the remainder of his college career. He therefore made his Major League debut on September 9, 1938, for the Indians, at the age of 21. He would appear in one Major League game as a pinch-hitter. In 1939, he would play for the Buffalo Bison's in the International League. Originally a catcher, he would be moved to shortstop and team with second baseman, Ray Mack. Both would be called up to the "big club" by mid-season. His first full season as a Cleveland Indian would occur in 1940. On April 27, in his first at-bat of that season, Lou would hit his first home run off of future Hall-of-Fame pitcher Hal Newhouser. He would also hit home run #2 in that same game, to help Cleveland beat Detroit 4-2. He was off to a tremendous start. Lou went on to hit a solid .295 with 101 RBI's and was named to the 1940 American League All-Star team. In December of that same year, he would be elected Rookie of the Year. Cleveland would struggle the next season under the leadership of manager Ossie Vitt, until he was fired in 1941. But on one particular July night in 1941, Lou would field a sharp-hit ground ball and throw out Joe DiMaggio of the Yankees, at first base. That play is still remembered in baseball history, because it was the night that DiMaggio's streak of safely hitting in 56 consecutive games ended. In 1942, at the age of 24, Lou Boudreau would become the youngest player to manage a Major League club. Lou would be instrumental in moving Bob Lemon from the outfield to the pitcher's mound and also move Larry Doby from the infield to the outfield. Both moves would produce Hall-of-Fame appointments for these players. He would personally lead all A.L. shortstops in fielding eight times, while also winning the batting title in 1944. Three times (1941, 1944, and 1947) he would lead the league in doubles hit during the season. In 1945, he would suffer a broken right ankle in a collision at second base with Dolph Camilli. As previously mentioned above, 1948 would be far and away Lou's best year; and he would be rewarded with a new 65,000 dollar contract in 1949. But as fate would have it, Lou's luck ran out after a nine- year stint in Cleveland. He was fired at the end of the 1950 season and replaced by another future Hall-of-Famer, Al Lopez. Lou would play for the Boston Red Sox during the 1951 season before returning to the player-management ranks in 1952. After four years in Boston, he would be asked to skipper the Kansas City Athletics in 1955.

After several lousy seasons in KC, he latched on as a color commentator for the Chicago Cubs, in 1960. All seemed well until Boudreau was asked to switch places with the current Cubs Manager, Jolly "Cholly" Grimm. So Lou came down from the booth to manage the Cubs and the talkative Grimm took his place in the booth upstairs. Of course it didn't work out. Grimm resigned the next year, and Lou went back to the broadcast booth for good. Boudreau would finish his managerial career with a record of 1,162 wins and 1,224 losses. On January 20, 1970, this seven-time All-Star received 232 of a possible 300 votes to gain admittance to the Baseball Hall of Fame. During his introduction, Baseball Commissioner Bowie Kuhn would say about Lou, "He was a human computer." Boudreau had made a science out of fielding. He studied the batters' tendencies and knew where they were most likely to hit the ball. He not only knew how to position himself in the field, but also his fellow players. Boudreau would be joined in the Hall of Fame by Ford Frick, Jessie Haines, and Earle Combs. "He was the greatest shortstop I ever saw," exclaimed Bob Feller. Lou would continue to talk about the game he loved and would spend nearly three decades broadcasting games for WGN. Before retiring in 1988, he would partner with the likes of Jack Quinlan, Vince Lloyd, Milo Hamilton, Harry Caray and Jack Brickhouse. His pals and players would always refer to him as "The Good Kid," while he was on the air.

On Friday, August 10, 2001, at the age of 84, Lou Boudreau passed away from cardiac arrest. He had suffered from circulatory problems associated with diabetes for many years. He was interred in Pleasant Hill Cemetery in Frankfort, Illinois. Lou had lived to see his uniform #5 retired by the Indians, as well as a street renamed in his honor, (Boudreau Drive) that ran next to Municipal Stadium in Cleveland. Fellow Hall-of-Fame shortstop Bill Mazeroski once said, "Being a shortstop in high school and a Cleveland Indians fan, Lou Boudreau was my boyhood hero. I thought he and the 1948 Indians were the greatest." He may not have been the greatest, but he was "The Real Deal."

Larger Than Life

In the beginning, he grew up a Red Sox fan with his favorite player being none other than Jimmie Foxx. At the age of sixteen, he started working on the docks in Cleveland and also began smoking cigarettes at the rate of two packs a day. He would continue for the next 53 years. Soon after, he was drafted into the United States Army and served in World War II. By 1943, he had been promoted to corporal and eventually participated in the crossing of the bridge of Remagen, into Germany. On March 15, 1945, during this battle, he received wounds in his left leg and forearm which would earn him a Purple Heart and a trip home with honors. He attended Ohio State University and majored in radio speech, while working at a gas station. At the end, he had spent forty-six years as the radio voice of baseball for the entire Midwest. He became a member of your family while you spent warm summer evenings on the back porch, listening to the radio with a glass of lemonade. That voice was deep, distinctive and well-known; maybe his smoking had something to do with it. Either way, you found yourself mesmerized at "hello." Radio was his forte, and he didn't care as much for TV. He was funny, down home, and a very giving man. Most would remember him as larger than life. He was pure baseball.

John Frances "Jack" Buck was born August 21, 1924, in Holyoke, Massachusetts. Jack was the third of seven children born to Kathleen and Earle Buck. Jack's father Earle died at the young age of 49. The Buck family moved to Cleveland, and it was there that Ohio State University offered Jack the opportunity to hone his radio skills by broadcasting their basketball games. By 1948, Jack had married his first wife, Alyce Larson, and together they had six children. By 1950, after college, he joined the St. Louis Cardinals organization, only to find himself in Columbus, with the Triple-A Redbirds. He was later moved to Rochester in 1953, to broadcast the International League Red Wings, another Triple-A affiliate of the Cardinals. His work was excellent, and he joined the Cardinals' broadcast team on KMOX radio at the beginning of the 1954 season. Baseball on the radio, as we know it, was about to change

At different times, he would partner with my friend Milo Hamilton, Joe Garagiola and the infamous Harry Caray. In 1959, Jack was excused from the broadcast by the Cardinals and replaced by Buddy Blattner. Jack would stay busy broadcasting the Saturday *Game of the Week* for ABC on television. Blattner would leave the booth at the end of the 1961 season, and Jack would be rehired. Garagiola would leave a year later, and Jack would share the booth now with only Harry Caray. Not only were they partners, but would become life-long friends. Both of them would undergo personal trials in 1969, as Caray was fired by the Cardinals and Jack's marriage to Alyce would end in divorce. Jack then married Carole Lintzenich, and they had a son, Joe Buck. Another daughter would follow later so, he would father eight children in all.

Jim Woods would join Jack in the booth briefly, during the 1970-71 seasons, before ex-Major League third baseman Mike Shannon joined Jack for the rest of his broadcast career, in 1972. For twenty-eight years they were the voices of the St. Louis Cardinals baseball. Shannon is still broadcasting for the Cardinals and speaks about Jack on the air with reverence. Most of Jack's children shared their father's and their Uncle Bob Buck's zeal for broadcasting; and his daughters Julie, Bonnie and Christine each have a job in broadcasting. His son Joe really needs no introduction, as he can be heard on Major League Baseball telecasts today and watched on FOX Sports TV during the World Series broadcasts. Jack's beloved Cardinals would also be World Series Champions in 1964, 1967 and 1982.

Jack also teamed with Hank Stram, calling NFL games. He started out in 1963 for CBS television, calling Dallas Cowboy football games, including the famous NFC Championship Game played in 1967, which became known as the "Ice Bowl." He was joined by Frank Gifford, Tom Brookshire and Ray Scott, for that broadcast. For almost two decades Buck and Stram would broadcast *Monday Night Football* for CBS on radio. I spent many Monday nights listening to them with the sound on my TV turned down. They were the best. Jack Buck also broadcast different football events at different times with many other announcers, like Bryant Gumbel, Keith Jackson, Verne Lundquist, Pat Summerall and John Madden.

Jack even broadcast some games for the St. Louis Blues of the National Hockey League and the St. Louis Hawks of the National Basketball Association. Along the way, Jack met and interviewed many other great athletes, such as Jackie Robinson, Ted Williams, Joe DiMaggio and Jessie Owens. Jack Buck called 11 World Series, 18 Super

Bowls, and four Major League Baseball All-Star Games. He would make his final appearance at Busch Memorial Stadium on September 17, 2001.

I met Jack Buck in Houston during a Cardinals-Astros game. He was kind enough to sign an autograph for me. He and his one-time partner, Milo Hamilton, were talking old school baseball. It was a pleasure to just sit and listen. Buck claimed his favorite baseball player to watch play was Willie Mays, while Milo always chose Stan Musial. It was quite an argument. It's amazing how many announcers say the same thing about Mays. Buck always said that the best part of the baseball season was spring training, unless your team was involved in post-season play. He believed that the first thing a baseball announcer has to tell the listener is that "The pitch is on the way," and everything else happens after that. He loved knowing that folks who could not see or that were in the hospital, could listen to the games he was broadcasting. He was known to soak his feet in a bucket of ice water during those hot summer broadcasts, because his booth did not have air conditioning. Later in his life he continued to mention the decline in the quality of play on the diamond. He blamed it on expansion and lack of Minor League experience. He hated old-timers games. "Sure they should be there to wave to the fans and sign autographs," he once said, "but don't make them play." He would rather remember them at their best.

During Jack Buck's time on the radio, his fame increased for several calls he made during play-off baseball games. Kirk Gibson's home run; in Game One of the 1988 World Series, Mark McGuire's 70th home run as a Cardinal, and Ozzie Smith's game-winning home run against the Los Angeles Dodgers, are replayed time and time again during the baseball season. My favorite was Kirby Puckett's walk-off home run in Game Six of the 1991 World Series. With the Atlanta Braves leading the Series three games to two, Twins centerfielder Kirby hit one out, and Buck simply ended the broadcast by saying, "And we will see you tomorrow night!"

Jack Buck, suffering from lung cancer, Parkinson's disease and diabetes was finally called home on June 18, 2002. The St. Louis community mourned their loss. Flags were flown at half-staff, local TV sports anchors all wore black suits on-air, and flowers were left at the base of his bust displayed outside Busch Stadium. He was 77 years of age. Buck had been the eleventh announcer to receive the Ford C. Frick Award of the Baseball Hall of Fame, in 1987. He was inducted into the Radio Hall of Fame in 1995 and received the Pete Rozelle Radio-Television Award for the Pro Football Hall of Fame, in 1996. Yes, it's true, little Jack Buck from Holyoke, Massachusetts had indeed become larger than life.

Take Your Pick, Williams or Wayne

Ted Williams (The Kid) is, was, and always will be, one of the greatest hitters that ever lived. Most people agree that he has forgotten more about hitting a baseball than most players will ever learn. Ted's temperamental, high-strung nature combined with his immense confidence in his beliefs propelled him to the top of the world of Major League Baseball. When Ted stepped into a batters box, he knew he had to be perfect. John Wayne (The Duke), on the other hand, was labeled "The Greatest Cowboy Star of All Time." His loyalty to this country and the American West made him a legend of the big screen. The power of his raw presence screamed the words American, honor, dignity, and strength. They were both American heroes in every sense of the word: One in real life and the other in the minds of the public.

They were both, tall, masculine, good-looking men. They each stood over 6'4". Both started their careers in 1939. One became famous on a movie set in Hollywood during the filming of "Stagecoach" and the other, on baseball diamonds across the country with the Boston Red Sox. One was shot down, for real, flying a plane in the Korean War, while the other was shot down on a World War II movie set in "Flying Tigers". Both were as American as baseball, apple pie, and Chevrolet. They both grew up in poverty during their early years and each received their formal education in California. They stood for justice, hard work, fair play, courage, patriotism and the American way. One earned two Triple Crown Awards in baseball and the other, two Oscar nominations in acting. One was selected into the Baseball Hall of Fame in 1966, and the other received a People's Choice Award for the most popular motion picture actor in 1976. One became an MVP in Major League Baseball, twice, and the other received his profession's highest honor in 1970, an Oscar. Both owned boats and loved to fish. They each were outspoken, controversial, admired, and revered as one of the best at their business. One has an airport named after him in Los Angeles and the other, a tunnel in Boston. They both were loud, had nicknames, and preferred those over their real names. One carried a gun most days to work, the other a bat. Both have museums honoring their lifetime accomplishments. They have both written books and had many books written about them, some good and some bad. Both were raised primarily by their mothers, but each had a male mentor (Tom Yawkey and John Ford, respectively) who helped them attain legendary status in their chosen professions. Their images appeared on many products over the years. Williams's image could be found on soft drinks, all types of Sears sporting goods equipment, baseball cards, and national magazines. Wayne's image was seen on lunch boxes, chocolates, cigarettes, playing cards, and comic books. One had a television show about fishing and the other, a radio show about detectives. One received the Medal of Freedom in 1991 from President George Bush, and the other received the Congressional Gold Medal in

1979 from Congress. One was elected to the All-Century Team; the other received a square on the Hollywood Walk of Stars. Both were very active in the fight against cancer. One helped finance the "Jimmy Fund" in New England, while the other supported the John Wayne Cancer Hospital in California. Both were married three times, and all ended in divorce. One has a life-size statue in the foyer of the Baseball Hall of Fame and the other, a life-size statue, on a horse, in front of the Great Western Bank Building on Wilshire Blvd. in Los Angeles, California. One hit a home run in his last at- bat of a Major League game and the other went out with guns blazing in his last film, "The Shootist." Both had the support of lifelong friends. Ted Williams had teammates Bobby Doerr, Dom DiMaggio, and Johnny Pesky, while John Wayne enjoyed the company of Harry Carey, Jr., Ward Bond, and Ronald Reagan.

Theodore Samuel Williams was born August 30, 1918. He became a professional baseball player, US Marine pilot, and fly fisherman. He died at the age of 84 of cardiac arrest, July 5, 2002.

Marion Robert "Duke" Morrison was born May 26, 1907. He became an actor, artist and patriot. He died at the age of 72 of lung cancer, June 11, 1979.

Throughout the years, as Ted grew older, he was asked by reporters, "How do you want to be remembered by baseball fans?" His answer was always the same, "When people see me walk down the street, I want them to say, 'There goes the best damn hitter that ever lived.'" It's a cinch that if he wasn't considered the best, it surely didn't take long to call roll. There is a great story of a blind man who came to every Red Sox game. When asked why, he said he came to see Ted Williams. He then went on the explain that he always knew when Ted came out to the on-deck circle, when Ted stepped into the batters box and of course when Ted hit, all by listening to the crowd. When Wayne was also asked the same question by reporters in his later years and he replied: "Feo, Fuerte y Formal," a Spanish proverb which means, "He was ugly, strong and had dignity." It appears that both men were greatly admired in the eyes of their fans. Wayne wanted very much to go to Annapolis and become an officer in the Navy; but after being denied, he chose to make movies and support the USO to fulfill his need for being a part of the American military. He even had an Army RAH-66 Helicopter named after him, "The Duke." Ted Williams on the other hand, actually lived the character that John Wayne portrayed in the movies. Ted served as a US Marine fighter pilot during both World War II and the Korean War, flying a propeller-driven F4U Corsair and a F9F Panther jet aircraft. Was one man any more famous than the other? I doubt it. Both will be remembered forever.

I never met Ted Williams or John Wayne in person, but I did visit the Ted Williams Museum during the summer of 1999. I also will never forget Williams' introduction before the All-Star Game in Boston that same summer. It would turn out to be Ted's farewell appearance.

Running Stop Signs

Before the hustle of Pete Rose to first base or Sammy Sosa's sprint to his outfield position before game time, there was Enos "Country" Slaughter. Old # 9 is one of five current Hall-of-Famers to be born in North Carolina. He was born in Roxboro on August 27, 1916, and died not too far away in Durham on August 12, 2002. It was a beautiful Monday morning and "Country" was about to turn 87.

Cardinal catcher, Joe Garagiola, used to say, "How do you keep them down on the farm when you've let them see the big city?" Enos was a product of the Branch Rickey farm system. A homegrown kid you might say who spent his first thirteen years in the Majors as a Cardinal. St. Louis manager Burt Shotten gave him his nickname "Country" and all you had to do was hear him speak to understand why. Enos played right field and almost did not make the big club because of an incident that happened in the Minors. As Enos walked to the dugout from his right field position at the end of an inning, Manager Eddie Dyer said, "Are you tired kid? If so, I'll get you some help." Enos said that he hit the top step of the dugout running from then on, coming and going.

Enos played in five World Series and hit over .300 in ten of nineteen seasons. Playing while hurt was his trademark, and he became famous for his hustle. During his playing career he overcame the flu, a broken collar bone, and other injuries to his fingers, shoulders, and knees. In no way did these setbacks diminish the fact that he was also a great player. He was a 10-time All-Star who twice led the National League in triples. Even three years in the Service during World War II could not slow down a Hall of Fame career, and Enos was inducted into Cooperstown in 1985. I had the pleasure to meet Slaughter on several occasions, always at a card show. He was always nice and very funny. He seemed to take an interest in each person who asked for his autograph as if he could not believe they wanted one. I loved hearing his Carolina accent. I grew up in Raleigh, North Carolina, not to far from Roxboro.

His most famous highlight occurred during the 1946 World Series against the Boston Red Sox. That was the first year that the Cardinals topped the one million mark in attendance. Not only did "Country" lead the National Leagues in RBI's with 130 but he also ran the Red Sox right out of town in Game Seven of the World Series as losers.

"He just outran the ball," said teammate Stan Musial. "Stan the Man" described Slaughter's "mad dash" from first base to home, with the game tied 3-3, on a double hit by Harry Walker. Slaughter had broken for second as Walker connected, and could see the ball streaking toward left-centerfield. Boston centerfielder Leon Culbertson had replaced Dom DiMaggio and was playing out of position for Walker. "He just ran right thru my stop sign," said Cardinal third base coach Mike Gonzales. Enos slid across home plate to score the eventual winning run, in the bottom of the eighth inning. Culbertson had fielded Walker's hit and relayed his throw to shortstop Johnny Pesky. Pesky in turn threw on to catcher Roy Partee, but not in time. Pesky would become the "goat" for the Red Sox fans in 1946, but I believe that the combination of Culbertson playing out of position and a perfect hit-and-run play by Slaughter and Walker gave Pesky no chance at home plate. In fact, Dom DiMaggio still claims he would have thrown out Slaughter at third if he had been in centerfield.

Enos would finish his career with the New York Yankees from 1954 to 1959 and see action in the 1957 and 1958 World Series. A statue has been erected of him in St. Louis outside of Busch Stadium insuring that he will never be forgotten. "Country" had come to town to stay.

Talk's Cheap — Let's Go Play!

It was said by his receivers that he was so accurate that if he threw you a pass in your gut, it meant catch the football and go down, because you were about to get hit. If he threw it up and out over your head, it meant you were wide open and you needed to run under it and score. If he threw it wide of you, it meant you needed to lay out for the catch or knock it down. Therefore, my favorite football player is, was, and always will be: Johnny Unitas. He played during a time when a different set of rules existed. His trademark crew-cut and golden arm set him apart, along with those black high-top cleats and bowlegs. Quiet confidence oozed from this quarterback, and his teammates swore they were in the huddle with God. So when Earl Morrall took over in a game for an injured Unitas and threw one up and out to Hall of Fame tight-end John Mackey, "I got hit so hard my teeth hurt," said Mackey.

Someone once said that the purest definition of leadership was watching John Unitas get off the team bus. Everyone looks for leadership, regardless of what we are doing in life. His ability to perform under pressure was uncontested. No high fives, no dancing or celebrating, and no finger pointing upward; that is not needed when you know you are No. 1. "You should only get emotional at weddings and funerals," said Unitas. "Football is a game."

Unitas was born in Pittsburgh on May 7, 1933, and was only five when his father died. His mother, Helen, worked two jobs to support four kids. He started playing football at age twelve and practiced throwing a perfect spiral though a swinging tire. After graduating from high school, where he had played against future Pittsburgh Steelers owner Dan Rooney, although he wanted to attend either Notre Dame or Indiana, he enrolled at the University of Louisville. The great Frank Leahy said he was too small. He started as a freshman. Drafted out of college in the ninth round of the 1954 draft by the Steelers, he was cut on September 6, 1955, before the season started. Jim Finks and Ted Marchibroda would be the Pittsburgh quarterbacks. He would spend the 1955 season playing semi-pro football for the Bloomfield Rams for six dollars a game and trolley fare. After receiving a letter from a fan raving about the play of Unitas, the Baltimore Colts offered him $7,000 a year to play, in 1956. Coach Weeb Eubank liked this skinny, stoop-shouldered kid with piercing eyes and the grit to back it up. Although he didn't look like an athlete, he was smart, clever and hungry. All Unitas ever wanted was a chance, and this time the Baltimore Colts got it right.

Unitas would go on to become the greatest quarterback to ever play the game. "He was better than I was," said Hall of Famer Sid Luckman of the Chicago Bears. During a time of true field generals, Unitas was a complete quarterback. Tough, smart and totally focused, he simply refused to lose. He was the first to call his own plays in the huddle, the first to audible at the line of scrimmage and the first to perfect the two-minute drill. Unitas said after his playing days, "I could never understand why a team would play you to a standstill for twenty-eight minutes with one defense, then change that defense the last two minutes and give up some things that would allow me to beat them." Ninety seconds for Unitas could last for days. His ability to read defenses and take command in the huddle was unmatched. He always thought he could score and wanted to go for the touchdown every time. He would even wave off the field-goal team as they trotted onto the field.

As for his records, Unitas was the first to throw for 40,000 yards and the only quarterback to complete at least one touchdown pass in forty-seven straight games. He was the most valuable player in 1964 and 1967. He played in ten Pro Bowls and led the Baltimore Colts to the NFL Championship in 1958 and 1959, and to the Super Bowl in 1970. He was also chosen Player of The Year three times. For eighteen years he wore the # 19, a horseshoe on his white helmet, and the look of an assassin on his face. Hell, even Joe Namath wore # 19 in high school. Everybody wanted to be "Johnny U". He was "the" Baltimore Colt. He would retire in 1973 with twenty-two NFL records and a broken and bruised body. His curved right arm was evidence of the thousands of passes, perfect passes, he threw. He limped from a torn Achilles tendon and many knee injuries. Everything about him was broken but his spirit. A torn muscle in his right arm rendered his hand almost useless in later years.

Of course, everybody knows about the 1958 NFL Championship game: The come-from-behind 23 to 17, overtime victory, over the New York (Football) Giants, and how Unitas threw time after time to Raymond Berry, to tie the game in regulation with a field goal and then orchestrate an eighty-yard drive for the winning score.

Not only was it the first championship game televised, but also the first to go into "sudden death." It was simply the greatest game ever played by the greatest quarterback.

He hated that the Colts left for Indy and even asked that his records be removed from the Indianapolis Colts Media Guide. His reason was simple: He never played in Indy...he played in Baltimore. There is even a statue of Unitas outside of the Baltimore Ravens stadium although he never played in that building either.

I met my hero in the summer of 1968. Unitas and fellow teammates held the annual Johnny Unitas All-American Sports Camp from June 23 through June 28 at Wingate College in Wingate, North Carolina. I was a junior in high school and was hoping to attract some attention from the college ranks. Many college coaches would be in attendance and what could be better than learning the finer points of playing football from the pros. There was a pro player from every facet of the game. Lou Michaels coached the offensive line and place kickers, Jimmy Orr worked with the receivers; Chris Hanburger worked with the defensive secondary; and Lenny Moore worked with running backs. Ed Emory coached the defensive line, and the man himself (Unitas) worked with the quarterbacks. We worked out three times a day, rested, talked football in between and watched game film at night. It was incredible. Can you imagine being in these guys' company, three times a day for six days? I still treasure the memories and all the guys' autographs, especially "Johnny U."

On Wednesday, September 11, 2002, at the age of sixty-nine, Unitas suffered a heart attack while working out in his beloved city of Baltimore. John had undergone a triple bypass in March of 1993 after his first heart attack, but there would be no reprieve this time. Johnny Unitas, the man, is dead but as long as somewhere a kid puts his hands under the rear end of the center for the snap, his legend will live on. Teammate Bill Curry once said, "Every Sunday when we were ready to take the field, our defensive Captain Fred Miller always said a few words, and then turned to John who was standing by the door. John always said the same thing 'Talk's cheap - - Let's go Play.'" Always! I wonder if they play football in Heaven... (Always)

Beyond Belief

Players who run like a jack rabbit excite people. Speed creates its own delights for your team and, of course, problems for the other guys. There is no doubt that fast players win games. So, can you imagine sitting in an NFL defensive coaches meeting, watching films of Bob Hayes? Imagine the looks of the coaches at each other. Eyes wide open, heads down and clasped between their hands, their minds racing. The question was always the same, "What are we going to do to stop this guy?" After watching him run by defensive backs like they were standing still, I'm sure you could see them talking to themselves and would hear them mutter a phrase like: that's not possible, he's scary, fear in cleats, nobody can run that fast, track speed, world-class speed, or we had better think of something else. "Bullet" Bob Hayes was a "weapon of mass destruction" for every defense in the NFL. Old-timers say he could outrun raindrops.

Coaches have always said you can't coach speed, so then how do you coach against it? Man-to-man defenses had always been good enough, but not now. We would begin to hear words like zones, cover-two and cover-three defenses. Bob Hayes' speed wasn't just ahead of his time; it was ahead of *all* time. There wasn't a quarterback in the league that could out-throw him. Sure there were other players with speed in the NFL, but they were few and far between. Hayes was even faster than they were. National Football League players like Bo Jackson, Deion Sanders and Cliff Branch were fast, and all were clocked at or below 4.2 seconds, in the 40-yard dash. That's barely human, crazy fast, a blur.

Unfortunately, there are no 40-yard times for Bullet Bob, but he did once run a 5.28 in the 60-yard dash, on a cinder track. It was the first time anyone had run under 6.0 seconds in the 60-yard dash. You think that's fast? Then imagine this: Bob Hayes was behind five other teams when he received the baton for the United States Olympic team, in the 4 x 100 meter relay of the 1964 Games, in Tokyo. Bob made up nine meters on the field and ran his 100-meter leg in 8.6 seconds to win his team the Gold Medal, by four meters. Some say he eased up at the end, that he could have gone faster if needed. Famed sportswriter, Jim Murray of the *Los Angeles Times,* called it, "The most astonishing sprint of all time. Hayes not only didn't drop the baton in the relay, he made up more ground than a cheetah after a square meal." The Starship Enterprise doesn't travel that fast. The sheer speed of Bullet Bob Hayes was "beyond belief." Hayes managed to travel where only a few men had gone before, to the end zone with a football in less than 10 seconds, in full pads.

Robert Lee "Bullet Bob" Hayes was born in Jacksonville, Florida, on December 20, 1942. He became a track star at Florida A&M and was chosen by the Dallas Cowboys in the seventh round of the 1964 draft, a sprinter with the ability to catch a football. Twelve touchdowns, 1,000 yards receiving with an average of 21.8 yards per catch, is how his stats would read at the end of his rookie season. When the Cowboys won the Super Bowl in 1972, Bob Hayes became the only athlete to win an Olympic Gold Medal and a Super Bowl ring.

Don't ever think that Bob Hayes was not a great football player, even in college. The backfield at Florida A&M included halfback Willie Gallimore, who became a Chicago Bear. The quarterback was Charlie Ward, who became the father of Heisman Trophy winner, Charlie Ward of Florida State; and the fullback Hewitt Dixon played for the Oakland Raiders. Hayes was the wingback. Coach Jake Gaither was once asked who was the finest Florida A&M football player *ever*? He paused and looked out into space as if he didn't hear the question. After a minute or so he answered, "Gallimore was terrific, but there could be another player like him one day. But Hayes...Hayes... *Nobody* ran that fast. Not possible. With those two, I would have had a chance against the greatest coach of my time, Bear Bryant. But then, if Bryant had Hayes...heh-heh... oh...my...God."

The 1964 training camp for the Cowboys turned out to be very interesting. Not only had the Cowboys drafted Hayes, but also Mel Renfro and Roger Staubach. Roger had a four-year commitment to the Navy before joining the Cowboys, but he was worth waiting for. Nice draft. "Hayes scared everybody in camp," said Fred Clarke. "He was so fast it was like he was melting in front of your eyes." Defensive backs were as nervous as cats in a room full of rocking chairs. Coach Tom Landry would only offer a tight-lipped smile when asked about Hayes. By 1972, the Cowboys would win their first Super Bowl, and Hayes had rewritten the Cowboys' receiving record book.

Bob Hayes is still the third-leading touchdown-maker in Cowboy history, with a total of 76. Only Emmitt Smith and Tony Dorsett, both running backs, have more. His eleven-year career had produced three Pro Bowls and many records. Someone once described his thighs as like Rolls-Royce jet engines. They were so big that people made fun of him. It was where the explosive power came from. The medical staff didn't even understand how to treat a pulled hamstring when it happened to Hayes. He refused any treatment that required a shot with a needle. His legs were his living.

After football, Hayes fell from grace. According to writer Jim Murray, "The only thing in the world that could ever keep up with Hayes was trouble. Trouble runs an 8.6 100." Hayes was convicted of being a drug and alcohol user, and a mule (someone who takes dope from one informant to another). Some say he was set up, gotten rid of, and taken out of the picture. He spent ten months in prison. Hayes never knew what to make of the 60's and 70's and spent some of the 1980's in jail. When he finally got out, the only thing waiting for him was the bottle. Hayes felt that the NFL and Cowboys had shunned him, so he gravitated to the only things that honored him, FAMU and the National Track and Field Hall of Fame. Finally in 2001, Jerry Jones made a well deserved space for Bullet in the Cowboys' Ring of Honor. On that day, Hayes admitted that he felt like an outcast by the NFL Hall of fame. He knew he belonged. I had a sideline pass for that game and got meet Bob Hayes and shake his hand. He was extremely humble and excited. I was also excited and he made me feel like a hundred dollar bill in a two dollar wallet. I feel sure he could still outrun everybody on the field that day.

At the age of 59, Bob Hayes died of kidney failure in Jacksonville, Florida, at the Shands Hospital on Wednesday, September 18, 2002 (1 week after Johnny Unitas). He had also battled liver ailments and prostate cancer. One of my favorite sportswriters, Ralph Wiley once wrote, "I'm surprised 'Death' caught Bob Hayes. He must have tricked him somehow; it would have been the only way to catch him." I sat near Ralph at the ESPY Awards in Los Angeles, at the Kodak Theater. He was some kind of writer, and he loved Bob Hayes.

There is a great story about the 1964 Olympics. Before the 4 x 100 relay finals, French runner, Jocelyn Delecour said to one of Hayes teammates, Paul Drayton, "You can't win; all you have is Bob Hayes." When it came to running, Bob Hayes is all anyone ever needed.

On Saturday, January 31st, 2009, Bob Hayes was finally forgiven and inducted posthumously into the NFL Hall of Fame. There is no doubt he belonged there. The next day, his sister Lucille Hester released a letter that Hayes had written three years before his death. In this letter, he thanked everyone for their votes and support for his election into the NFL Hall of Fame. Hayes knew there was a chance that he would not live to see his election. He ended the letter by saying, "I love you all." Writer and friend, Ralph Wiley, is no longer with us either, but he would have been pleased. If there is a place in heaven where you can run, I'm sure that is where you will find Bob Hayes. There is no doubt that he had been touched in a special way here on earth. Even though there had been set backs in his life, he ended up where he belonged. God keeps opening and closing doors, not only to guide us, but until we get it right.

Bottom Rail on Top

He had been in many clubhouses, perhaps hundreds, but this one in Chicago felt different. Shock and contempt filled the air. It was July 5; the middle of the 1947 season, and the skipper was introducing him to his new teammates. Most refused to look at him or stir from their pre-game preparations. He walked down the row of lockers and offered his hand to each player. Many accepted this rookie's hand shake but some did not. He was only twenty-three but now felt like he was fifty. His size could not have been an issue for he stood six feet, one inch tall and weighed one hundred eighty pounds. In fact, he was bigger than most of them. He had even attended college, so intellect was not an issue. Quiet, fair skinned, and moody, this guy could play. He was a second baseman who could also play shortstop or outfield if needed, but the real reason he was there was because of the thunder in his bat. He was what the scouts called a natural-born hitter. So why did his new teammates look past him as if he were not there? Why had some of them refused to shake his hand? There are times in your life when you sense something is about to happen, and then you realize it already has. He knew the answer, knew there would be resistance to his presence. He was the only man in that clubhouse who was not white. Welcome to the big leagues, Larry Doby. Welcome to history.

Some wise person once said, "The key to life is not getting what you want, but wanting it after you get it." Doby may have been undecided at that moment. He was handed uniform # 14.

The Indians were now ten games behind the Yankees, after losing three of their last five ballgames. It was July 3, 1947, and Skipper Lou Boudreau found his club in fifth place. He had just met with Indian's owner Bill Veeck and was unaware that Veeck had signed a black ballplayer. "What the hell is Veeck doing?" thought Boudreau. It's got to be a gimmick, a publicity stunt, a way to sell more tickets. "Larry Doby will be a great player; you'll see," shouted Veeck. Still, Lou was confused. Doby had no minor league experience and he played second base. The Indians had Joe Gordon, one of the best at the keystone bag. "Give him a chance," said Veeck. "This kid can hit and play anywhere." It was now up to Lou to make it work. Doby had signed his contract only eleven weeks after Jackie Robinson. There would now be a black baseball player in both the National and American Leagues. Some would say, "Bottom Rail on Top."

Veeck and Doby had hit it off immediately. "Call me Bill and I'll call you Larry," said Veeck. They both loved jazz and baseball. From the minute Doby had signed his Major League contract, they were both in this venture together.

Lawrence Eugene Doby was born in Camden, South Carolina, on December 13, 1924. His family later moved to New Jersey, where Larry achieved All-State status in football, basketball and baseball, at Patterson East High School. His father had been a semi-pro baseball player but had died when Larry was only eight. While growing up in a racially mixed neighborhood in New Jersey, Larry learned to be quite an athlete by being aggressive and intense. His play was fueled by lots of fire and spirit, yet he remained sensitive and hated being kidded or ridiculed by his high school teammates. At graduation, Larry enrolled at Long Island University and continued to play baseball in the Negro Leagues, under the name of Larry Walker, to protect his amateur status. World War II would change his world and L.D., as he was now called, would serve two years in the service of the US Navy. Doby would later marry Helen Curvy.

Doby would rejoin the Newark Eagles in 1946, after the war. It was here that L.D. would make a name for himself, with his bat. The Newark Eagles, run by Effa Manley, would become the Champions of the Black World Series, in seven games. They had beaten Josh Gibson and Buck Leonard of the Homestead Grays, winners of nine straight pennants, and then upset Satchel Paige and Hank Thompson of the Kansas City Monarchs. The great 1-2-3 punch of Newark, Larry Doby, Monte Irvin, and Johnny "Cherokee" Davis, would prove too much for Kansas City to overcome. While looking down at the ground in disgust, Wilmer Fields, pitcher of the Homestead Grays said, "Doby, hit me hard."

The 1947 season would open with the debut of Jackie Robinson for the Brooklyn Dodgers. This move by Branch Rickey would open the door for many black players like Doby. The bench was where Larry spent the first half of the 1947 season with the Indians. Doby remembered, "It was the worst time of my life. I wanted to play nine innings." Doby was even asked to play first base one time, but he had no first baseman's mitt. Doby asked teammate Eddie

Robinson if he could borrow his glove and was told no. Eventually, he was moved from the infield to centerfield after fellow Negro Leaguer, Biz Mackey, urged Indians General Manager, Hank Greenberg, to move the temperamental Doby. He would spend thirteen years out there.

Nineteen forty-eight, would be a great year for the Indians and Doby. He would be joined by the immortal Satchel Paige and represent the American League in the World Series. Doby had hit .156 in 30 games as a second baseman the year before, but 1948 would find Larry with a .301 batting average, along with 14 homeruns and 66 RBI's in 121 games.

On October 10, 1948, 81,897 people watched Cleveland pitcher Steve Gromek jump into the arms of Larry Doby. The photo that was taken of this union ran the next day on the front page of the Cleveland Plain Dealer sports section. It is believed to be the first photo printed showing a white man and a black man celebrating together. In the fourth game of the World Series, Larry Doby had hit a homerun to give the Indians a 2-0 lead over Johnny Sain and the Boston Braves. It would be the decisive run in a 2-1 win for Cleveland and Gromek. Doby would continue to hit all the Braves pitchers while compiling a .318 batting average for the 1948 World Series. For his efforts, he and his teammates could receive $6,772.00 each; the winners' share of the 1948 Series and the largest pay-out in baseball history at that time. Doby and Paige had become the first Negro Leaguers to play in a World Series and Doby, the first to hit a homerun in a World Series game.

In 1949, Doby would find him self barnstorming with Jackie Robinson, after another great season with Cleveland. Both black and white players had been taking the game down South for years.

Doby not only continued to hit, but would become one of the premier outfielders in the American League, for virtually the entire decade of the 1950's. He would lead the League in homeruns in 1952 and 1954, and won his only RBI title in 1954 with a career high of 126, on the way to a record of 111 regular-season wins. On August 2, 1950, Larry would hit three homeruns in one game, and June 4, 1952 would find him hitting for the cycle against the Red Sox. He owned pitcher Virgil "Fire" Trucks of Detroit and smoked the "Fireman" for eight homeruns in his career. Effa Manley, of the Newark Eagles, would be heard to say, "Jackie Robinson can't carry Doby's glove." Doby would attend Robinson's funeral in October of 1972.

In the late 1950's, you could follow Doby in Chicago with the White Sox or in Detroit with the Tigers. During 1957, 1958, and 1959, he would be passed around like a bag of chips from Cleveland to Chicago, Chicago back to Cleveland, Cleveland to Detroit, and then Detroit back to Chicago.

Early in the 1957 season, Doby exploded with his fist, as well as his bat. After being "beaned" twice in a three-game series with the Yankees, Larry had simply picked himself up and trotted to first base. Throwing inside was an accepted part of pitching in the forties and fifties, and feared hitters expected to get "dusted" every now and then. Game three would find Yankee pitcher Art Ditmar unleashing a high-and-tight wild pitch that would send Doby to the dirt in a hurry. Doby had come to the plate with two outs, two runners on base and a bat in his hand. Ditmar's throw was so wild it even eluded Yankee catcher Elston Howard. As both base runners advanced on the throw, Ditmar rushed in to cover home plate as Doby was getting up. Words between the two preceded the perfectly executed left hook by Doby that flattened Ditmar. Veteran Yankee outfielder Enos Slaughter said, "This was the best baseball fight in twenty years." Although profanity accompanied punches throughout the brawl, race never entered into the fight. American League President, Will Harridge, fined white and black players alike. It appeared that the emancipation of Negro players on the field was complete.

Following his playing career, he coached and worked in the front offices for the Indians, White Sox, and Expos, and became the second black manager in the Major Leagues after Frank Robinson. He would win 37 and lose 50 in 1978 while enforcing his only two rules. Play as hard as you can on every play and keep yourself in top condition. Cleveland would retire Doby's uniform # 14, in 1994.

On June 18, 2003, Larry Doby passed away quietly, at his home in Montclair, New Jersey. He was 78. He had played in both worlds, but always said the Negro National League was a great League. The only difference between the two was bench strength. The Majors carried 25 players to only 16 for the Negro League teams. He had played with such Negro stars as Monte Irvin, Don Newcombe, Leon Day, Ray Dandridge, Biz Mackey, Satchel Paige and Max Manning. He had participated in seven All-Star games and two World Series. Doby hit 253 homeruns and over 100 RBI's five times. His career batting average of .283 had proven Bill Veeck to be correct. "Larry Doby will be a great player, you'll see," shouted Veeck. He was inducted into the Baseball Hall of Fame in 1998.

Doby and I met briefly at a baseball card signing show before he was inducted into the Hall of Fame. Larry Doby was a fine man. He was nice, soft spoken and seemed to appreciate the attention. I think he was aware of his place in baseball history and knew it was only a matter of time. In a lot of ways, Doby deserved as much credit as Jackie Robinson for opening doors for fellow Negro League players.

Never Played a Down

He did as much as anyone to shape today's NFL. Instant replay, sideline radios in quarterback helmets, and wind-direction strips were some of his ideas. He also championed the idea of a more stringent scouting combine by using computer technology. He advocated the six-division, wild-card playoff concept. His place during the AFL-NFL merger in 1966 was not only significant, but some say absolutely necessary to get the deal done. He was the original chairman of the league's competition committee and participated from 1966 to 1988. He worked tirelessly to make the game more exciting, but never at the expense of the players' safety. To speed up the excitement of the game, he convinced the committee to start the play clock immediately after the previous play, while making the sideline borders wider to help eliminate injuries. Heck, how many of you know that this guy not only gave Pete Rozelle his first job in pro football, but he also hired Pat Summerall to broadcast New York Giants football games? His pal Don Shula said, "I truly believe he had as much, or more, to do with the success of professional football as anyone who has ever been connected with the league."

Although he never played a down, "Tex" Schramm was the man.

Texas Earnest Schramm was born on June 2, 1920, in San Gabriel, California. Tex was named after his father and, interestingly enough, his mother and father did meet each other in the great state of Texas. Tex also married his high school sweetheart, Martha Anne Snowden, in 1941. He received a journalism degree from the University of Texas and became a sports writer after serving time in the Air Force. Tex worked for the Los Angeles Rams from 1947 to 1956. He worked his way up from Publicity Director to General Manager before being hired as an executive for CBS-TV Sports. It was here at CBS that Tex learned how to mesh pro football and television into a multi-billion dollar industry. The league is still enjoying the fruits of his labor.

In 1960, at the age of 39, Tex Schramm was hired by owner Clint Murchison to oversee an expansion team that had not yet been approved by the NFL. From 1960 to 1989, Tex was the President and General Manager of the Dallas Cowboys. "Bum" Bright became the Cowboy owner from 1985 to 1989, and then sold the team to current owner Jerry Jones. Tex was so well-respected by both Murchison and Bright that he even held the voting rights at league meetings for the Cowboys (a right usually reserved for team owners). The first move Tex made for the Cowboys was to hire Coach Tom Landry. Even though Dallas did not win a single game in their first season, Tex stood by Landry, as this legendary coach would produce 20 straight winning seasons, 18 playoff appearances, 13 division titles and five Super Bowl appearances. "Tex was the ultimate football-minded man," said Bob Lilly. "He loved the game and he had a flair about him of show business." Bob Lilly was

Schramm's first ever draft-pick for the Cowboys and he became a Hall-of-Fame defensive tackle.

It turns out that Schramm's real genius lies in his ability to market the Cowboys world-wide, and that made them one of the world's most recognizable teams. This phenomenon began in 1966, when he volunteered to host a second NFL game on Thanksgiving Day. Turkey and Cowboys became a tradition. In 1972, Tex struck gold with two more innovations. He would change the sidelines forever by introducing the Dallas Cowboys Cheerleaders, and he developed the largest radio network any sports team has ever had. The Dallas Cowboys games could be heard on 225 stations in 19 states, plus a Spanish speaking network that included 16 stations in seven states and Mexico. Tex struck again as he led the charge to use replacement players during the 1987 NFL players strike. "Once the players saw the league could go on without them, that was the end of the strike," said Schramm. Gene Upshaw, executive director of the NFL Players Association, had this to say about Schramm: "He was a competitor and loved to argue, but he had a lot of class and you always knew he was trying to do what was best for the NFL." Schramm also created the Cowboys famous Ring of Honor, where the best of the best would be enshrined forever.

Tex would leave the Cowboys in 1989, two months after the firing of head coach Tom Landry by the new owner, Jerry Jones. He claimed he left to become the commissioner of the World League of American Football, but I think he saw the writing on the wall. The strained relationship between Schramm and Jones was noticeable. Even though Tex Schramm was inducted into the NFL Hall of Fame in 1991, it was not until 2002 that Jerry Jones announced that the following season, Schramm would be placed in the Cowboys

Ring of Honor. Schramm would attend the press conference during the announcement and spoke with his eyes full of tears. "I never gave up hope," said Schramm. "Things that should happen to people that deserve them, usually do happen." Jones said that by having Schramm's name on the façade, "His spirit will be honored for years to come. This organization and its fans will forever be the beneficiaries of Tex Schramm's spirit and vision." Unfortunately, Tex Schramm would not live long enough to see his name placed in the Cowboys Ring of Honor.

At the age of 83, Tex Schramm, the man who invented "America's Team," left us quietly. The date was July 15, 2003 and he was at his home in his beloved city of Dallas, Texas. His wife Martha (Marty) had preceded him by seven months. "The NFL family has lost one of its giants," said Paul Tagliabue, NFL commissioner. "Tex Schramm was one of the visionary leaders in sports history—a thinker, doer, innovator and winner with few equals." I never got to meet Tex, but I did meet Tom Landry, Bob Lilly and Jerry Jones. All three men spoke about Tex with reverence.

Soft Hands

The day he was born, the doctor told his mother he would not live through the night. He had come into this world weighing only one pound, 13 ounces. It was 1931 in rural Texas, and there were no incubators to be found. Still his grandmother had hope for his survival. She would place him in a shoebox, turn her oven on and place the box on the open oven door. It was here that he would defy the odds. Not only did he survive, but he would spend the rest of his life going places where no one had gone before. He would climb aboard the backs of 40,350 different horses during his forty- plus years of racing. He would also set the record for visiting the winners circle 8,833 times, including 1,009 Stakes races and 11 Triple Crown races. His profession would take him to 48 different race tracks all over the world including Germany, Sweden and England. His horses earned an astounding sum of 123 million dollars in purses. Life at the race track was good, and he was considered the most successful jockey in the world. At a time when jockeys kicked, whipped and pulled hard on the reins of their mounts, this gentle little fellow became known for his "soft hands." His riding skills were unmatched, and it appeared as if he were one with the horse. Some folks said that he was so relaxed while on the back of a horse that he could go to sleep with a fly on his nose.

William "Bill" Lee Shoemaker was born on August 19, 1931, in Fabens, Texas. Although everyone in his family grew to normal size, "Shoe" would top-out at 4 feet, 11 inches and weighed 96 pounds. Some folks said he was so small that he could sit on the edge of a dime and still swing his feet. His parents divorced when he was ten, and Shoe moved with his father to California. Not big enough to participate in football or basketball, Shoe became a high school champion in wrestling and a Golden Glove boxer. Shoe was introduced to the world of thoroughbred horses on a ranch, by one of his high school buddies. He quit school after the eleventh grade and, with the help of trainer George Reeves, won his first horse race at the age of 17. The date was April 20, 1949. The rest, as they say, is history.

Shoe won the Kentucky Derby four times: Swaps (1955), Tomy Lee (1959), Lucky Debonair (1965), and Ferdinand (1986). He won the Preakness Stakes twice: Candy Spots (1963), and Damascus (1967). He claimed the Belmont Stakes five times: Gallant Man (1957), Sword Dancer (1959), Jaipur (1962), Damascus (1967), and Avatar (1975). In 1981, Shoe became the first jockey to win a one-million-dollar race when he rode John Henry in the first Arlington Million. One of the few mental mishaps by Shoemaker occurred in 1957 while riding Gallant man in the Derby. Shoe was in the lead down the stretch when he misjudged the finish line and stood up in the stirrups to celebrate. He ended up finishing second by a nose to rival Bill Hartack aboard Iron Liege. He was suspended from racing for 15 days. Embarrassed yet undaunted, Shoe rode

Gallant Man to victory a few weeks later in the Belmont Stakes, in New York.

Shoemaker's success did not come without a price. In 1968 his horse went down and Shoe got a broken leg when he was hit by the hind leg of another horse. In 1969, two days before the Kentucky Derby, his horse flipped backwards and fell on Shoe, breaking his pelvis, ruptured his bladder and caused nerve damage in one of his legs. Still, time and time again, Shoe had refused to quit the one thing he loved the most, horse racing. He was inducted into the National Museum of Racing and Hall of Fame in 1958.

There is a story I would like to share that was told to me by Roy Davis, a friend from South Texas. Roy loved, owned and raced horses. He also knew how to bet them. Roy once attended a charity event in Oklahoma City and the guest speaker was none other than Bill Shoemaker. A reporter from the local media, who was not very knowledgeable about the sport of horse racing, confused Spectacular Bid with Secretariat. He assumed that Shoe had ridden Secretariat and asked Shoe what he remembered most about Secretariat. Shoemaker's answer was priceless. "The thing I remember most about Secretariat", said Shoe, "was that she had the smallest rear-end of any horse I have ever seen and the longer I chased her, the smaller it got." Roy said Shoemakers' answer brought the room down with laughter.

Shoe always claimed that Spectacular Bid was the best horse he ever rode. Other notable horses ridden by Shoemaker included Round Table, Northern Dancer, and Silky Sullivan.

Finally, in 1989, Shoe decided to retire from active horse racing. His final win came at Gulfstream Park in Florida on January 20, 1990, aboard Beau Genius; and his last race occurred on February 3, 1990, at Santa Anita Race Track, where 64,573 fans turned out to cheer him on. After his retirement, Shoe became a trainer; but bad luck still seemed to follow. On April 8, 1991, he lost control of his Ford Bronco and caromed 50 feet down an embankment. Shoemaker was left paralyzed from his neck down. From a wheelchair, he would continue to consult as a horse trainer until 1997, while also becoming a spokesman for the rights of disabled persons. His advice for the disabled, "Never give up."

On October 12, 2003, when the man with the soft hands known as Bill Shoemaker finally rode into the winner's circle of life, he was 72. Dying of natural causes, he left behind three wives: Ginny, Babbs and Cindy; also a daughter Amanda, and million of fans. His awards from racing are too numerous to list here. One of his last public statements went like this: "I have always believed that anybody with a little guts and the desire to apply himself can make it, can make anything he wants to make of himself."

I read once where somebody said, "The joy of a raindrop is when it finds the river." That was the joy of Willie Shoemaker; he had found his river in the "Sport of Kings," horse racing.

No Guts

He was once accused by manager Casey Stengel of having no guts, because he refused to brush back a hitter. "The pitcher only needs two pitches," he would say. "The one they're looking for and the one to cross'em up." He only hit forty-one batters in 5,244 innings pitched in his entire career. You see, there was a time in baseball when you were not considered a great hitter unless the pitchers threw at you once in a while. They called it keeping the batter honest. Most pitchers hated when a batter "dug in" at home-plate. Pitchers thrive on intimidation. When a homerun was hit off a pitcher it was not uncommon to see the next hitter thrown at, in retaliation. All the great hitters were "dusted" in the Forties and Fifties. This pitcher did not need to hit batters. His high-leg kick, deceptive speed, southpaw delivery and tenacity kept the hitters guessing. In fact, he won 202 games in the 1950's, more than any other pitcher in the Majors during that time. "Hitting is timing and pitching is upsetting that timing," he was quoted as saying. Manager Charlie Dressen called him "my go-to-sleep pitcher," meaning Charlie always got a good night's sleep the night before he pitched the next day.

It has been said that the loneliest place on a baseball diamond is the pitcher's mound, but this fellow felt right at home. Pitchers are at the very center of the contest. They come in all shapes, sizes, temperaments and ages. This twirler stood six-feet tall and was a lanky 183 pounds. He had a long, sad face with enough of a nose to mind everybody's business. His delivery from the mound seemed perfect, as if his body turned over from ground level. He had a tremendous pick-off move to first base and once caught Jackie Robinson leaning the wrong way twice in one game. He could change speeds, and hitters swear that no two pitches looked the same or arrived at the plate in the same spot. Not only did he have a moving fastball, but he also had command of the curve, slider and change-up. Some say he could even change speeds on his change-up. "I just ignored the middle twelve inches of the plate," he would say. As the years wore on, he developed a screwball when his fastball faded. As part of his routine, he always threw batting practice two days before each start. Pitchers never do that anymore.

One of the myths about left-handers is that they are notoriously wild. Because of this, he would often shake off the catcher simply to confuse the hitter. Manager John McGraw hated left-handers. He once said that, "If you split open a southpaw's head, all that would fall out would be bases on balls." "He was a left-hander!" teammate Johnny Logan once said. "As a left-hander, you never knew what he was going to do." For twenty-one Major League seasons he would keep them guessing

He was known as one of "The Originals," one of thirty-two players who arrived in Milwaukee from Boston as the Braves, in 1953. As far as the fans were concerned in Milwaukee, they were all-stars, and Milwaukee County

Stadium would never be the same. Have you guessed who I'm talking about yet? Sure you have. Warren Edward Spahn was born in Buffalo, New York, on April 23, 1921. He was one of six kids born to a father who sold wallpaper and had a passion for baseball. Warren played amateur ball in Buffalo at the age of nine and became a first baseman before entering high school. He switched to pitching shortly afterwards, because there was already an all-city player at the first base bag. At the age of eighteen, Spahn would sign with the Boston Braves in 1940 for eighty dollars a month. He was invited to spring training after he won 19 games in the minors, in 1941. He would debut with the Braves in 1942, but was sent back to the minors after refusing to brush back Pee Wee Reece in a game with the Dodgers. Stengel would later call that decision the worst mistake he ever made. It was at this time that Casey told the press, "Spahn has no guts". Spahn would miss the next three years, while serving in the First Army Corps of Engineers in Europe during the war. He would return a hero and the only Major League player to receive a battlefield commission for bravery in combat. More than 500 Major League players served the U.S. during World War II. Spahn would also receive the Bronze Star and a Purple Heart. So the man with no guts stood up to Casey, Hitler and the German army.

He would finally reach the big leagues to stay at the age of twenty-five, and boy did he stay. In 1947, he would wear the number 21, a tomahawk-fronted uniform, and emerge as one of the best pitchers in baseball. He would go on to pitch 665 games, winning 363, which is tops for a left-hander. Spahn also recorded 2,583 strike-outs. He is fifth all-time in wins behind only Cy Young, Walter Johnson, Christy Mathewson, and Grover Cleveland Alexander.

Spahn won 20 or more games in a season, 13 times in his career, which is more than anyone else. He threw 63 shut-outs and recorded a 3.09 ERA. Spahn won the 1957 Cy Young award, and he also led the National League in wins eight times. He became a 14-time All-Star and a World Champion in 1957. Interestingly, the great Willie Mays hit his first homerun off of a Warren Spahn pitch. When ask by reporters about the pitch, Spahn said, "Gentlemen, for the first 60 feet that was one hell of a pitch." Spahn also hit 35 homeruns, a National League record for pitchers, which allowed him to stay in ballgames late when offense was needed. He would pitch two no-hitters at the ages of 39 and 40. Spahn would receive the nickname "The Meal Ticket," for his ability to consistently win; yet he never earned more than 100,000 dollars a year. In fact, the Los Angeles Dodgers once named their new pitching machine "The Warren Spahn," because of its consistency. In 1948, the Boston Braves starting pitchers won 44 regular season games; Warren Spahn and teammate Johnny Sain won 39 of them. On September 14 of that year, this one-two punch of the Braves would cause Boston sports editor Gerald V. Hern to pen this poem.

> "First we'll use Spahn, then we'll use Sain,
> Then an off day, followed by rain.
> Back will come Spahn, followed by Sain,
> And followed, we hope, by two days of rain."

His two best seasons were 1953 and 1963. He would record an identical 23-7 win-loss record at the ages of 32 and 42. Spahn was a tough old bird who hated to lose. On September 29, 1956, after battling for 12 innings against the St. Louis Cardinals, Spahn threw a slow curveball to

a hitless Stan Musial. Musial promptly hit the right centerfield wall with that pitch, for a double. Clete Boyer
received an intentional walk, to set up the double-play. Rip
Repulski lined into a sure-fire double play that caromed
off of Eddie Mathews' knee into left field. Musial trotted
home with the 2-1 win. As "Spahnnie" walked from the
mound that day, there were tears visible from both eyes.
A photographer approached Spahn to capture the moment.
Spahn threw his glove at the man and continued into the
dugout. After winning his 300th game, reporters ask him
how bad he had wanted to win that game. Spahn replied, "I
wanted this one. I wanted the last one, and I want the next
one." Spahn gave his catcher Joe Torre his glove when he
won his 300th game.

By 1965, Spahn didn't know it, but he was at the end of
his career. He was a pitcher and pitching coach for the New
York Mets, skippered by none other than Casey Stengel.
Spahn was now forty-four and wanted to pitch more. Casey
wanted to move him to the bullpen. Spahn wanted no part
of that and was fired by Stengel. "I played for Casey before
and after he was a genius," laughed Spahn.

"I don't think Spahn will ever get into the Hall of Fame
because he won't stop pitching," said Musial. He would
be elected in 1973, in his first year of eligibility, receiving
nearly 83 percent of the votes. He would also be elected by
the fans to baseball's All-Century Team and be honored by
the Atlanta Braves with a 9-foot-high bronze statue in the
plaza outside of Turner Field.

I will never forget meeting Warren Spahn in Houston
at a baseball card show. He was late and most of the folks
standing in line with me were becoming agitated. One
older gentleman in front of me was pacing back and forth
and beginning to grumble about the wait. Finally Spahn

showed up and happened to walk right by this fellow. As Spahn passed by, realizing he was late, he said in jest, "Who you guys waiting for?" This older fellow looked him directly in the eye and answered without a smile, "Cy Young." The whole place broke up in laughter including Spahn. I guess he thought waiting for Spahn was like waiting for the dead. I would get to visit with Spahn on several occasions. He was a bit of a hard case, especially when talking about who should or should not be elected to the Hall of Fame. You could still feel the competitive fire inside him as he spoke. My dad always referred to him as a southpaw.

On November 24, 2003, Warren Spahn would throw his last pitch in life. His pitcher's mound was in Broken Arrow, Oklahoma and for 82 years he had kept them all guessing. Is it a slider or a change-up? Who needs guts when you can throw like that?

Poetry in Motion

He always made them pay on the outside. He brought style and grace in large doses to this game. During the 1930's, the game of football had become a grind'em out contest of brute force and strength, a test of wills. The flying wedge had been abolished because of the injuries it produced, so three yards up the middle and a cloud of dust became the norm, with an occasional forward pass. For the most part, field position was determined by the kicking game, but then along he comes and suddenly the whole football field is being used, especially the outside. Not only could he run like the wind but his agility was uncanny, as if he could see in all directions at the same time. He was some kind of runner, faster than most and could not be contained. When he ran, it was as if you could see the earth breathing beneath his feet. He was so fast he made cheetahs jealous.

He and his twin brother had been discovered at Bonita High School in La Verne, California. That stadium would later be named after him. They participated in every sport possible and excelled. Some sources say he won between 13 and 16 letters in four sports. Their dream was to attend USC together and play football, but things have a way of changing. He ended up playing one year at Cal Poly Pomona before a Congressman from California, named Jerry Voorhis secured an appointment for him at West Point. He refused to go without his brother. He would attend West Point only if his twin brother could go. They enrolled together, in 1943.

"Mr. Outside," as he would later be nicknamed, was Christened Glenn Woodward Davis on December 26, 1924. He was born in Burbank California. Davis had won numerous awards in high school. He would be named the 1942 California High School Player-of-the-Year, while scoring a record 236 points for Bonita. In 1943, he would win the Knute Rockne Trophy for the best track star in California.

His plebe (first) year at West Point would be tough in the classroom, but on the gridiron he put on a show. As a fullback, Davis ran the football 144 times and amassed 1,028 yards rushing while leading Army to seven wins, two losses, and one tie. He was described as poetry in motion. Davis also needed constant tutoring in his classroom work, especially in math. Still, that same year, he failed mathematics and was expelled from West Point after his first term. Glenn Davis had no choice but to return to California and attend Webb School for Boys. After passing an intense four-month course at this prep school, he was readmitted to West Point for the 1944-45 school year. It was here that Davis would meet the other half of what became known as "the Touchdown Twins," Doc Blanchard. These two would form a backfield tandem that was unequaled until a few years ago. Davis would switch positions to halfback as Blanchard took over the duties at fullback. Davis scored a record 59 touchdowns while at Army and still holds the all-time record for most yards averaged per carry in a season (1945), with 11.5 yards. Davis, now known as "Mr. Outside" and Blanchard who was nicknamed "Mr. Inside" teamed up to score 97 touchdowns in their college careers. Their combined touchdown record was not broken until 2007, by USC running backs Reggie Bush and LenDale White. These two scored 99 touchdowns to set the new record. Davis would be named All-American three times in football, while also starring in basketball, baseball and track at West Point. Davis played on three of the best Army teams ever. Davis would win the Maxwell Award, the Walter Camp Trophy as best player-of-the-year, and the 1946 Heisman Trophy. He finished his career with 6,494 yards on 637 carries and averaged a touchdown every nine plays. This great athlete also graduated in 1947, ranked 305 out of a class of 310. Running with a football was a breeze; adding and subtracting, Davis found a little tougher.

After graduating from Army he was offered $75,000 dollars to play baseball for the Brooklyn Dodgers, but he had his sites set on professional football. Davis and Blanchard appeared in a cheap B-movie film about their lives and football heroics entitled *Spirit of West Point*. It was a flop, but the two players got paid $25,000 each for their part in the film. After he was discharged from the United States Army in 1950, Davis got his chance to play pro football. He spent two seasons with the Los Angeles Rams. He had 42 catches for seven touchdowns and passed for two more, while leading the Rams to the 1950 NFL Championship against the Cleveland Browns. Davis also made the Pro Bowl. In 1951 he re-injured a knee, and his career came to an end. It had been quite a ride for Mr. Outside.

Davis now headed to Texas to work in the oil business. In 1953, he tried a comeback with the Rams, but the knee would not hold up to the grind. He would take a job with the *Los Angeles Times* as their special events director. Glenn Davis retired from that job over 30 years later, in 1987. He had been married three times and had one son, Ralph, and a stepson, John Slack III.

In La Quinta, California, on March 9, 2005, Mr. Outside passed away. Even though he had once run the hundred-yard dash in 9.7 seconds, Glenn Davis was not able to outrun prostate cancer. Cancer runs a 9.6. Davis was 80 years old. His pal Blanchard would now take all the carries.

Worth the Price of Two

The year 1945 would find him playing baseball in Kansas City with the Monarchs. His roommate would be none other than the great Jackie Robinson. His career in the Negro Leagues would have him catch and pitch with the likes of Leroy "Satchel" Paige, Bobby Robinson, Josh Gibson, Oscar Charleston, Jud Wilson, Turkey Stearns, Hilton Smith, Smokey Joe Williams and his brother Alex. This six-time All-Star would reportedly play or manage for more than 15 teams in 32 years, but it seemed that his real talent lay in his ability to tell stories. My father used to say," There's a difference in telling stories and story-telling." So, pull up a chair and sit back and listen while I tell you about one of the most-quoted baseball players of all time. Man, this guy led the league in talking.

Theodore Roosevelt "Double Duty" Radcliffe was born on July 7, 1902, in Mobile, Alabama. He was given the name "Double Duty" by writer Damon Runyon, who saw Ted catch for Satchel Paige in the first game of a double-header, during the 1932 Negro League World Series, and then pitch a shutout in the second game.

At the age of seventeen, Ted hitchhiked with his brother Alex north to Chicago, to join another older brother. He would eventually sign a contract to play semi-pro base-ball for 100 dollars a month and 50 cents a day, meal money. Several years later, in 1928, Radcliffe would sign with his first Negro National League team, the Detroit Stars, and start a career that would last well over 32 years. Unfortunately, because of the times, there are only eight years of his career documented. Those statistics show him hitting .273, with a top mark of .316 for the 1929 Detroit Stars. As a pitcher in the 1930's, he won 33 games and lost 17. Ted also saved seven games and appeared in the East-West All-Star game six times, three as a pitcher, and three as a catcher. He became known right away for his fast talking. Brash and full of spunk, Ted was a colorful character if there ever was one! He spoke with a slight lisp and kept everyone "in stitches" with his stories. Ted loved baseball and loved talking about it even more. He still claims to be the only player to strike out Josh Gibson and hit a home run off of Satchel Paige, but it could never be documented. Ty Cobb once said that in an exhibition game, Ted wore a chest protector that said, "Thou shalt not steal." Ted had a strong throwing arm, good catching reflexes, and called a clever game from behind home plate. He had a short, squatty body at 5 feet 9 inches tall and weighed 210 pounds.

"We used to fill that Mack Park up on Sundays," said Ted, who played three seasons for the Detroit Stars. "They'd be lined up on the streets when we opened the gates. We could only get seven or eight thousand in the place, but there were many days that we'd outdraw the Tigers."

In 1992, Ted gave an interview where he talked about Negro players from the past. "There were a lot of great ballplayers came through Detroit with the Stars. I guess the names don't mean much now. Seems to me, a man can play ball that good, he ought to be remembered." He was talking about Norman "Turkey" Stearns. "Turkey Stearns hit the facing of the outfield upper deck at old Comisky Park, with a 450-foot blast," exclaimed Double Duty, "and it was still going when it hit." Ted thought Stearns was a great player and in fact picked him over "Cool Papa," Bell as the best Negro League centerfielder of all time. "Everybody knows that Cool Papa Bell was the fastest man," said Radcliffe; "but he couldn't field with Turkey Stearns." Radcliffe believed Stearns to be one of the best "ever" and would always end the conversation with, "You can talk all you want about the players from the Negro Leagues that made the Hall of Fame and they deserved all of it; but unless Turkey Stearns is in there, too, ain't none of them should be there. He played in Detroit at the same time as Ty Cobb, Harry Heilmann, Heinie Manush, and Charlie Gehringer were with the Tigers and all four of them ended up in Cooperstown. But I saw him play and, back then, Turkey Stearns didn't have to care for nobody."

Ted also considered Jud "Boojum" Wilson a better hitter than Josh Gibson. Ted should know because he split time behind the plate with Gibson when Josh was a rookie catcher with the Homestead Grays. "He didn't hit as many home runs, but he hit so many doubles and singles. That's why they called him 'Boojum,' from the sound of his line drives rattling off the fences," laughed Radcliffe.

Ted would show his humor in stories like when he called Wilmer "Red" Fields "the man who integrated the Homestead Grays." You see, Fields was a very light-skinned man, but he was an African-American. Duty also talked about how Emory Osborne showed him and team-mate Chet Brewer how to throw a scratched ball. "Didn't have to cut it, just scratch it a little," said Radcliffe. Another funny story that Ted liked to tell was how Josh Gibson hit a homer against the Memphis Red Sox, in 1938, which bounced into a passing freight train heading to St. Louis, Missouri. "It was a 500-mile home run," said a smiling Radcliffe. While playing in Cuba during the winter, he was asked if he had seen a young Fidel Castro play baseball. "Couldn't play a lick," laughed Ted. Double Duty did catch a no-hitter by Satchel Paige and swears that Paige's control was so good that he saw him throw a clam shell and kill a butterfly. Ted also said about Satch, "One season his arm was so sore he couldn't throw it across the street." I said, "Just roll it up there. They're ascared of your name; they ain't gonna hit it." About the speed of Cool Papa Bell, Ted would say, "You had to see him to believe it. He'd take a little walk off the base — and forget it, he was gone." Ted also believed that Newt Allen of the Kansas City Monarchs was the best second baseman on the team, ahead of Jackie Robinson. "We called him 'Colt,' because he was so young," said Ted, and many claimed he wouldn't even look at first base on the pivot. Ted laughs out loud when talking about the time he pitched the last six innings of a ballgame with a broken finger for the Birmingham Black Barons. "I had to pitch with these three fingers," he said. While pitching in Mexico, Radcliffe said, "Every time I hit a home run, they gave me a watch and a suit of clothes." He hit 17 home runs, sold most of the watches and became one of the best-dressed men in Mexico.

Radcliffe always said, "The three greatest men in Negro baseball were Posey, Wilkinson, and Abe Saperstein of Birmingham. They operated like big-league teams. They were the only ones had four or five sets of uniforms, the rest of them had two; you had to dry your uniform overnight on those other teams." Double Duty always swore that when the Negro teams played against the white teams in an exhibition game, "We were playing against the nine ballplayers and two umpires." It was during one of these exhibitions that Radcliffe claims that Josh Gibson hit a home run off of St. Louis Cardinal right hander Bill Doak that traveled out of Sportsman's Park, and onto a front porch, sending the startled family running for cover. In 1947, Double Duty remembers being in the clubhouse when Clyde Sukeforth and George Sisler, Branch Rickey's top two scouts, came in to take Jackie Robinson to the Knickerbocker Hotel after a game. Jackie would return to his room at 1:00 pm that night, a member of the Brooklyn Dodgers' farm club in Montreal.

The game has changed since he retired in the fifties. Throughout his career, Double Duty had to endure seg-regation in every city except St. Paul, Minnesota. He has been inducted into the "Yesterday's Negro League Players' Wall of Fame," at County Stadium in Milwaukee, received the Illinois Historical Committee's Lifetime Achievement Award from Mayor Richard Daley, and has also been the guest of three U. S. Presidents at the White House. "Heck, even 94-year-old Buck O'Neil called me an old man," said Ted before he died; "I was so old, I couldn't vote." Approaching his 100th birthday, you could find Ted sit-ting in an easy chair next to a window facing a sandlot. His worn-out, twisted, broken hands were the proof of a catcher's life in baseball. He would be surrounded by bats, gloves, plaques, and posters from those long-ago days. "It ain't like it used to be. There used to be some good pitchers. There aren't ballplayers like there used to be. It's a shame," exclaimed Radcliffe. His apartment, in a retire-ment center, was about a half mile from old Comisky Park, in Chicago.

On August 11, 2005, the most-quoted man in baseball, Ted "Double Duty" Radcliffe, finally stopped telling stories. He had made people smile for 103 years. When you live that long, there is a lot to talk about! "Double Duty shared such a love for baseball and a passion for life," said White Sox owner, Jerry Reinsdorf. "We all loved to see him at the ballpark, listen to his stories, and share in his laughter. He leaves such a great legacy, after experiencing so much history and change during his long life. He will be missed by all of us with the White Sox." He certainly gave us our money's worth!

On Deck

Eighty-eight-year-old Phil Rizzuto is now up. That's right: He was on deck, as they say in the world of baseball. He was batting second behind Al Lopez. Rizzuto is the oldest living member of the Baseball Hall of Fame, now that Al Lopez has passed away. So how old was Al, you ask? Heck, Al Lopez Jr. is sixty-three. Al was so old that he played for the Brooklyn Robins, later to be called the Dodgers. Oh yeah, and remember the Boston Braves? I didn't think so. He played baseball with them too, before they left for Milwaukee. Alfonso Ramon Lopez had just turned 97 on August 20, 2005. In fact, prior to his death on October 30, 2005, Al was also the only living major leaguer to play during the 1920's. His first game as a major leaguer occurred on September 27, 1928.

Al was born in Tampa, Florida in 1908, the last time the Chicago Cubs won a World Series. Henry Ford was building his first Model T automobile, Theodore Roosevelt was in the White House, The Panama Canal was being built and the Wright Brothers had managed to tame the science of flight in Kitty Hawk, NC. He was born before Wrigley Field or Fenway Park was built. There was no Baseball Hall of Fame, infield fly rule or designated hitter.

Radar guns, uniform numbers and the National Anthem were not even part of the game yet. Heck, Arizona wasn't even a state. At the age of 10, Al was knocked unconscious when he was struck in the face while playing baseball. This accident required treatment to repair broken bones, but it would never sour Al on the game he was growing to love. Al wanted to be a part of this game, a very big part.

Lopez, or "Senor" as he was called by his teammates, would squat behind home plate for nineteen years in the big leagues. When he retired, he held the Major League record for most games caught (1,918). That record would stand for almost forty years before Bob Boone and Carlton Fisk finally caught him.

At 5'1", 165 pounds, Lopez was not much of an offensive threat, and he only hit higher than .275 three times in his career. When Brooklyn manager Wilbert Robinson spotted newcomer Al Lopez at spring training in 1928, he exclaimed, "They're sending me midgets. He's too small and skinny." As it turned out, Uncle Robbie was wrong and Al developed into an excellent catcher in spite of his unimposing dimensions. Eight was his career high in dingers (1936 and 1939), while 57 RBI was the most he accomplished in 1930. His great value was found in his endurance, and for 12 years he caught 100 or more games to lead the National league. In 1941, he tied a Major League record of 114 games caught without a passed ball. He also led all catchers in assists three times and fielding average three times, as well. But one very interesting batting fact stands out for old Al Lopez. On September 12, 1930, he became the last Major League player to record a homerun on the bounce. That's right, Al smoked a fastball over the head of Cincinnati left-fielder Bob Meusel, and the ball bounced into the bleachers in Brooklyn's Ebbets

Field for a homerun. The National League would change its rules the next year, making Al's homerun just a double.

Lopez would call the signals behind home plate for some of the best pitchers in the game. Bob Feller, Dizzy Dean, Hal Newhouser and Dazzy Vance would hurl their best stuff at Lopez with the confidence that their pitches would be caught for a strike. Lopez would also spend hours telling folks how as a teenager in 1925 he had a chance to catch the "big train" himself, Walter Johnson. "He wasn't firing like he used to, but he was still very fast and had good control," Lopez said. "All you had to do was hold your mitt around the strike zone, and it'd be right there." For 45 dollars a week at the age of 16, Al would catch baseball fever. He had no way of knowing then that baseball would be his life.

Al Lopez would go on to become a two-time All-Star while playing for four different clubs from 1928 to 1947. He would wear uniform numbers 10, 7, 8 and 12, but would be most recognized by the number he wore as a manager, 42. He would put on the tools of ignorance for some of the best managers of the game. Casey Stengel, Frankie Frisch, Lou Boudreau, Max Carey, Bill McKechnie and Wilbert Robinson would all leave their managerial marks on Lopez. Those marks would serve him well.

As a manager, which got him elected to the Hall of Fame in 1977, Lopez won 1,422 games while losing 1,026, for a .518 winning percentage. In fact, he won more games (1,381) then any other manager in Major League Baseball from 1951 – 1965, including Walter Alston, Casey Stengel and Paul Richards.

Many experts ranked his 1954 Cleveland Indians team as one of the greatest of all time as they set an American League record by winning 111 games out of 154. With hitters like Larry Doby and Bobby Avila, Cleveland led the American League in homers. But it was on the pitcher's mound that the Indians thrived. Bob Feller, Bob Lemon, Early Winn, Mike Garcia and Art Houtteman made up one of the most talented pitching staffs in history. Don Mossi, Hal Newhouser and Ray Narleski chewed up the remaining innings from the bull pen. It has been written that Al was a complete manager. He just knew when to gamble and when to play the percentages. His work with pitchers was exceptional, and his clubs consistently had the best pitching in the American League. May 2, 1969, Al Lopez resigned as the White Sox manager because of health problems. Al moved to Tampa, Florida and lived alone after his wife, Connie, passed away in 1983. He is survived by one son, three grandchildren and nine great-grandchildren.

Lopez would be inducted by a special veterans committee, into the Baseball Hall of Fame on January 31, 1977 along with Amos Rusie and Joe Sewell.

With Rizzuto now batting for Lopez, Bobby Doerr is on deck.

Too Short

On March 14, 1960, he became the last of nine born in a small apartment on the south side of Chicago. The corner of State and 43rd Streets was located in the Robert Taylor Homes section of town, otherwise known as "the projects." He was a momma's boy if there ever was one. Both his parents worked long and hard and, in fact, his dad had two jobs, which kept him busy and away from home most of the time. He rarely saw his father who was said to have been a pretty fair left-handed pitcher in the old Negro Leagues. So his mom, like most, became the guiding force in his life. Growing up in the projects came with all sorts of disadvantages, but love and laughter would sustain this family through the rough times. It was said that if you came out of these projects with a number on your back, it was more than likely issued by the state prison and not some sports team. Still, many fine people lived in these homes all their lives.

His allowance was one dollar per week, and it was used to purchase candy and little rubber balls for 10 to 15 cents apiece. There was no little league in the inner city, so wadded-up aluminum foil; old socks or rubber balls were used to play baseball. At every turn, you could see mysterious squares painted on the sides of buildings. These of course were used as strike zones. If he was lucky enough to find four or five guys to play ball with at the same time, then they would move to a nearby asphalt field, complete with painted bases. This would be his daily routine until he entered high school.

Calumet High School would introduce him, at the age of fifteen, to organized baseball. With his love for the game, a God-given talent, and a little coaching, he would become a high school All-American at third base. His arm strength was magnificent, and he could always hit a fast ball. Summers would find him playing ball with several semi-pro teams throughout town. Playing ball with the bigger kids helped hone his skills; but no matter how well he played, he was always told by the scouts and others that he was "too short" or too small to play baseball. His five-foot eight-inch height and roly-poly body were deceiving in regard to strength and speed. He looked more like a football player than a third baseman. Even though he could not bend down and touch his toes, he could run the sixty-yard dash in 6.3 seconds and throw what the old guys called a "frozen rope" to first base. After high school, he would not be drafted by the pros. Yet still he dreamed and all the while he could hear his mother say, "You can make the Major Leagues, Kirby".

Ford Motor Company dismissed Kirby Puckett in the summer of 1980, after his high school graduation. With no job, he had wanted to take a summer off, but he was offered a full scholarship by Coach Dewey Kalmer of Bradley University to play baseball. With tears streaming down his face, he accepted. Bradley was great. It was only two or more hours away from home by bus, and besides he would get to play baseball.

Sometimes life has a way of handing you some bad news with the good. He had only been in school a month when his dad died. After staying with his mom for a month, she insisted that he return to school. "I have too much money tied up in bats, gloves and balls," she would say. When he returned to Bradley, he was moved to the outfield. Seems that Coach Kalmer had an all-senior infield and nowhere for Kirby to play. He would receive a crash course on playing centerfield. Kirby would make the All-Missouri Valley Conference team hitting .400 and leading the team in home runs and stolen bases. Things still didn't feel right to Kirby, and he decided to leave Bradley at the end of the school year. More semi-pro ball would lead to lots of baseball, and scouts from the Twins began to take notice. Kirby enrolled at Triton College, not aware that he had been taken in the January 1982 draft by the Minnesota Twins. Kirby Puckett would be their first pick and the third pick overall in the draft. The Twins sent Tom Hull to Kirby's house with a two-thousand-dollar signing bonus. He had made that in a month at Ford installing carpets in cars and politely said, "No, thanks." Hull returned a few weeks later with a six-thousand-dollar offer and was sent away again by the stubborn Puckett kid. Then more bad news reared its ugly head. Tom Hull died suddenly from a heart attack before he could meet with Kirby again. Kirby would continue with school and college baseball. Kirby would own the Junior College World Series with his play, as scouts continued to watch.

Ellsworth Brown of the Twins offered Kirby a twenty-thousand-dollar signing bonus at the end of that school year, and the six month holdout was over. In 1984, Kirby would find himself playing with the Toledo Mud Hens. It was in the Minor Leagues that he received his first real nickname, "Shoes." That's right! You see Kirby loved shoes, and growing up poor he had learned to take care of the few shoes he had. He was constantly shining his spikes. Shoe companies like Nike, Reebok and Adidas offered him new baseball shoes in an effort to have him sign with their company. Instead of signing, Kirby simply collected duffle bags of shoes. He loved it, but finally signed with Adidas.

He had only been in the minors for two years and had skipped double-A ball entirely, when on May 7, 1984 a few weeks into the season, "Puck" arrived in Anaheim, California. The dream had come true. He had finally made it to the Major Leagues.

The rest of Kirby Puckett's career is all there in the baseball books. How on May 8, he became the ninth player in MLB history to collect four hits in his first Major League game. How he went on to become one of the greatest players ever to don a Twins uniform. How in twelve short years he led the club in hits (2,304), doubles (414), total bases (3,453), at-bats (7,244), and runs (1,071). He collected six Gold Gloves, five Silver Slugger Awards and was a 10-time All-Star. How he would dominate the 1991 World Series with his play against the Atlanta Braves. All he did was scale the outfield walls, and hit a walk-off home run, all while carrying the team on his back. All you had to see of "Puck's" career was Game Six of that series, to know he belonged in the Baseball Hall of Fame. He was also honored with the Roberto Clemente Award in 1996. Sadly, his career was cut too short when he developed glaucoma in his right eye which caused him to lose his sight. All in all, Kirby never dwelt on his adversity. He loved baseball and his enthusiasm was contagious. Always laughing and enjoying life, he kept telling everybody, "If you believe in yourself and you work hard, anything, and I'm telling you anything, is possible." The Twins would retire Kirby's number 34 in 1997 and place him into their Hall of Fame in the year 2000. The ultimate honor in his game would take place in 2001 when he became a first-ballot inductee into the National Baseball Hall of Fame.

I met Kirby in Phoenix at a spring training game. He was kind enough to sign two Hall of Fame Perez-Steele cards for me. I also heard a story that Bob Costas named his son Kirby after Kirby Puckett. What an honor.

On March 6, 2006, at the age of 45, Kirby Puckett's life was cut too short by a stroke. After he had retired from baseball in Phoenix, Arizona, his weight would balloon up and, with heart disease a big part of his family's history, Kirby's health became a question mark. Signs, flowers and baseballs were laid out in front of the Metrodome in his honor. He will always be remembered as being a winner and a champion, and also for that infectious laugh. He was simply a joy to watch. Kirby Puckett was too short; too short to play, had too short a career and too short a life. There was nothing ever really too short about "Puck".

Ladies and Gentlemen

Every Friday night at 10 pm, I would beg my father to stay up and watch the "Gillette Friday Night Fights." It was the mid nineteen-fifties and that night always started the same way. I would sit on dad's lap as he lay back on our sofa. Our black and white Motorola TV would begin to warm up with a white dot in the center of the screen. As the picture began to appear there would be several very bright lights hanging over the square canvas surrounded by a ring of three ropes. You could see the ringside announcer, judges, reporters, cameramen, and the bell located on the front row, but then darkness would prevail and the crowd behind them all but disappeared. The murmur that ran through the crowd would tell you that this was a big fight.

Then it happened, the part I remember most as a kid. He always seemed to be a very short, round man with almost no hair. As he approached the center of the ring, a microphone that was hanging on the end of a cord would slowly be lowered down toward him. "Where does that microphone come from," I would ask my dad. It always seemed that the man had to stand on his tip-toes to reach that microphone. He would place the microphone in front of him and say these words: "Ladies and Gentlemen, tonight, live, from

Madison Square Garden, the heavyweight title elimination bout." The roar of the crowd would send chills down my spine. The winner of this fight would take on the champion, Archie Moore, for the heavyweight championship of the world. As the announcer spoke, his words would sometimes echo three or four times before fading away, as if one word began before the last one ended. Boy was it exciting. Then the man would continue with his introduction. "In this corner, wearing the white trunks with black stripes, standing 5'11" tall, weighing 182 and 1/4 pounds, and with a record of twenty-nine wins and one defeat, twenty-one of those wins by way of knockout, Floyd Patterson." Then he would repeat the last name again, "Patterson." Now his opponent would be introduced. "In the other corner, wearing black trunks, standing 6'3 1/2" tall, weighing 211 pounds, and with a record of twenty-one wins and three defeats, ten of those wins by way of knockout, Tommy "Hurricane" Jackson, Jackson." Then, as you have seen hundreds of times before, the two fighters and their trainers would meet the referee in the center of the ring for the final instructions of the fight. It was June 8, 1956.

"The Rabbit," as Muhammad Ali nicknamed him, would finally get his chance at the heavyweight title, if he could just win this fight. Patterson would decision Jackson in twelve rounds. Later that same year, on November 30, Patterson would knock out "The Mongoose", Archie Moore, to become the youngest man to hold the heavyweight title at the age of 21.

Patterson had been born into poverty on January 4, 1935 in Waco, North Carolina. As the last of eleven born, this rough-and-tumble kid would face many challenges on a day-to-day basis. He emerged from a troubled childhood that included petty theft and persistent truancy while growing up in Brooklyn, New York, and ended up in a reform school for boys by age ten. It was there, at the age fourteen, that he learned to box and ended up training in the now-legendary Gramercy Gym, under Cus D'Amato, the same man who would later train Mike Tyson. Patterson took to boxing like a duck takes to water. Patterson would win the New York Golden Gloves title in both 1951 and 1952. At age seventeen, Patterson would represent the United States in the 1952 Olympics held in Helsinki, Finland, and won the Gold Medal as a middleweight. His unique fighting style would find him boxing with his gloves held high in front of his face while springing forward with vicious hooks and jabs that most often caught his opponents off guard. This little guy packed a big punch in both hands. The speed of his hands and feet had never been seen before by most fighters. "He was very quick; next to Ali, he was the fastest guy I fought," claimed George Chuvalo. Patterson was considered small for a heavyweight, even during those days in boxing. He never fought at a weight over 188 pounds and had to be quick to avoid the beatings of much larger opponents. Still he would go down 21 times in a total of 64 fights. "They said I was the fighter who got knocked down the most, but I also got up the most," Patterson once said.

Patterson fought some of the best on his way up the ladder. Toughs like Dick Wagner, Alvin Williams, and Jimmy Slade would prove to be no match for Patterson. Joey Maxim was the exception and defeated Floyd Patterson in eight rounds on June 7, 1954. There would be no rematch between these two. After winning the vacant World Heavyweight Title over Moore, Patterson would fight several exhibitions, including three major fights with Roy Harris, Brian London, and a rematch with Tommy

Jackson. He would retain his title in all three fights only to lose it in his next fight, to Ingemar Johansson, on June 26, 1959. Johansson would embarrass Patterson by knocking him down seven times in three rounds, and the fight was stopped by the referee on a technical knockout. A year later, June 20, 1960, Patterson would stop Johansson cold in five rounds, to regain his title in the heavyweight rematch. Those results would make Patterson the first man in the history of boxing to regain the heavyweight title. The third and final bout between these two fighters would take place in Miami Beach, Florida, on March 13, 1961. Patterson would win again with a knockout of Johansson in the sixth round, to remain the World Heavyweight Champ. He would knock out Tom McNeeley in December of 1961, before facing Sonny Liston on September 25, 1962. That first Liston fight would be the beginning of the end for Floyd Patterson as heavyweight champ. Liston would knock out Patterson in the first round and embarrass the former champ and good guy, to the point of wearing fake glasses and a beard in order to avoid being recognized in public. The same results occurred ten months later in a rematch with Liston. For another ten years after that first Liston fight, Floyd Patterson would continue to do the only thing he knew he was good at, boxing. He would get three more shots at the title but never regain it. Patterson would go the distance but lose each fight to Muhammed Ali, Jerry Quarry, and Jimmy Ellis, for the titles in 1965, 1967, and 1968. That 1965 fight with Ali became famous, as Ali kept screaming at Patterson throughout the fight, "What's my name?" Patterson had insisted on calling Ali by his given name, Cassius Clay, which infuriated Ali. The two fighters would not become friends until after Patterson had retired. Although he would score a few more big wins over fighters like Henry Cooper, Terry Daniels, and Oscar Bonavena, Patterson would never wear the title belt again. His last fight and loss would be a rematch with the great Ali on September 20, 1972.

Overall, Floyd Patterson would finish his career with a 55-8-1 record including 40 knockouts. He would be inducted into the U. S. Olympic Committee Hall Of Fame in 1987 and the International Boxing Hall of Fame in 1991. After retiring in 1972, Patterson would remain close to his beloved sport by serving twice as chairman of the New York State Athletic Commission. In a 1998 interview, Patterson said, "If it wasn't for boxing, I would probably be behind bars or dead." On May 11, 2006 Floyd Patterson would go down for the final count. Alzheimer's disease and prostate cancer would finally take his life. He had fought the good fight for 71 years.

Hall-of-Fame trainer Emanuel Steward would say of Patterson, "That was my first true hero."

A Means to An End

He was a rancher, always had been. The smell of fresh-turned dirt and sunshine made him feel good; made him smile. Tending the land, not the *pin* was his passion. Raising cattle and growing things were his specialties. He was what the old-timers called "salt of the earth," some would say. To him, *eagles* flew over the ranch, *greens* were something you ate for dinner, a *drive* was something you took Sunday afternoons after church, *irons* were used for branding and a *hook* was used to catch a fish. He had no idea you could make that much money hitting and chasing a little white ball around a golf course. Every time he played, he could think of nothing more than making enough money to buy more land, a new tractor or more cows. His enjoyment came from ranching, but he played some golf too. Golf was his way to come up with the grub-stake; but don't ever be mistaken, the ranch came first. Golf was just a means to an end for him. Little did he know that it would be history that kind of got in his way!

John Byron Nelson, Jr. was born on a ranch near Waxahachie, Texas, on February 4, 1912. His family moved to Fort Worth, Texas, when Byron turned 11 years old. A severe case of typhoid fever cost him nearly half his body weight and almost his life. He would barely survive, but lost his ability to father children. It was in Fort Worth that he began to caddy at the age of 12, at a local golf course known as Glen Garden Country Club. Initially, caddies were not permitted to play at the club, so young Byron would practice after sundown, by placing a white handkerchief over the hole so he could find it in the dark. A few years later, in 1927, the country club would change its rules and witness a match, during the Glen Garden Caddie Tournament, where the 14-year-old Nelson would defeat by a single stroke, his fellow caddy and future golf great, Ben Hogan, in a nine-hole playoff. After he graduated from high school, Byron worked as a file clerk in the accounting office of the Fort Worth and Denver Railway Company. As the Great Depression of the early thirties occurred, like most folks, he became a casualty and lost his job. Since real jobs remained scarce and because no other line of work was available in 1932, he decided to turn to the business of professional golf. He would leave quite a legacy. Byron Nelson started out with hickory shafts, competing against Gene Sarazen, and would live to see Tiger Woods play with titanium heads. In between, history was made.

His first win on the PGA Tour happened in the 1935 New Jersey State Open, and he would celebrate his second win one year later at the Metropolitan Open. In 1937, the world of golf would begin to take notice of this young, gentle man from the State of Texas, when Byron would win the big one, "The Masters." In 1939, Nelson won four tournaments including the prestigious U.S. Open, which would be his tenth victory overall. He would capture the PGA Championship in 1940 with a one-stroke win over Sam Snead and win "The Masters" for the second time, in a playoff against Ben Hogan in 1942. In 1944, he won 13 of the 23 tournaments he played. The following year, he won 18 times in 31 starts. Are you listening? That means he won 31 of the 54 tournaments he entered in two years. Incredible! Eleven of those victories came in a row, still the all-time record today. Nelson would also finish second 7 times in 1945 and never placed out of the top 10. He shot under 70 a remarkable 19 times, consecutively. One of those wins in 1945 came in the Corpus Christi Open played at Oso Beach Golf Course, a course that I have played many times. He also won a second PGA Championship that same year, which gave him a total of five major championships. He was voted AP Male Athlete of the Year in both 1944 and 1945. His last year of serious golf would be 1946. He would continue to play occasionally, but his 673-acre ranch in Roanoke, Texas began calling him back. Remarkably, at the age of 34 he decided to retire. The six victories he recorded in 1946 would bring his total victories on tour to 52. His last win occurred in the 1951 Bing Crosby Pro-Am Championship. Only five players have more victories than Nelson: Sam Snead, Jack Nicklaus, Ben Hogan, Arnold Palmer, and now Tiger Woods. Nelson once said, "Every great player has to learn the two C's: how to concentrate and how to maintain composure."

Byron Nelson also played on the prestigious U. S. Ryder Cup teams of 1937 and 1947. He later captained this same team in 1965. Byron played in the British Open on two occasions and finished fifth in 1937. Nelson is still the only professional golfer to have a PGA tour stop named after him, the EDS Byron Nelson Championship. His swing has been described as long and fluid with perfect balance. His coordination, from his feet up, was all synchronized. "You've got to feel your swing through your sight," he once said. "The mechanics of my swing were such that it required no thought," Nelson said. "It's like eating. You don't think to feed yourself." "Byron Nelson was, without question, one of the greatest players our game has ever seen," said Jack Nicklaus. "I only won $182,000 in my whole life," said Nelson laughing. "In 1937, I got fifth-place money at the British Open—$187—and it cost me $3,000 to play because I had to take a leave of absence from my club job to go." In the 1960's he became one of golf's earliest TV announcers.

Most folks my age did not get to see him play golf and will mostly remember the stories and remember watching Byron Nelson join "Slamming Sammy" Snead and Gene Sarazan at the Masters Tournament in Augusta, Georgia. Those three always began the tournament by hitting the ceremonial first balls. In fact the bridge at Hole #13 at Augusta is named for Byron. Something else you may not know is that three of golf's greats, Nelson, Snead and Ben Hogan, were all born in 1912, about 6 months apart.

He was found dead at their home on a Tuesday, September 26, 2006. He was lying face down on the back porch. "He had told me before I left home for Bible study, 'I'm so proud of you,'" said his wife, Peggy. Byron Nelson was 94 years young and passed away from natural causes. He was buried the following Friday in Irving, Texas. Byron Nelson was elected to the PGA Hall of Fame in 1953 and to the Golf Hall of Fame in 1974. There have also been many streets, parkways and highways named after him, and on October 16, 2006, President George W. Bush awarded Nelson posthumously the Congressional Gold Medal, the highest award that can be bestowed upon a citizen by the Legislative Branch of the United States government. Tiger Woods called Nelson "the greatest ambassador golf has ever known." Through it all, he never complained. He always remained grateful and gracious. His courtly manners inspired others to call him "Lord Byron," a nickname he received from Atlanta sports journalist, O. B. Keeler. I think the most humble thing I ever heard Byron Nelson say was during an interview with The Associated Press in 1997. It went like this: "I don't know very much. I know a little bit about golf. I know how to make a stew and I know how to be a decent man." Being a gentleman may have been the thing he did best.

If Only That Cap Could Talk!

On a hot afternoon in Houston, Texas I approached the autograph section of a Tri-Star show. The entire bottom floor of the George R. Brown Center was filled with card dealers, collectors, and autograph and memorabilia seekers. There could have easily been a thousand people or more, on hand. To my left sat Hall-of-Fame players Reggie Jackson and Warren Moon, signing autographs, while Brooks Robinson signed to my right. I was astounded because no one was in line for the guy signing autographs in the middle section. There he sat quietly with the biggest grin you have ever seen. It was if he knew something you didn't...and he did. His hands were folded together in front of him as if he were in prayer. With sparkling eyes, he looked lost in thought. I was here to see him and held three of his newly-released books under one arm and a picture of him in the other hand, to be signed. I was excited to meet him and could not understand why others were not as interested in his autograph and stories as I was. His line was empty. Perhaps they did not realize who he was. It was then that I became distracted. You see, on his head sat a cap that may have been as old as he was. He was already pushing 85 years of age by now, and this cap looked every

220

bit as old. It wasn't so much the look of the cap that caught my attention, as it was the names that were on that cap. It must have been signed by at least fifty players.

Recently, he had been made quite famous after starring in Ken Burns' documentary on "The National Pastime," baseball. Millions of people had now seen him on their local PBS channels. Were they not paying attention or did they just not care? This guy "is" the ambassador of Negro League baseball. You have probably heard the saying, "Been there, done that." Well, he may have invented that saying. Not only was he one of the last of the greatest generation, but he was also one of the few left of a dying breed, a Negro League baseball player and manager. He also oversees the Negro League Hall of Fame in Kansas City, Missouri.

As I approached, his face lit up like a roman candle. I laid down my picture and stuck out my hand and said, "Hi, Mr. O'Neil, my name is Andy Purvis, and I want you and me to have lunch sometime and you can tell me about every one of those players who autographed your cap." He smiled even more and said, "I can do that." That's right; he was non-other than Buck O'Neil. Of course we never had that lunch, but I'm still available. Man, if only that cap could talk!

Buck O'Neil is a fascinating guy who has spent his lifetime in baseball. His smooth delivery of stories and incredibly sharp mind lure you into another world where baseball is life. He could deliver decades of baseball knowledge at the drop of that cap. Baseball is his religion. His voice reminds you of your grandfather, telling tales on the back porch, on a breezy night in October. White-haired, a bit slumped over and wrinkled, when talking baseball he is still as full of life as a new baby boy. It was as if he could tell you anything and you would nod with approval. I once saw him on a televised Major League Baseball game which was hosted by ESPN's Jon Miller and Joe Morgan. Miller asked Buck, "Was Josh Gibson really as great as they say?" Buck smiled and said, "Oh, he was better than that." Wow! I may never forget that answer. How clever of this old man to leave the listener with the thought that however great you thought Josh Gibson might be as a player, he was really even better than that.

John Jordan "Buck" O'Neil was born November 13, 1911 in Carrabelle, Florida. It's quite possible that he was born in a dugout with a baseball bat in his hands. He was introduced to the game of baseball at a very early age by his father, who played for several local teams. "I loved it," said Buck. The family would later move to Sarasota, Florida where Buck, at the age of twelve, would work in the celery fields. One hot day Buck's father overheard him say, "Damn. There's got to be something better than this." His thoughts then turned to baseball. Living in Sarasota not only enabled Buck to work in a celery field, but also to see real Major League baseball played by professional teams which came south for spring training. With his chest stuck out, Buck said, "I saw Babe Ruth, I saw John McGraw, I saw Connie Mack—I saw all the great ballplayers of that era; and now my eyes are wide open seeing these people play baseball at a level that I never imagined it could be." Buck knew at this early age that the game of baseball was his way out of that celery field for good.

So you see, if those names on his cap could talk, they would tell you the life story of Buck O'Neil. This cap would tell you about a fellow, who has played, coached, managed, and scouted for seven decades in the game of baseball. Hall-of-Fame players like Satchel Paige, Jackie

Robinson, James "Cool Papa" Bell, Larry Doby, Oscar Charleston, and Monte Irvin would tell you about Buck O'Neil, who was denied a high school education because of racial segregation. They would tell how he would leave Florida in 1934 and after playing some semi-pro ball for a few years, he would join the newly- formed Memphis Red Sox in 1937, as a first baseman. In 1938, a year later, his contract would be sold to the Kansas City Monarchs. These players would describe how his cat-like reflexes and soft hands allowed him to make terrific catches, on even the worst of throws, to the first sack. Buck had always been able to catch a baseball, even at a very early age. How his genuine love for people and the game made him easy to be around and a great teammate. Regardless of the segregation laws of that era, he was strong-willed, determined, and first and foremost a baseball player.

Guys like George "Mule" Suttles, Leon Day, Hilton Smith, Quincy Trouppe, and Lorenzo "Piper" Davis would confirm what a fine hitter Buck was in the late 1930's and 1940's; and how Buck's 1946 batting average of .353 was the highest in the entire Negro Leagues and he followed that year with a .358 mark, in 1947. Four times he would hit over .300 and finish with a .288 lifetime average. He was an excellent clutch hitter. Great eyesight and terrific bat control allowed him to place the ball in play with the best hitters of his day. He was also as fast as most of them. Hitting sometimes goes into a slump, but speed never takes a day off.

Other players like "Nap" Gully, Raleigh "Biz" Mackey, Bill "Fireball" Beverly, Jimmy Crutchfield, and Sam Bankhead had also autographed that cap. They would tell you about the countless number of games in which Buck played during the Negro League barnstorming days of the Thirties and Forties. Where playing all day, riding a bus all night, and pinching pennies was a way of life. Barnstorming was a way to bring the game of baseball to the South where most of these players had grown up and also provided African-American players the opportunity to test their skills against the white Major League players. Everyone could bunt, steal a base, hit for average, and run to first base in under four seconds. "It was like having nine, Rickey Henderson's on your team, at the same time," laughed Buck. There was always lots of talking and bragging on the field, while little tricks of the game became commonplace. Thousands of fans turned out to see the Negro League players. "They were proud, very proud," said O'Neil. "That was the era of dress-up. If you look at a picture taken from those games, you see the men have on ties, hats (everybody wore hats then), and the ladies had on fine dresses," exclaimed Buck. Their game was exciting, entertaining and on the cutting edge of professional baseball.

Other names on that cap like Ted "Double Duty" Radcliffe, Willard Brown, "Crush" Holloway, Wilmer Fields, and Bill "Ready" Cash would witness Buck's play in three Negro American League All-Star games, as well as two Negro American League World Series games. O'Neil would bat .333 with two homeruns in those series. His career would then be briefly interrupted from 1943 until 1945, while he served time in the U.S. Navy, during World War II. In 1948, as Buck's playing days began to wind down, he was so well-respected by management that he was offered the opportunity to be a player-manager for the Kansas City Monarchs. He would continue to manage until 1955.

It was during these years that he would have an impact on the careers of many future Major League players like

Don Newcombe, Sam Jethroe, Elston Howard, Luke Easter, Vic Power, Hank Thompson, and Minnie Minoso. During this time, Buck also helped guide the Monarchs to five pennants while managing the East-West All-Star teams from 1951 to 1954. Buck claims that managing the Monarchs was simple, because he had some of the greatest players who ever lived.

In 1956, Buck signed on as a scout for the Chicago Cubs. He is credited with signing Lou Brock to a Minor-League contract and discovering Lee Smith and Joe Carter. Although Buck had some dealings early on with Ernie Banks, it was actually "Cool Papa" Bell who signed Banks for the Cubs, two years before Buck became a scout. In 1962, O'Neil became the first black coach hired by a Major League team, the Chicago Cubs. After many years as a coach and scout for the Cubs, O'Neil would join the Kansas City Royals in 1988 as one of their scouts. He was also named "Midwest Scout of the Year," in 1998.

In 1990, Buck O'Neil became the driving force behind establishing the Negro League Museum in Kansas City, Missouri. He still serves as the honorary Board Chairman. Although I have never visited this museum, I understand that here you can learn all about the Negro Leagues including the careers of other players like Max Manning, Connie Johnson, Willie Pope, Verdell Mathis, Gene Baker, and, Mahlon Duckett. You will also find out how great players like Hank Aaron, Roy Campanella, Willie Mays, Frank Robinson, and Joe Black got their start in the Negro League ranks. The question most often asked Buck O'Neil is, "Who was the greatest baseball player that you have ever seen play?" His answer has always been, "The best Major League baseball player I ever saw was Willie Mays, but the best BASEBALL PLAYER was Oscar

Charleston. We old-timers knew that the closet thing to Oscar Charleston was Willie Mays." O'Neil also served as one of the 18 members of the Baseball Hall-of-Fame Veterans Committee from 1981 to 2000. The induction of eight Negro League players during that time was a reflection of his role on that committee. Buck O'Neil himself was nominated in 2006 but failed to receive the necessary votes to gain admission.

My favorite interview with Buck O'Neil occurred with film producer Ken Burns. Burns asked Buck if the game of baseball would always survive. Buck responded "Yes, somebody or something will always happen to keep the interest of the game alive." Then he told this story: "I heard Ruth hit the ball. I'd never heard that sound before, and I was outside the fence but it was the sound of the bat that I never heard before in my life. And the next time I heard that sound, I'm in Washington DC, in the dressing room, and I heard that sound of a bat hitting the ball – sounded like when Ruth hit the ball. I rushed out, got on nothing but a jockstrap – rushed out – we were playing the Homestead Grays and it was Josh Gibson hitting the ball. And so I heard this sound again. Now I didn't hear it anymore. I'm in Kansas City. I'm working for the Cubs at the time, and I was upstairs and I was coming down for the batting practice. And before I could get out there I heard this sound one more time that I've heard only twice in my life. Now, you know who this is? Bo Jackson. Bo Jackson was swinging that bat. And now I heard this sound... And it was just a thrill for me. I said, here it is again. I only heard it three times in my life. But now, I'm living because I'm going to hear it again one day, if I live long enough." He just might be correct.

The last time I saw Buck O'Neil in person was in July at the Fan Fest of the 2004 All-Star Game. I was standing with a friend of mine, Mike Patranella, at the Negro League Baseball Hall of Fame display. I was telling him and few others about some of the players that were pictured there in the display. I had just finished talking about Buck O'Neil when in he walks, as big as life. Again he had been able to move through the crowds without being recognized. I said hello, shook his hand and asked him how he was doing. His smile was still contagious, there was still a twinkle in his eyes and his warmth filled the room as he answered, "Wonderful." It was then that I turned to the folks standing there and said, "Ladies and Gentlemen, Mr. Buck O'Neil." I left him there surrounded by well-wishers and admirers. I still smile when I think about that cap.

Buck O'Neil had been denied induction into Baseball's Hall of Fame by the voting process. Most fans thought it an injustice but it didn't seemed to bother him. He just loved being a part of the game.

On Friday night, October 6, 2006, my friend Buck O'Neil passed away peacefully in his sleep. He had entered the hospital on September 17, in his hometown of Kansas City, at the age of 94. He will be missed. I remember a quote from Buck that he read at his friend Satchel Paige's funeral, Buck said, "Don't feel sorry for us. I feel sorry for your fathers and your mothers, because they didn't get to see us play." He was right again. Maybe now he can hear that sound again in Heaven.

Nothing Was Complicated

He wasn't very tall nor did he weigh very much, a little guy by most people's standards; but when he walked into a room, it was as if royalty had appeared. His very presence demanded attention and people would stop what they were doing with hopes of catching his eye, in order to pay their respects. Whether you saw him at 6:15 in the morning or 10 o'clock at night, he would make you feel like he was there only to see you. Being in the same room with this guy was like being in a movie scene and everyone called him "coach." He held nothing back, remembered everything, and the only time he grinned was right before he nailed someone.

He was born in the Jewish section of Brooklyn, NY, on September 20, 1917. Arnold "Red" Auerbach would spend hours each day running the streets and playgrounds with his kid brother, Zang, who was four years younger. His passion for basketball would later lead him to Seth Low Junior College and then on to George Washington University, where he would spend three so-so seasons, scoring 334 points in 56 games. Red was the first in his family to go to college and received his first coaching job at the prestigious St. Albans School in northwest

Washington, DC. It was about this time that he met his bride-to-be, Dorothy Lewis, and they were married in 1941. His next coaching job would find him at Roosevelt High School in Washington. Suddenly, World War II would force all young men to make a choice and Red choose the Navy. Although he never had to travel overseas, he did get to meet his Navy buddies Phil Rizzuto, Yogi Berra and eventually Joe DiMaggio. He would grow to love coaching basketball, Chinese food, playing gin, racquetball, smoking victory cigars, telling marvelous stories and, oh yeah, for all practical purposes he was the guy who invented professional basketball. He was also the world's worst driver, but no one seemed to care as long as his team kept winning championships.

Mike Uline was in the hockey business and owned an arena named after him in Washington. It was here that Uline would witness Red coaching a basketball game between the Washington Redskins and the Philadelphia Eagles. That's right; the greatest coach in basketball history began his professional career, coaching football players to play basketball. Uline would be one of eight men who gathered together to form the Basketball Association of America. The coach Uline chose for his newly founded team, the Washington Capitols, was...you guessed it... Red Auerbach. Red's team would post a 49-11 mark and make the playoffs in their first year. By 1950, Red's recent success in Washington landed him in Boston with the title of Celtics Head Coach. He would win 39 of the 69 games played that year and never experience a losing season as coach in his 16 years on that bench. His last game as coach was on April 28, 1966. He had won nine NBA Championships, eight in a row. He would now become the General Manager of the Celtics.

Winning is what his teams did, a lot, and most would agree that as the Boston Celtics Head Coach and General Manager, he was directly responsible for sixteen NBA Championships in thirty years. Smoking his signature victory cigar (his words, not mine) was what he did each time, after his team won a game; therefore, he smoked a lot of cigars: Nine hundred and thirty-eight regular season wins to be exact. That number of victories would make Red the winningest head coach in NBA history until Lenny Wilkins passed him in 1995. The one thing you may not know about Red is that he never smoked a victory cigar after a win on the road—*never*. He thought that would be insulting to the other team and their fans. But smoking that cigar was the first thing most people mentioned when they spoke about Red. There is a true story from the 1980's about Red lighting up a cigar in one of Boston's great seafood establishments, Legal Seafood. He was soon after approached by a female customer who screamed at him, "You can't smoke in here! It says so on the menu!" Red politely told her to go look at the menu again. The menu actually said, "No cigar smoking in here...except for Red Auerbach." Makes you smile, doesn't it? I wonder if he grinned before answering her. In 1969, his records and accomplishments would be honored with his induction into the Basketball Hall Of Fame.

You should have seen his office. The Basketball Hall of Fame would be jealous. His walls are lined from top to bottom with framed photos, newspaper clippings, and Celtic memorabilia. He apparently saved everything, and these treasures are not just your run-of-the-mill stuff. Players, presidents, and heads of state all took their place on these walls. His office was different from most and not just for the obvious reasons; but you see, there were no fax machines, computers, or cell phones. He almost never used his VCR. The only electronic device he liked and used was his DirecTV hook-up, which allowed him to watch his beloved Celtics and as many college and NBA games as possible. You could find him many nights at home in his Washington, DC condo, watching basketball being played on the West Coast until one o'clock in the morning. His thinking was, he never knew when he might be asked about a draft pick or a trade.

He still made it to Boston six or seven times a year to watch his Celtics play and always sat in the same seat (Section 12, Row 7). "I don't sit in the luxury boxes with all that food and all that stuff in there...I like to hear what the people say, even at my age," he spouted. As for today's NBA, he hated luxury taxes, salary caps, and escalating trade kickers. Nothing riled him up more than players helping opposing players up from the floor during the game. "And what's all this hugging after a game?" he shouts. "They're the enemy! We never did that...We ran straight into the locker room after the game was over. Show a little class." He also hated all the stuff that went on during team introductions and timeouts. Worst of all for Red was the scoreboards imploring fans to make noise. "Nobody's gonna tell me when to holler," yells Red. When ask by an NBA official what the Celtic's halftime entertainment would be, he answered, "Ball boy rolls ball rack to center court." It was that simple. For Red, it was about basketball. He yearned for the good old days when one G.M. called another and said, "I need a big guy, you got one? I got a guard that you can use. Great, let's make a trade," and the deal was done. You see, nothing was complicated for Red. He did everything when he was coaching. When the Celtics needed a logo for their team, Red asked his brother Zang, who was a cartoonist for the Washington Star, to design and paint a logo at center court. It can still be seen today at the Fleet Center, where the Celtics now play. Besides being head coach, at the age of thirty-two, he was also director of basketball operations, team president, general manager and head scout. That's right he had no assistants. What he did have, he called birddogs (friends) in every part of the country where he could pick up a phone and say, "You got anybody down South that I need to look at?" Red once drafted a kid named Sam Jones out of North Carolina A&T before he ever saw him play. But his friend, ex-player and coach at Wake Forest, Bones McKinny, had seen him play, and his word was good enough for Red. I believe that judging talent may have been Red's greatest asset. It was also said that Red didn't see players as black and white, only green and white (Celtic colors). He traded for Bill Russell, Robert Parish, "Tiny" Archibald, and Bill Walton. He drafted "Hondo" Havlicek, Kevin McHale, Dave Cowens, "Cornbread" Maxwell, "Satch" Sanders, Danny Ainge, Tommy Heinsohn, "Jo Jo" White, Bill Sharman, Reggie Lewis, and the Jones boys (Sam and K.C.). He even drafted Larry Bird a year earlier than he was eligible. Now there's a list of names that gets your attention, not to mention the Hall of Fame. Even with all that talent, some will tell you that a little piece of Red died the day Lenny Bias died. Red had followed the career of Bias at the University of Maryland for three years and then drafted him with the Celtics first pick. Lenny Bias died of a cocaine overdose before he ever played his first game for the Celtics. It was at this point in Red's life that he began to scale back his involvement with the team and started spending more time in Washington, DC with his family. Still the results of those names equaled 16 NBA Championships.

His favorite current non-Celtic player was Los Angeles Laker forward, Kobe Bryant, and he would also admit to watching Shaq, Kevin Garnett, Jason Kidd and Allen Iverson, if you pressed him. When asked "Who is your favorite Celtic?" His response is always, "Russell [Bill] is my boy, and we're very close, even today…but if you had to pick the greatest player of all time, you might go with Michael [Jordan]. If you're starting a team, then it's debatable."

The relationship between Russell and Red was one of true friendship. They had both been successful before they joined together, therefore neither of them needed to prove anything to one another. Red never told Russell how to play basketball and Russell never told Red how to coach. They were very much like father and son. Their friendship continued to grow even after the Celtics. Russell tells a terrific story about Red and their relationship when Red died. Red's daughter called Russell about two hours after Red passed and when Russell picked up the phone and said "Hello," Red's daughter said, "We just lost daddy!"

Of course the fun side of Red was in his story telling, and believe me, he had a lot of stories. He was like a slot machine, put in a quarter, pull the handle and out comes a story. Some of these stories are legendary, like the parquet floor in Boston Garden having dead spots that only the Celtics knew about, or how Red had the hot water turned off in the visitors' locker room every time the Lakers came to town. Red's response: "Let them think what they want to; if they think that, then good for us." Teams also complained about the heat in the Boston Garden, until Red explained that his team always played on the end that was air conditioned. He loved telling the story of how he used the Ice Capades and a trade to draft Hall-of-Fame center, Bill Russell. Red gave St. Louis two good players, Ed Macauley and Cliff Hagan, for the second pick in the 1956 draft; but he needed to insure that the team with the number-one pick, Rochester, would not take Russell. Then Red had the Celtics owner, Walter Brown, who also owned the Ice Capades, call the owner of the Rochester Royals club, Les Harrison, and offer to send the Ice Capades to Rochester for a week, if they didn't draft Russell. They didn't, Red did, and the rest is history. Another story has Red being chased by none other than Wilt Chamberlain. "He was the most unbelievable physical specimen ever," says Red about Wilt. "He was so strong it was frightening, but there was only one thing he could not do on a basketball court; he couldn't beat us!" exclaimed Red. The Celtics would run Wilt so crazy that one night he tried to get at Red while at courtside. The only thing that saved Red was Russell stepping in between him and Wilt. "I actually liked the guy," said Red. "He flew all the way across the country to come to my eightieth birthday party. After all those years, that meant a lot to me." Red was also known to stretch the truth to keep his players happy. He told his guys that when they traveled, the top berths on the train were three inches longer than the bottom berths, therefore the taller guys should sleep up top. No one ever measured or questioned his story. He also loved to tell how in his first year as head coach, he got Bob Cousy. "Picked him out of a hat," laughed Red. Cousy had been drafted by the Chicago franchise which had folded. Three players, which included Cousy, went into a dispersal draft to the three worst teams in the league. It would be the best pick of Red's career. Another story Red tells is about the time he borrowed a buddy's car; and when he brought it back he said, "You should have this thing checked out; it shimmies when it goes over 100 mph." Johnny Most, legendary Celtics announcer during the glory years, was one of Red's best friends until Red started a summer basketball camp for kids. Johnny attended with his kid but was eventually asked to leave because he wouldn't shut up; once an announcer, always an announcer. This last story pertains to Red's team rules. He had only one. Why? Because he thought lots of ironclad rules would take away his flexibility with the team and hurt the other members who did nothing wrong. Can you guess what his one rule was? Never in a million years! Here goes...no one was allowed to eat pancakes on game day. Red thought they would sit in your stomach and slow you down on the court. He actually caught Bill Russell and Sam Jones eating pancakes at an IHOP at one o'clock in the morning, with a game to play that night, and fined them five dollars per bite. He said laughing, "I've got one damn rule and you two can't even follow it."

Arnold "Red" Auerbach died of a heart attack Saturday, October 28, 2006. He was 89 and survived by two daughters, three grandchildren, and three great-grandchildren. Red was special. He made jewels out of stone, or simply stole other teams' talent like a wolf in sheep's clothing. He intimated officials, other coaches and players. His powers were mystical yet enchanting. He instituted rule changes that helped his team compete, like alternating possessions instead of the jump ball each quarter. Ever wonder why the Celtics always wore black sneakers? "They stay cleaner," said Red. "You don't have to change them as often." It was Red's idea to have giveaways at the games to help with attendance. "We gave away baseball bats one year," says Red. "You couldn't do that today; one bad call and the court would be full of baseball bats." It was a different time then. Everything the Celtics became and are today was because of him. He invented the word "dynasty" and he never forgot a favor. When asked about his favorite Celtics title, "The first one in 1957, always the first time you win." Was he the greatest basketball coach of all time? His records make it debatable, but the facts made him a legend.

Leading with His Chin

Don't be mistaken; he was a tough guy, a bully at times, someone who intimidated the dickens out of you. And, as bullies do in times of trouble, he would stick out that chin as if he were daring you to hit him. He wanted you to hit him so he could show you how a real man should react. His whole body would scream unhappiness during game time when things weren't going his way; but that face, that face would become wide and distorted and, yes, it would stick out. His face resembled a cross between Vince Lombardi and "Bum" Phillips. His imposing presence was continually fueled by his intensity. He just looked mean. No one messed with his boys or his team. With clinched fist, he would pace the sidelines like a tiger ready to pounce onto his prey. He could smash a headset quicker than you can say "Wolverine." You would swear that the big yellow M on his cap stood for "Mad." He looked like the guy who ran the Titanic into that iceberg. He could be downright rude to officials, with his finger pointing, ranting and raving. He was "old school," reared during a time where the tough got going when the going got tough...a time when people stood up and fought back when the breaks went against them. "Football is the

American game that typifies the old American spirit," he said. "It's physical. It's hard work. It's aggressive. It's kind of a swashbuckling American sport. Football is not going to die. It is our American heritage."

He was Glenn Edward "Bo" Schembechler, football coach, a "Michigan Man" if there ever was one. That's just one of the unusual things about this guy. He was actually born in Barberton, Ohio, on April Fools Day, 1929. He was educated and graduated from Miami of Ohio in 1951; he also received his Master's degree from Ohio State University in 1952. So how did this born-and-bred Buckeye end up being a "Michigan Man?" In 1969, when Bo became the head football coach of the Michigan Wolverines, he had already been the head coach at Miami of Ohio for six seasons. Before that he had played football as an offensive lineman, at this same school, under the leadership of Coach Woody Hayes. After a stint in the Army, Bo would serve as an assistant coach at Bowling Green University and then Northwestern. Bo then followed Woody to Ohio State as his assistant for five years, before returning to Miami of Ohio as Head Coach in 1963. In six seasons at Miami of Ohio he would win two Mid-American Conference titles. The Ohio State football program at that time was one of the best in the country. It made perfect sense to the Michigan folks to hire their new head coach from their arch rival. So, Bo pulled on the maize and blue sweater and became a Wolverine. He would find a football program that had fallen far away from its glory years, under coaches Fielding Yost and Fritz Crisler. The 100,000-seat Michigan stadium was seldom filled and the marching band found fewer occasions to play their fight song, "The Victors." Bo went to work right away, not only to rebuild a fine football program, but to also beat his mentor Woody Hayes, from Ohio State. As luck would have it, it didn't take long for Bo to put his stamp on the rivalry with a 24-12 upset win over a #1 ranked and undefeated Ohio State team on November 22, 1969, and start what would become known as "The Ten Year War" between these two schools. "It was everything I lived for," he said, sticking out that chin. "Win and you were in heaven, Buckeyes against Wolverines, and Woody against me." So, from 1969 until 1978, these two football powerhouses would battle for the bragging rights of The Big Ten Conference. These games were as much about the two coaches as it was the game. Don't misunderstand, Bo and Woody were very close but their friendship was placed on hold when Bo took the Michigan job. Schembechler, the winningest coach in Michigan football history, held a slight edge over Hayes with a record of 5-4-1. Woody Hayes would be asked to resign after the 1978 football season. That's how Bo became a "Michigan Man."

Bo's other accomplishments as coach read like a Hall-of-Fame plaque. In 21 seasons at Michigan, he took his team to 17 post-season bowl games, including 10 Rose Bowls. He won or tied for 13 Big Ten Championships while filling the "Big House" Michigan stadium, to capacity each week. The sound and meaning of "GO BLUE" could be heard again across the country as Bo restored "Football Saturday" in Ann Arbor, Michigan. "He told me many times, 'Football should be played in the afternoon,'" recalled Jim Brandstatter, a former player. "He would not stand for a 3:30 start or an 8 o'clock start. Therefore, ladies and gentlemen, toe meets leather at 1:14 exactly." Bo was voted Big Ten Coach of the Year 7 times and also voted once as the National Coach of the Year, in 1969. He believed that running the football and playing neck-breaking defense won football games and he recorded a 234-65-8 record, tops for any NCAA Division I coach then active. In fact, he never had a losing season. Fifteen times, his Michigan team finished in the Associated Press Top Ten and his 1985 team finished second in the nation. We must remember that he did all the above with a clean slate, not a hint of scandal. He was an amazing communicator and the power of his commitment and confidence was contagious. His only disappointment was that his Wolverines never won a national championship under his leadership.

Bo was inducted into the Miami University Hall of Fame in 1972, the State of Michigan Sports Hall of Fame in 1989, the University Of Michigan Hall Of Honor in 1992, the Rose Bowl Hall of Fame in 1993, and finally the National Football Foundation College Hall of Fame in 1993. When we think of Bo's teams, names like Jim Harbaugh, Rick Leach, Butch Woolfolk, Rob Lytle, Leroy Hoard and Anthony Carter come roaring back into our memories. And Bo loved his offensive linemen as if they were part of his family; just ask Reggie McKenzie or Dan Dierdorf. I knew Reggie McKenzie fairly well. We spent hours together and on the air talking about Coach Bo and the Michigan teams. My friend and radio partner of 13 years, Shane Nelson, had played in the NFL with Reggie while with the Buffalo Bills, and we were introduced on the air and then in person. When we met, Reggie had already left the Buffalo Bills for the Seattle Seahawks. Reggie, an offensive guard at Michigan from 1969-71, had nothing but kind words to say about his old college coach but made it a point to remind me of how tough Bo could be. "He almost made me quit," said Reggie. "He preached "team" from day one and it's still being taught now." Even after his first heart attack, before the Rose Bowl in 1970,

Bo's combativeness never dimmed. "He made me an All-American," said McKenzie. Reggie McKenzie was also inducted into the College Football Hall of Fame in 2003, as Bo stood by and grinned. Bo Schembechler understood that there is something in good men that really yearns for discipline and the harsh reality of head-to-head combat. As the Michigan coach, Bo lost his last game to USC, 17-10, in the 1990 Rose Bowl. Bo loved coaching but grew to hate other aspects surrounding the game. He hated drugs, sports agents and recruiting. "Recruiting is the worst part of college football," he wrote. "I no longer look forward to it. I can't wait till it's over. It makes me feel like a pimp."

Bo also served as the Athletic Director at Michigan from 1988-90 and during this tenure he is most remembered for this statement, "A Michigan man will coach Michigan, not an Arizona State man." This comment was made when Bo found out that the current Michigan Basketball Coach, Bill Frieder, had accepted a job on the eve of the NCAA Tournament to coach at Arizona State the following year. Bo was so angry that he refused to accept Frieder's 21-day notice and replaced him with Assistant Coach Steve Fisher. Michigan would win the 1989 NCAA Basketball Championship, coached by Fisher, another "Michigan Man." Bo stepped down the following year and then became the President of the Detroit Tigers from 1990-92. From 1992 until the present, Bo engaged in speaking tours and hovered over the Michigan program as if he were their guardian angel. Although he had quit traveling to the away games because of his health, he still made it a point to speak with the team before each game.

On Saturday November 17, 2006, Bo collapsed in the bathroom of a Southfield television station, WXYZ, just minutes before he was to tape a show on the eve of this year's biggest game, between #1 Ohio State and #2 Michigan. Bo was 77 years of age, and had fought heart disease and diabetes for 40 years. "His heart just stopped," said Dr. David. He was survived by one son, Glenn III and his second wife, Cathy. Bo left us the way most of us would prefer. He just wanted to live until he died. No one wants to go through the process of dying. Bo will always be tied to Woody in thought and in the stories that will be told in the years to come. It reminds me of what a great soldier, who had fought many battles against his worthy adversary, once said, "Under any other circumstance, I feel I could call you friend." After Bo died, current head football coach, Lloyd Carr reminded folks of a story from the early 1980's, when Bo was offered to be the highest-paid football coach in the nation by Texas A&M University. Bo called his staff together to ask what they thought about the opportunity. "The staff was divided about whether to go or whether to stay," Carr recalled. "At the end of the meeting, with a tear in his eye and a crack in his voice, he said, 'Yes, but you don't have to tell those players you're leaving.'" Ah, yes, a "Michigan Man" until the end.

The Foolish Club

One day while flying across the country in coach class, he began to scribble on a piece of airline letterhead. He was a geologist by trade, but on this day, rocks and land formations were not what were on his mind. He was nicknamed "Game" as a child, because of his passion for inventing new games and scoring systems. Nothing was out of bounds and he always looked to change or make up new rules to make competition better and make the game better for the fans. He played college football at Southern Methodist University and loved the game of football. He also enjoyed the sports of tennis and soccer. Some folks referred to him as a dreamer but he thought of himself as a visionary, a leader, and an innovator. Someone once said the true definition of a leader is someone who propels other people to a new level that they could not have achieved on their own. On that piece of stationary that he was scribbling on, lay the foundation and plans for the American Football League, a rival to the very well established National Football League. This new league would begin to play against each other in 1960 and eventually agree to merge with the NFL in 1966. This AFL-NFL merger would be agreed upon in a car parked at Love Field in Dallas, Texas. This gentle, thoughtful man was named Lamar Hunt, son of billionaire H.L. Hunt. Lamar Hunt and Tex Schramm were in that car, and they became the architects and "founding fathers" of the multi-billion dollar business that is today known as the National Football League.

Lamar Hunt was born with a silver spoon in his mouth, August 2, 1932, in El Dorado, Arkansas. By the middle of the 1950's, Texas oil had made his family one of the three or four richest in the United States according to "Fortune Magazine," but Lamar always played down his wealth. He wanted to be like most other people: hard-working, down to earth, and appreciative of the things he had. I think that's why he was riding in the coach section of that airplane. "He was the kind of guy you wished all people of wealth would be like," said a friend of mine, Dale Bowers. "He always wore charcoal grey trousers and a blue blazer, I never saw him in anything else." Mr. Bowers was in the advertising and television business and a Kansas City Chief season ticket holder for many years. During his time in Kansas City, Dale had the opportunity to sit and chat with Lamar on several occasions. "He was so humble, you would never know that he was wealthy," said Bowers. "He will be missed."

In 1959, at the age of 27, Hunt tried to purchase an NFL team but was told by the League that they had no desire to have more than 12 teams. So Hunt joined together with seven other men who shared the same impossible dream (to own a professional football team) and formed what was called "The Foolish Club". This club would create the foundation of the original AFL. Hunt's team would become known as the Dallas Texans of the AFL, later to be moved in 1963 to Kansas City and renamed the Chiefs. Those eight original teams were known as the Boston Patriots, Dallas Texans, Houston Oilers, Buffalo Bills, Oakland

Raiders, New York Titans, Denver Broncos, and San Diego Chargers. Interestingly enough, none of the original AFL teams has folded and only two have moved; the Dallas franchise to Kansas City, Missouri, and the Houston franchise to Nashville, Tennessee. Professional football had officially arrived in Texas, Colorado, California, and the New England area, compliments of the AFL. Four other cities obtained NFL franchises as a direct result of competition created by the AFL. Those teams became the Dallas Cowboys, New Orleans Saints, Minnesota Vikings, and the Atlanta Falcons

This new league not only created salary competition for the current NFL players but it also made a place for many other players from small colleges, the Canadian Football League, and African-American schools. A whole new source of talent lay hidden in the rural areas of America. No more three-yards-and-a-cloud-of-dust; this new game would be a brand of football unseen in the NFL. "Goodbye Bronko Nagurski," and hello, "George Blanda." The AFL took advantage of the growing popularity of football in the Sixties. They offered a flashier game where words like "The Bomb" became commonplace. Players with names like Len Dawson, John Hadl, and Daryle Lamonica would be discussed around kitchen tables on Sunday nights. More colorful uniforms and logos were worn by the teams and their names were sewed on the backs of their jerseys for identification, all compliments of Lamar Hunt. It was also Hunt's idea to implement the two-point conversion, place the game clock on the scoreboard so fans knew how much time was left, and use the growing power of television to promote the AFL. Many other players like Joe Namath, Don Maynard, Lance Alworth, Jack Kemp, Babe Parilli, Buck Buchanan and Cookie Gilchrist would all make their mark in pro football with the AFL. In the minds of the American public and the NFL, the classic televised 1962 double-overtime American Football League Championship game, between the Dallas Texans and the defending champion Houston Oilers put this league on the map. The old lion was forced to take note. This league was here to stay.

As for Lamar Hunt, God's blessing of great wealth was not wasted on him. He never flew first class, never meddled in other people's business, never sought the spot light, and he was never heard to raise his voice. After the U.S. Congress approved the AFL-NFL merger in 1966, Hunt's Kansas City Chiefs played in the first AFL-NFL Championship game in January, 1967, against the Green Bay Packers. In 1969, this game would be named "The Super Bowl" by you guessed it, Lamar Hunt. Hunt thought "this" game should be special and different from the conference championships. Hunt would also convince NFL Commissioner Pete Rozelle to use Roman numerals to give this game "more dignity." In 1970, as luck would have it, Hunt's very own Kansas City Chiefs would defeat the Minnesota Vikings to win Super Bowl IV. It would be Kansas City's only victory in a Super Bowl during his life time. In 1972, for his contributions, Mr. Lamar Hunt, at the age of 39, would be the first AFL figure elected into the Pro Football Hall of Fame and the trophy awarded to the American Football Conference Champion would also be named after him.

Hunt did continue to retain his interest in the oil business but also branched out into real estate. He helped develop amusement parks known as Worlds of Fun and Oceans of Fun. He was also involved in professional sports beyond football. He had big dreams for a little guy. He was one of the founding investors in the Chicago Bulls of the NBA.

He was the founder of the World Championship Tennis Tour which helped legitimize the game and he helped bring about the North American Soccer League. In fact his family still owns three Major League Soccer franchises: the Kansas City Wizards, F.C. Dallas, and Columbus Crew. His passion and motivation for these other sports would result in his induction into the U.S. Soccer Hall of Fame in 1992 and into the International Tennis Hall of Fame in 1993. He loved to travel to the World Cup Soccer events and collected artifacts from carnivals like fortune-telling machines and strength meters.

Lamar Hunt passed away in Dallas, Texas on Wednesday December 13, 2006 at the age of 74. The cause was complications of prostate cancer and a collapsed lung. He is survived by his wife Norma, four children and 13 grandchildren. Right up to the end he fought for changes in the NFL. He wanted to loose the hold by Detroit and Dallas on the Thanksgiving Day game and in fact a third game was added this year in Kansas City, where it may stay permanently. In short, the NFL adopted virtually every pioneering aspect of the American Football League except its name. He was one of the three original AFL owners still heading their franchise, the others, Ralph Wilson of the Buffalo Bills and Bud Adams of the Tennessee Titans, formerly the Houston Oilers. I can't imagine the number of people he touched during his lifetime. His vision and the drive to always make things better for the fans were Lamar Hunt trademarks. You would be hard pressed to find anyone else that has made a bigger contribution to modern professional sports in America. Lamar Hunt did something else, he kept the piece of stationary with notes he had written while on that plane.

Center of Attention

His given name at birth was Leslie Lynch King, Jr. He was born on July 14, 1913 at 3202 Woolworth Avenue in Omaha, Nebraska. His father, a wool trader, married and separated from his mother only 16 days after he was born. Dorothy, his mom, then gained full custody of Leslie through a divorce that was finalized by December of that same year. His father had been abusive towards his mother and had hit her many times. By 1916, he had moved to Grand Rapids, Michigan with his mom, to live with her parents. Dorothy met a fellow and remarried, and Leslie was given his new father's name although he was never formally adopted and did not legally change his name until December 3, 1935. He did not find out about his real parentage until he was told by his mother, on his seventeenth birthday. He would grow up in East Grand Rapids with three half-brothers, sons of his new stepfather's first marriage; and there were also three half-siblings from his biological father, who also remarried. He would have sporadic contact with his real father until his death. Early life in Michigan was grand; his days were filled with chores, sports and scouting. By 1929, he had become an Eagle

Scout with the Boy Scouts of America, an award he would cherish his entire life.

The name that you would recognize this fellow by today is Gerald R. Ford, the 38th President of the United States of America. Ford became a star athlete at Grand Rapids South High School and captain of the football team. That's how he made it in this book. In 1930, he was selected to play for the All-City team where he drew the attention of many college recruiters. His choice for higher education was the University of Michigan, who had one of the finest football teams in America during the twenties and thirties. Ford would start at offensive center and linebacker on defense for the Wolverines and help lead them to undefeated seasons and national titles, in both 1932 and 1933. The 1934 season would find Ford the star of a team that won only one game his senior year. But still, he would capture attention in a game against the University of Chicago. In this game, Ford would be the only future U.S. President to tackle Jay Berwanger, a future Heisman Trophy winner. Also in that same season, Ford and a teammate, Cedric Sweet, played their hearts out on defense against the eventual national champion, University of Minnesota. In a scoreless tie at the end of the first half, assistant coach Bernie Oosterbaan said he had tears in his eyes, he was so proud of them. He said years later, about that game, "I always felt Gerry was one guy who would stay and fight in a losing cause." Ford himself later recalled, "During 25 years in the rough-and-tumble world of politics, I often thought of the experiences before, during, and after that game in 1934. Remembering them has helped me many times to face a tough situation, take action, and make every effort possible despite adverse odds." He would be voted the team's most valuable player in 1934. His outstanding play earned him a spot on the

Eastern team of the East-West Shrine game played in San Francisco, on January 1, 1935, and also a place on the 1935 Collegiate All-Star football team. Ford had become one of the nation's finest college football players. That game was played against the Chicago Bears at Soldier Field. He would later be offered a player's contract for $200.00 a game by the Detroit Lions and Green Bay Packers. Ford turned down both offers because he wanted a law degree and began at Yale Law School in 1938. He would continue to coach boxing and his first love, football at Yale. He would graduate in the top twenty-five percent of his class in 1941. The rest of his military and political career is in the history books.

One of the best offensive centers in college football, he released his final public statement on November 12, 2006.

"The length of one's days matters less then the love of one's family and friends. I thank God for the gift of every sunrise and, even more, for all the years he has blessed me with Betty and the children; with our extended family and the friends of a lifetime. That includes countless Americans who, in recent months, have remembered me in their prayers. Your kindness touches me deeply. May God bless you all and may God bless America." Gerald Ford

Gerald Ford passed away on December 26, 2006. Ford had become the longest-lived President by surpassing Ronald Reagan by 45 days. He had lived for 93 years. Ford also became the second President to die on December 26, the same day as Harry Truman. Old age had finally caught up to Gerry. Bouts of pneumonia, two minor strokes, a heart that required a pacemaker, and finally an angioplasty procedure, were all signs that Ford's body was slowly failing him. All of Betty and Gerald's kids visited their parents to say their goodbyes before Christmas, and most where at his bedside when he died. On December 30, Ford would become the 11th United States President to lie in state. It seems funny that this fine athlete and scholar would be criticized so much by the media for being clumsy. Even popular television shows like Saturday Night Live would make fun of him. He more than likely outlived his critics. Gerald Ford was also the last living member of the Warren Commission and the only man to hold the office of Vice President and President of the United States without being elected by the public for either. There is no doubt that for 93 years he always remained the center of attention.

Swapping Paint

This fellow loved his sport and all the people who made it go. In return, they loved him back. His voice was smooth and easy to listen to. One of his many gifts was his ability to explain to people what they were actually seeing as it happened. Sometimes he was referred to as "The Professor" because of his straightforward delivery and down-home manners. You could find him most days sitting on a pile of tires telling stories to others. He looked like a school teacher and could talk you right through all the nuts and bolts of his sport. The equipment he used weighed about 3,500 pounds and for most of the folks like himself, they would farm all day and build these cars at night, in their sheds. He spoke about automobile racing like your grandma talked about recipes. His home-spun rifts made camshafts and push rods sound like corn-bread and sweet potato pie. His weekends were spent on small remote playgrounds in towns like Rockingham, Martinsville, Darlington, Riverside, Concord and Bristol. He made most of his money going around in circles and getting in and out of car windows. Why, because he was a race car driver and a darn good one! He spent a lot of time pushing down and turning left on race tracks all across the country. On a good day he could get four new tires and a tank full of gas in less than 16 seconds. He would swap paint each week against some of the best drivers in the world. Names like Richard Petty, Cale Yarborough, Junior Johnson, Buddy Baker, and Bobby Allison would haunt him in his sleep. To be a professional driver, all that was needed were nerves of steel, cat-like reflexes, 360-degree vision, and a wheelbarrow full of chips on your shoulder. One mistake could cost you the race, your life, or both.

Benny Parsons was built on July 12, 1941, in North Wilkesboro, NC. All that it required was a bit of racing fuel for blood, some sheet metal for hide, a little oil pressure for a pulse, and a heart the size of an 8-cylinder motor. He was born dirt-poor and hungry. He was reared by his great-grandmother near a community called Parsonsville. This rural home had no running water or electricity. At the age of 19, he moved to Detroit, Michigan. His father worked at a gas station in Detroit and owned a cab company. Therefore, Benny received his driving lessons on the mean streets of the "Motor City." About two months after arriving in Detroit, Benny was introduced by his dad, to two guys who owned a race car. Benny tells the story like this: "I met two guys my dad knew who had a race car. I started going to the track, into the pits. Three years later, in 1963, one of these guys stopped by Dad's station and asked me if I'd like to drive a car. I said I thought so. He said he had a car he'd give to me, a Ford. We went to his garage, and the first thought I had was that we got cheated. It was torn all to pieces. We fixed it, though, and I ran my first race, a figure-8 feature on a quarter-mile dirt track, and spun out. Twelve years later, I was the Daytona 500 Champion."

In 1964, Parsons drove his first race in NASCAR's top-level Grand National series, now called the Nextel Cup series, but didn't land a fulltime ride until 1970. "Money was scarce at the start," said Benny. "In 1965, my first son was born and somehow I had $75 to start him a bank account. About this time, the rear end cooler pump broke on the race car. A new one cost $99," laughed Benny. Parsons withdrew the $75 and borrowed $24 elsewhere, got the pump and went on to success. Benny continued to drive and eventually won two A.R.C.A. titles in 1968-69 before making the decision to move back to Ellerbe NC. His goal was to become a fulltime NASCAR driver, and he was often kidded about listing "taxicab driver" as his occupation on race entry forms. In 1973, against all odds and with limited funding, Parsons drove a non-sponsored Chevrolet to the Winston Cup Championship, while winning only one race out of 28. Locked in a close-points race with Cale Yarborough for first place, Benny crashed his car in the series finale at Rockingham Speedway. Just as his hopes seemed to all but disappear, members of several rival teams hurried to find replacement parts, helped put the car back together and got it back out onto the race track just in time for him to earn enough points to claim the championship. "What they did was a real miracle," he recalled. In 1975, Parsons would win the sports premier event, the Daytona 500. "It's been over 30 years and I'm still introduced as the winner of the Daytona 500," Parsons said recently. In 1978, he finished first at Riverside International Raceway; and he won twice at Ontario Motor Speedway, in 1979 and 1980. The trophy for the World 600 at Concord NC would also rest on Benny's mantle, in 1980. In 1982, he would become the first driver to qualify for a race at over 200 miles an hour. His time of 200.176 mph was recorded at the Winston 500, which was run at Talladega Super Speedway in Alabama. From 1964 to his retirement in 1988, Benny qualified for the pole position 20 times and won 21 of the 526 races that he started. He also ended his career with 199 top-five finishes and placed 283 times in the top ten. He estimated that he made 134,870 laps while earning almost 4.5 million dollars in prize money. By 1989, Benny had moved into the broadcasting booth of ESPN and won a Cable Ace Award for best sports analyst in his first season. He is still the only driver to have won season championships in both the Automobile Racing Club of America, (a Midwestern stock-car circuit), and NASCAR's top circuit, the Winston Cup, (now the Nextel Cup). Parsons was inducted into the International Motorsports Hall of Fame in 1994. Benny was inducted into the National Motorsports Press Association's Stock Car Racing Hall of Fame in 1995 and also won an Emmy Award for broadcasting with ESPN in 1996. In addition, he was named one of NASCAR's 50 greatest drivers in 1998, a title well deserved.

Besides driving a racecar, Benny loved talking about racing, playing golf and owned an appetite as big as all outdoors. He absolutely loved ice cream and, in fact, his ESPN segment called "Buffet Benny," about food available at the race track, literally launched his popularity as a broadcaster. "Wanna stop and get a bite?" may have been his six most favorite words. In the old days, when the announcers had to walk through the grandstands to get to the booth, Benny would have to stop several times on the way up in order to collect all the snacks, cookies and goodies he was handed by the fans. "It led to the crew having a smorgasbord of treats to snack on during the race," said fellow driver and announcer Ned Jarrett. "Everybody looked forward to his stories during his pre-race stroll through the garage," said Doug Yates. "You'd see him coming and right away the whole mood would pick up." Yates said. One of Benny's favorite stories occurred during his first trip to Daytona. "I couldn't afford a racing suit," said Benny. "So I bought a painter's suit. I finished a lap down, but thought I had won the race. I thought they just didn't want to recognize me as the winner because of my painter's suit," laughed Benny.

On Tuesday, January 16, 2007, Benny Parsons, a guy who was too nice to be a race car driver, made his last pit stop at the age of 65. Although he had not smoked in 29 years, he suffered from lung cancer. Chemotherapy and radiation treatments since his cancer was discovered in July of 2006 had cost Benny the use of his left lung, but still he showed up at the track with his oxygen tank in tow. He continued to call races for NBC and TNT during his treatment. Unfortunately, after being declared cancer free, the doctors discovered a blood clot in his right lung. He would enter the hospital in Charlotte, NC on December 26, never to recover. He is survived by his wife Terri, two sons, Kevin and Keith, and two granddaughters. Current driver, Michael Waltrip summed up everybody's feelings about Benny Parsons this week by decorating his car during testing at the Daytona International Speedway with these words, "We love you, BP."

Clinched Fist

He was as strong as a wet rawhide strap; darn near invincible, no doubt about it, and tough with a capital "T." In fact, his nickname was "Bruiser." No one played as hard as he or gave as much to the game of baseball. Compared to his previous employment, breaking up a double play at second base was sheer joy. Playing baseball was a piece of cake, compared to spending thirty-two months in combat. During World War II, he had commanded a platoon of sixty-four United States Marines that landed on the Japanese-held island of Okinawa, in the Pacific. After 53 days of savage fighting, only six men including him self had survived. It took a hit from a large piece of shrapnel in his thigh, to send him home. With him, he carried home a case of malaria, 11 campaign ribbons, two Bronze Stars and a pair of Purple Hearts. He was serious, strong as a blacksmith, and a natural-born leader. He was proud to have served his country and even prouder to have come out alive. He wore that intensity on his face in such a way that Los Angeles Times sportswriter Jim Murray once wrote, "He looked so serious that his face resembled a clinched fist." Of course that broken nose he received in high school contributed greatly to his fierce appearance.

He always seemed to be in the right place at the right time. If he had not listened to his older brother Herm and signed that Minor League contract in 1941, for less money than he was making as an iron worker, he would have never played Minor League baseball. If it had not been for the wound he received on Okinawa in 1945, he may have died on that island. After the war, if he had not stopped by that bar on the way home from work where another brother Joe worked, he would have never met New York Yankee scout, Danny Menendez. If he had not signed that contract with the Yankees for $175 a month, he would have never returned to professional baseball. If he had not made the team in 1948, he would not hold the World Series record for hitting safely in 17 consecutive games, and he would not have participated in nine pennant winners and seven World Series championships in ten years. Without his experience, knowledge of the game and excellent play, he would not have received the opportunity to manage the Baltimore Orioles to their first World Series title in 1966. Hall of Fame broadcaster Mel Allen summed it up best when he coined the phrase, "Hank Bauer, the Man of the Hour." Sometimes in life, timing is everything.

Henry Albert "Hank" Bauer was born in East St. Louis, Illinois, the youngest of nine children, on July 31, 1922. His hard-nosed Austrian parents had little money, and Hank was sometimes forced to wear hand-me-downs or clothes made from old feed sacks. His father became a bartender, after losing a leg in an aluminum mill accident. Hank played basketball and baseball at East St. Louis Central Catholic High School. It was there that Hank received his permanently disfigured nose from an elbow thrown on the basketball court. After he graduated from high school in 1941, his brother Herman was able to get to get him a tryout with a Class D baseball team in the Wisconsin State League, located in Oshkosh. Hank made the team as a catcher with a strong right arm and a pretty good eye at the plate. Herman had spent some time in the Chicago White Sox Minor League system. In January, 1942, one month after the Japanese attack on Pearl Harbor, along with his brothers, Hank enlisted in the Marine Corp. Hank saw action in many of the battles fought in the Pacific, such as Guadalcanal and Okinawa, and lost his brother Herman in France. He was discharged from the service in 1946 and signed with the Yankees minor league affiliate in Kansas City, Missouri. He spent one year with the team in Quincy and one year with the Kansas City Blues. Hank hit over .300 both seasons and was called up to the New York Yankees club in September of 1948, for good. He was now one of the Bronx Bombers, or was he? The Yankees had Charlie Keller, Joe DiMaggio, and Tommy Henrich in the outfield; where would Hank fit in? Bauer proceeded to bang out three singles in his first three at-bats and thought, "Man, this is going to be easy." He finished the season with a .180 average. In 1949, things begin to work out for Hank. Manager Casey Stengel introduced platoon baseball, and Bauer began to split time with Cliff Mapes in right field. In 301 at bats, Hank hit 10 home runs and batted .272. He was a dead-pull fastball hitter and once said, "If I hit a ball to right field, it was an accident." Yes, he was now indeed considered a Bronx Bomber.

He started in three straight All-Star games from 1952-1954, and he played in 53 World Series games. Hank was one of nine players to help establish the Major League record of 11 home runs hit in one game. He contributed two of the eleven home runs against the Tigers himself, on June 23, 1950. In Game Six of the 1951 World Series, Hank tripled home three runs with a 402-foot shot, to clinch the title against the New York Giants. He scored the winning run from second base in the 1953 World Series, on a single hit by Billy Martin. Bauer powered the Yankees with his bat, again in the 1955 World Series, by hitting at a .429 clip. His 26 home runs in 1956 were a surprise; but the RBI single he hit during Game Six of the World Series was more important and helped protect the lead for Don Larsen, who went on to pitch the only perfect game in World Series history. In 1957, Hank led the American League in triples with nine, but it was his home run in the seventh inning of Game Six that defeated the Braves. On June 2, 1958, Bauer hit two home runs against White Sox pitcher Jim Wilson. They both were hit out of the stadium in Chicago. That same year, Hank had his best overall series, but Game Three against Braves pitcher Don McMahon stood out. With the Yankees down two games to none, Bauer drove in all four Yankee runs to whip the Braves. It was also in this series that Hank's 17 consecutive games, hit streak in World Series play came to an end, against pitcher Warren Spahn. That date was October 5, 1958. On December 11, 1959, Hank Bauer, Don Larsen, Norm Siebern, and Marv Throneberry were traded to the Kansas City Athletics for Roger Maris and two other players. Hank was 37 and had returned home. In fact, he never did move his family to New York during the 11 years he played there.

For the next two years, Hank was a player-manager for Kansas City. On June 10, 1961, Bauer hit an inside-the-park home run over his buddy Mickey Mantle's head at Yankee Stadium. They would laugh about that for years to come. On June 19, 1961, Kansas City owner Charlie

Finley hired Hank Bauer fulltime, to skipper the A's as the manager. November 19, 1963, Bauer was named Manager of the Baltimore Orioles; he replaced Billy Hitchcock. In 1964, Hank would be named the American League Manager of the Year. Behind Hank's guidance, the O's would find themselves in the 1966 World Series, where they would sweep the L. A. Dodgers, 4-0. It was Baltimore's first World Series title. Hank Bauer and Gene Stallings of the 1914 Miracle Braves are the only two managers to have 4-0 records in World Series play. Bauer would again be given the Manager of the Year award. "He was my first manager in the Major Leagues. He gave me my first opportunity in 1965, when he could have kept other people. I was lucky he was a Jim Palmer fan. You can't get into the Hall of Fame without your first chance," stated Palmer. On July 10, 1968, Bauer was fired by the Orioles and replaced by Earl Weaver. Hank would then be hired to manage the 1969 A's, but this time it was in Oakland, California. It would be his last stop, as he was fired on September 19, 1969. For the next 18 years, Hank would scout for the Yankees and the Royals. He would retire from baseball for good on July 9, 1987. His career totals included a batting average of .277 with 164 home runs and 703 RBI's in 1,544 games. It appears that every one of his hits came at just the right time. "Maybe I bore down a lot more in the Series," Bauer told a Kansas City Star reporter. "I played for the right organization."

Hank's toughness followed him into the Yankee clubhouse, and it was once told how he had berated a young Mickey Mantle for not running out a ground ball. "Don't fool with my money," he would scream, referring to the additional World Series checks the Yankees had become accustomed to receiving each year. He would even crawl up on top of the Yankee dugout and search the stands for the fan who was yelling racial slurs at teammate and catcher, Elston Howard. When asked about it, he responded, "Ellie's my friend." No one messed with Hank. He was also present at the famous Copacabana incident in New York City, where he and several fellow Yankee teammates got into a fight with local patrons. Hank was blamed for starting the fight. The case ended up going all the way to the grand jury, but Hank never had to testify. When asked by Stengel if he had hit the alleged victim, Edward Jones, who suffered a concussion and a broken jaw, Hank's response was, "I wanted to, but I didn't." Only the fellows who were there will ever know the real truth. He was also part of the melee that occurred with Clint Courtney of the St. Louis Cardinals. "What I remember," Said a smiling Hank, "is Clint crawling out from under the pile looking for his glasses, but he couldn't find them. That's because Bob Cerv ground them into the grass with his cleats."

After a lengthy battle with cancer, Hank Bauer passed away on Friday, February, 9, 2007. The 84-year-old tough guy lived in Shawnee Mission, Kansas. "I am truly heart-broken," Yogi Berra said in a statement about his death. "Hank was a wonderful teammate and friend for so long. Nobody was more dedicated and proud to be a Yankee; he gave you everything he had." I met Hank on two occasions, both times in Houston, Texas at a baseball card convention. The first time was in the mid-eighties, and Hank was traveling with his two best friends, Mickey Mantle and Moose Skowron. Now there's a trio to talk baseball with. He still wore that Marine Corp crew cut and had that gleam in his eye. It seems that Mickey took care of his two best friends by always including them in any card-signing contract that he agreed too. The second time I met Hank he was there only with Moose. He was always nice in a hard-nosed kind of way; I just think he had a hard time being friendly. He was still scouting for the Yankees and Royals, and also attending an Old Timers game every now and then. I had him sign several things, including a 1958 World Series program. Bauer led the Yanks over the Braves in seven games during that series, while hitting .323 with four home runs and eight RBI's. Hank shared that home run record with Lou Gehrig, Babe Ruth, Duke Snider and Gene Tenace. Only Reggie Jackson's five home runs in the 1977 World Series eclipsed that mark. He may not have been considered a Hall-of-Fame player, but he was a great Yankee, and was also the link between the great teams of the forties and the even greater teams of the fifties and early sixties. In five years, he had played in five consecutive world championships, still a record today. The last time I read anything about Hank Bauer, before his death, was in 1995 when it was announced that he would be a pallbearer at the funeral for Mickey Mantle. Hank Bauer lived during one of America's greatest generations. He was a good person, a very good baseball player, and an even better American. Looking back at his entire career, Mel Allen was right. Hank Bauer was indeed the man of the hour.

Underhanded Royalty

S ome baseball scribe once wrote, "Sometimes I feel like I will never stop, just go on forever. Till one fine morning, I'm gonna' reach up and grab me a hand full of stars. Swing out my long lean leg and whip three hot strikes, burning down the heavens. Look over at God and say! *How About That!*" There is only one athlete I think about whenever I read that statement. He was an ex-marine with a bulging right arm and an attitude as big as all outdoors. This World War II vet had a crew cut that was so flat it looked as if you could land a plane on top of his head. As a trouble-making child, he had been thrown out of school in his early teens. Records show, he had been abandoned at birth and placed on the doorsteps of a Catholic Hospital in Walla Walla, Washington. There he would be sent to a new home with a new mom, who would give him the name, Myrle Vernon King. Along the way, while growing up, this tough son-of-a-gun discovered he had a talent. He could throw a softball faster than anyone one else he knew. He was clocked at 104 mph to be exact. Armed with this newly found talent, he decided to start a new life with a new name. He took the name Feigner from his mother's side of the family and Eddie from a good friend of his, and became Eddie Feigner, the "Greatest softball pitcher" that ever lived.

Eddie Feigner was born on March 26, 1925. He returned from overseas and took up where he left off before the war, striking out batters in record numbers with a softball. In 1946, after his team had defeated a popular local team from Pendleton, Oregon, he was challenged to play again. Eddie, feeling invincible, stated, "I would play you with only my catcher but you would walk us both." So, it was decided that Eddie would pitch and play the other team's nine with his catcher, a shortstop and a first baseman. That day, on a dare, Eddie Feigner laid down the foundation of the greatest softball team ever assembled, "The King and His Court." Meanwhile, the other three players wondered how they would go about getting ready for this game. It was springtime in the Pacific Northwest and the local parks were all taken. Eddie requested permission to practice and play some of the prison teams inside Washington State Prison. His request was granted, and many curious inmates watched as these four athletes perfected their skills. Eddie practiced pitching from the mound, located the standard 46 feet away from home plate, and from second base. He threw underhanded, between his legs, from behind his back, from his knees, from centerfield, and blindfolded. No one had ever witnessed anything like this. A week later, 400 locals turned out to see "The King and His Court" play the local nine. It was the first time, officially, that a game of four verses nine had ever been played. For seven innings, Feigner pitched a perfect game while striking out 19 of 21 batters. One pitch was hit to the shortstop and one to the first baseman. Both resulted in outs. Eddie's team won 7-0. And you thought Nolan Ryan was good!

For the rest of his life, Eddie Feigner would tour this country and most of the world while showing off that cannon of a right arm and raising millions of dollars for children's charities and the Armed Services. His numbers are staggering. It has been written that from 1938 to 1998, Eddie pitched in 11,125 games, winning 9,743 and tying 310. He recorded 930 no-hitters, 238 perfect games, 1,916 shutouts and struck out 141,517 batters with 8,698 of those strikeouts occurring while pitching blindfolded. His right arm would take him to all 50 states, over 100 different countries, 300 military institutions and would entertain more than 20 million fans during his lifetime. His team would travel an estimated 3 million miles while barnstorming all over the world and achieved widespread fame similar to that of the Harlem Globetrotters. Interestingly, he is most known for striking out six Major League baseball stars in succession, during a nationally televised exhibition game at Dodger Stadium, in 1964. They are as follows: Willie Mays, Willie McCovey, Brooks Robinson, Maury Wills, Harmon Killebrew, and Roberto Clemente. Eddie's team would continue to play in other ballparks across the country, including Yankee Stadium and also appeared on many national television shows. These shows included *The Today Show, I've Got a Secret, Tonight Show, What's My Line?* and *CBS Sports Spectacular.* On the *Tonight Show,* Eddie had Johnny Carson hold a bat across home plate. Feigner hit Carson's bat while pitching blind folded in his very first try. Then in an effort to top that, he convinced Johnny to hold a cigar in his mouth. Feigner promptly knocked the cigar out of Johnny's mouth without so much as a scratch on the Late Night TV star. Eddie also claims he struck out a young leftfielder from Cuba known as Fidel

Castro, ate dinner with big band director Tommy Dorsey, and watched movies with Elvis Presley in his basement.

Eddie Feigner, the greatest softball pitcher who ever lived, died Friday February 9, 2007, in Huntsville, Alabama. He was 81. He had been confined to a wheelchair by a second stoke in 2000 that had officially ended his playing career at the age of 75. The day before his stroke you could have found him throwing out the first pitch for the women's softball competition in the Sydney, Australia Olympics. For over 60 years, Eddie took his turn firing a softball under-handed at speeds untouched by any Major Leaguer. He was simply unbeatable. He is revered as one of the greatest pitchers of all time, with the likes of Walter Johnson, Sandy Koufax, Bob Feller, and Christy Mathewson. Eddie is sur-vived by his wife Anne Marie, son Eddie Jr., who played for his dad for 25 years, daughters Shirley, Carol and Debbie, nine grandchildren, and four great-grandchildren.

Although Eddie has now left us, the "King and His Court" still awe the public with a brand of softball that defies imagination. The current members are as follows: Dave Booth, catcher; Jason Fisher, utility man; Russ Fittje, shortstop; Rich Hoppe, pitcher; and Jack Knight, team captain and first baseman. Last but not least, the honor of the oldest living member of the team goes to 85-year-old Mike Meilicke. Mike still gets a gleam in his eye when speaking about Eddie Feigner. "He wasn't too bashful," Meilicke said about Feigner. "He'd look you right in the eye and say, 'I can strike you out.'" Striking people out was what "The King" did best.

Rough Waters

He was no sailor. Never skippered a boat or navigated the open seas. In fact, he was far from the leather-skinned, sea-faring captains of his day. He was prim and proper with wire-rimmed glasses. Educated by the best schools in this country and he stood up as straight as an arrow, all 6-foot-5 of him. He was Ivy League with a capital I. He was called a "stuffed shirt" and "pompous" by his shipmates. He was a New York lawyer with a chip on his shoulder as big as the Pacific Ocean. He was at the head of many controversial decisions and fought with a baseball union that besieged him with lawsuits, grievances and work stoppages. Integrity became his middle name and he fought to preserve the difference between right and wrong. He became admired and hated all at the same time. He was labeled "the village idiot" by some owners and a "Hall of Famer" by others. For 15 years, he steered, prodded, pushed and jerked this game into the wind and through a great deal of change and controversy. No one would rest, on his watch. He was called insensitive and judgmental. He sailed the American pastime through rough waters; but, as I said above, he was no seaman. He was a sports administrator who believed in the idea that any activity that did not meet the "not in the best interest of baseball" logic was to be scuttled and sunk. It was a rough, but amazing voyage.

The fifth commissioner of Major League baseball was born Bowie Kent Kuhn on October, 28, 1926, in Takoma Park, Maryland. He grew up in Washington, D.C. and graduated from Theodore Roosevelt High School. As a kid he operated the manual scoreboard at Washington's Griffith Park and became a baseball fan. He attended Princeton and graduated with honors in 1947, with a Bachelor of Arts degree in Economics; and then he earned a law degree at the University of Virginia, in 1950. Bowie also served on the board of the law review, while at the University of Virginia. His accomplishments would land him a job with a New York City law firm known as Willkie, Farr & Gallagher. This firm represented the National League of Major League Baseball. Bowie would find a home working in baseball's legal affairs and would serve as a counselor in a lawsuit brought against the National League by the City of Milwaukee, Wisconsin, when following the 1965 season; the Braves announced that they were moving to Atlanta, Georgia. In 1968, the owners of Major League baseball forced then current commissioner William Eckert out of office, and Kuhn seemed like the best-suited replacement. Bowie Kuhn would take charge on February 4, 1969. Little did the owners know that the forty-two year old Bowie Kuhn would be no push-over.

From 1968 to 1983, the attendance at Major League games almost doubled. In fact, it increased from 23 million a year to over 45.5 million. In addition to the increased number of fans, several very lucrative television contracts were implemented. This was an absolutely amazing accomplishment in the face of several labor strikes, numerous player suspensions for drugs and gambling, and the end of baseball's reserve clause. Owners' anger reached an all-time high with Kuhn, especially during the strike in 1981.

Here are some of the waves that Kuhn had to navigate through. At the end of the 1969 season, the St. Louis Cardinals traded Tim McCarver, Curt Flood, Byron Brown, and Joe Horner to the Philadelphia Phillies, for Dick Allen, "Cookie" Rojas, and Jerry Johnson. Curt Flood refused to report to the Phillies and demanded that Commissioner Kuhn declare him a "free agent." Kuhn denied Flood's request, citing the reserve clause which held language in his contract that stated Flood could not play for another team, even after his contract had expired. Flood, in return, filed a lawsuit; and the case ended up in the Supreme Court. The case, *Flood v. Kuhn* was ruled *stare decisis*, "to stand by things decided," upholding a 1922 ruling in the case of Federal Baseball Club v. National League. Flood would forfeit his 100,000-dollar contract and retire from baseball. In 1970, Tigers' star pitcher Denny McLain was suspended for gambling, and Jim Bouton's book titled <u>Ball Four</u> was declared detrimental to baseball, by Kuhn. In 1971, night-time World Series games occurred for the first time. Kuhn thought that the game would attract a bigger audience in prime time, as opposed to afternoon games. An estimated 61 million people tuned in to watch Game 4 on NBC, and Kuhn was proved correct, as all World Series games are now broadcast in prime time. In 1971, the decision was finally made to include Negro League Players into the Baseball Hall of Fame. Kuhn caused a public outcry when he deemed it necessary to place their plaques in a separate wing of the Hall of Fame because they were not true Major League players. Since the Hall of Fame is a separate entity from Major League Baseball, it is under no obligation to abide by the Commissioner's rulings. All plaques now hang together in the same wing. In 1976, Kuhn butted heads with Oakland A's owner, Charles Finley, when he disallowed several deals of Finley's to sell several of his players to the New York Yankees and the Boston Red Sox. Kuhn blocked them on the grounds that these deals would be bad for the game. Kuhn also became involved with Hank Aaron's chase of Babe Ruth's all-time home-run record, in 1974. Atlanta opened the season with a three- game series in Cincinnati, but Atlanta Braves management wanted Hank to break the record at home in Atlanta. Bowie declared that Hank would have to play at least two games in Cincinnati. The result was that Hank Aaron tied Ruth's record with home run number 714 in his first at-bat, with the commissioner in attendance, but hit no other home runs while in Cincinnati. Aaron would later break the record in Atlanta with home run number 715, off of Al Downing of the Los Angeles Dodgers. Kuhn was criticized for not being in Atlanta. A prior engagement was Kuhn's answer. In 1979, Kuhn issued a notice to all clubs that all reporters, regardless of sex, would have access and be treated equally in the locker rooms. In 1980, during the Iranian hostage crisis, Kuhn thought up the idea of a life-time baseball pass, which was later given to all 52 hostages upon their return from Iran. Both Willie Mays (1979) and Mickey Mantle (1983) were barred from baseball, because of their involvement with gambling casino promotions. Both were later reinstated by Kuhn's successor, Peter Ueberroth, in 1985. Also in 1983, four players from the Kansas City Royals, Willie Wilson, Jerry Martin, Willie Mays Aikens, and Vida Blue, were all found guilty of cocaine use. That same year, Steve Howe of the Dodgers was also suspended for drug use. Other players like Keith Hernandez, Dale Berra (son of Yogi Berra), Dave Parker, and Ferguson Jenkins admitted to having problems with drugs during their careers. It has also been said that Kuhn added Carl Yastrzemski's name to the 1983 All-Star roster in "Yaz's" last year, but had failed to do the same for Willie Stargell in 1982.

As you can see, it was rough seas for Bowie Kuhn. It seemed like there was always a problem at every turn. Five of baseball's eight work stoppages occurred on Kuhn's watch. He fined and suspended owners Ray Kroc, Ted Turner and George Steinbrenner, for tampering with players' contracts. No fish was too big to be hooked by Bowie Kuhn. Yet he had overseen a sport that transformed itself into a business of free agents with multimillion dollar contracts. From 1975 until 1984, baseball revenues grew from 163 million to 624 million dollars; and the players wanted their cuts. Players' salaries rose from an average of 19,000 per player to over 300,000 dollars. All in all, I think he liked being the commissioner. On his watch, he allowed the infamous designated-hitter rule of 1973, for the American League, to begin; and prior to that he allowed divisional play for both leagues to start in 1969. Finally, he was forced out by the owners, after the 1984 season. On October 1, 1984, Peter Ueberroth took Kuhn's place. Kuhn returned to the law firm of Willkie, Farr, & Gallagher. He would later undergo open-heart surgery just days before his 78th birthday, and he survived.

On Thursday, March 15, 2007, Kuhn would finally be confronted by a deal he could not win, death. He had been hospitalized for several weeks with pneumonia, which eventually led to respiratory failure. He died at St. Luke's Hospital in Jacksonville, Florida. He would be survived by his wife Luisa, son Stephen, daughter Alix Bower, and stepsons Paul and George Degener.

"I wanted to be remembered that I was commissioner during a time of tremendous growth in the popularity of the game," Kuhn said, "and that it was a time in which no one could question the integrity of the game." I think he got his wish.

Putting People in His Pocket

Why is it that most folks only say nice things about a person after they have died? He was an honorable man and he took pride in living a clean, God-fearing life. Many words have been used to describe him these past few days: pioneer, teacher, and gentleman, admired, father figure, motivator, old school, good citizen, good American, and of course, coach. He always said that his only real accomplishment in life was that he had one job and one wife, for over 50 years. He really cared about all of his players and tried to mold them into productive citizens. He was able to recruit the kids who usually went to LSU, Arkansas or Alabama. He personally never talked about winning or losing, but win was all that his teams did. Knowing that he had an impact on his players' lives meant more to him than any of the victories. He didn't just talk about X's and O's. He spoke about drugs, going to class, studying, and what kind of men they would grow up to be. He wasn't just about football; he was about human beings, and because of that, over 80 percent of his players graduated. He had known that he wanted to coach ever since he was in the fourth grade. Seems that a local high school football team visited the elementary school where he was attending. "The other kids wanted to be players, but I wanted to be like that coach," he said with a grin. "I liked the way he talked to the team, the way he could make us laugh. I liked the way they all respected him." He also was fond of saying, "I have a piece of every teacher I ever had and a piece of every player that ever played for me." I guess that's what he meant when he said he liked putting people in his pocket and of course winning football games was also a way to end up in his pocket. "I try to coach each player as if he wanted to marry my daughter," he exclaimed. He believed that if you surrounded yourself with good people, then you became a little part of them and they a little part of you. The result was excellence. "Coaching is a profession of love," he once said. "You can't coach people unless you love them." He was more concerned about his players being good men than good athletes, yet he placed over 200 of them in professional sports.

Sixty-five miles east of Shreveport near the Arkansas border, Eddie Robinson began his coaching career at a tiny, all-black school known as Louisiana Negro Normal and Industrial Institute. His career started in 1941, before Japan attacked Pearl Harbor, and spanned the terms of 11 presidents, several other wars, and the civil rights movement. He was able to take this small school, known today all over the country as Grambling State University, and transform it into a football powerhouse for over 50 years. Born in Jackson, Louisiana in 1919, Robinson was raised by a father who was a sharecropper and mother who was a domestic servant. Eddie played football for Leland College located in Baker, Louisiana, and then took a job for 25 cents an hour working in a feed mill. Robinson met Dr. Ralph W. Jones, President of Louisiana Negro Normal and Industrial Institute, because Eddie's sister and Dr.

Jones' wife were friends. Dr. Jones was not only President but also the baseball coach, and he decided to hire Eddie Robinson as the football coach. This quiet, hard-working new coach produced an undefeated team in only his second year. Robinson began his career with no assistants, no groundskeepers, no trainers, and very little equipment. He made sandwiches for his players to take on road trips because they could not eat in "white only" restaurants. He also had to line the field himself before game time. He was never bitter and often said that he enjoyed being an American and that you didn't have to be white to be an American. In 1946, this college would change its name to Grambling State University and produce the university's first Black College All-American and National Football League player. His name was Paul "Tank" Younger and he would help Robinson win 35 of the 46 games that he played in during his four seasons at Grambling. Younger was drafted by the Los Angeles Rams and would go on to become the first of four Grambling football players coached by Eddie Robinson, to be elected into the Pro Football Hall of Fame. The other three are Willie Brown, Buck Buchanan and Willie Davis.

There were many other Grambling players whose names are just as familiar, like Ernie Ladd, James Harris, Sammy White, Cliff McNeil, Charlie Joiner, Roosevelt Taylor, Everson Walls and Doug Williams. Football Saturday in Central Louisiana became a big time event. The NFL began referring to Grambling as the cradle of pro players and Sports Information Director, Collie Nicholson took advantage. During the sixties, Grambling would travel to play some of the best football teams in the biggest arenas in the nation. Yankee Stadium, the Sugar Bowl and the Cotton Bowl were some impressive places on their schedule. "I can remember when blacks were not even allowed to sit in the Sugar Bowl," said Robinson. Grambling State also played in the first college football game ever played outside the United States. The Tigers defeated Morgan State 42-16 in Tokyo, Japan, in 1976. And don't forget the Grambling Tiger Marching Band. That band and the Grambling Tiger football team were promoted like a circus in those days. He often said, "There's more than football at Grambling. We have a great show band. You can be killing us on the field, but people aren't going to leave until after the half." His team and his band would make the Bayou Classic an annually televised event.

It was a crisp Saturday night October 5, 1985, in Dallas, Texas, when a crowd of over 36 thousand watched Eddie Robinson's Grambling State Tigers defeat Prairie View A&M, 27-7 to earn his 324th victory. That win gave him the most victories of any college football coach in history. He was 66 years old and was coaching his 44th season. After the game, instead of celebrating, he spent time in the locker room apologizing to his players for the many recent absences from practice which had occurred leading up to this game. Demands of his time from the media had been exhausting. He had been good copy, as the news cronies would say.

It's safe to say that starting in 1941; Eddie Robinson did for the South what Jackie Robinson had done in 1947 in the North, for the pride of the Black American. He may have been one of the most important figures in the history of college football. He opened the door for thousands of black players and coaches. As a role model, he was to college athletics what Dr. Martin Luther King was to civil rights. Coach Rob's teams won or shared 17 Southwestern Athletic Conference championships, were black national champions nine times and appeared in the I-AA playoffs three times. He had only eight losing seasons during his tenure and was the first black coach to win the Bobby Dodd Award. Eddie Robinson has been inducted into every Hall of Fame for which he has ever been eligible.

On Tuesday, April 3, 2007, in Ruston, Louisiana, Football Coach Eddie Robinson called his last play. He was 88 years old, had suffered from Alzheimer's disease for the last several years, and had been in and out of nursing homes since 2004. He was survived by his wife Doris, son Eddie Robinson Jr., daughter Lillian Rose Robinson, five grand-children, and four great-grandchildren. He spent 57 years at Grambling State University and compiled a win-loss record of 408-165-15. This record included the two years during WWII where the university did not field a team. With 408 total victories, Robinson surpassed Bear Bryant, in 1985 and remained the winningest college football coach until 2003, when Coach John Galiardi of Division III St. John's University of Collegeville, Minnesota broke Robinson's record.

On Monday April 9, 2007, Coach Robinson's casket lay in state at the Louisiana Capitol in Baton Rouge. It is believed that he is only the fifth person to receive that honor. The renowned Grambling band played the National Anthem as more than six thousand people paid their respects. His wife placed a football in the coffin before it was closed. His body was then returned to Grambling for a wake and then burial on Wednesday. Once, when asked how he would be judged after his coaching days were over, he responded, "You can't un-ring a bell. I played as long as I could play, whenever I could play, and as hard as I could play. How else can you judge me, except for what I accomplished?" Well done, Coach Rob; well done!

Just Sign Right Here

It seemed like he was always there. Sitting or walking behind the signers. I must have noticed him several times before I actually spoke. I wondered who he was, what was he doing, and how did he know the players so well. He didn't look like an athlete; was he just hanging out or was he working? Turns out that almost every weekend for fourteen years he was there, somewhere in the background, looking out for his players. He was a sports agent and one of the best. They invented the word pioneer for guys like this. He handled over 350 players from baseball, football, basketball, boxing and hockey. But the thing he did best was represent Hall of Fame players. No one messed with his guys while they were on the autograph signing tours, and he expected them to receive the VIP treatment at every show. Just ask life-long friend, Hank Aaron. He always looked out for his players' best interests and his prowess became known and respected by all.

Anyone who knows me will tell you I'm not shy, especially when it comes to sports athletes. So, I introduced myself to Mr. Bob Allen, Sports Agent.

Bob Allen, like most boys, wanted to be an athlete when he grew up. A bout with rheumatic fever during his childhood caused Doctors to advise him to sit out. But, like most guys, Bob didn't listen; and he became an All-American in track and field for the University of Marquette, in 1954. In fact, while in college, he came up a few strides shy of winning the NCAA two-mile title. "I convinced the track coach to let me run," said Allen, "But there I was. A skinny kid, sick my whole life, I beat all. I exploded on the scene." It was this kind of determination that would be at the forefront in all of Allen's success. There was one other thing that stayed in the thoughts of Bob Allen, baseball, the game he loved most. Growing up in Milwaukee, afforded Bob the opportunity to see some of the games' very best, play baseball. He would raise the money he needed to attend games by collecting bottles for cash. His passion was so great that he began to keep all the stats on every player. Later on, Allen would use this baseball knowledge to acquire a job with the local newspaper, Milwaukee Journal, in their sports department. His work impressed the sports editor and soon an introduction to the Milwaukee Braves front office was in order. Bob now dreamed of being connected with the Major League club. He would not take "no" for an answer. Bob would do anything to be associated with the club. He ran errands, scrubbed floors, cleaned the club house, all while not being paid. "The first time I went down to the club house and there sat Warren Spahn, I was so excited," he recalled. Eventually he caught on and stayed 13 years as a publicist for the Braves. Of course the World Series appearances in 1957 and 1958 against the New York Yankees were the highlights of Allen's time in Milwaukee. Those winning years with Milwaukee gave Allen lots of exposure to many of the games' greatest players, and he continued to develop those friendships for years to come. "So how lucky can you get?" exclaimed Allen as he sat in the dugout of an All-Star game with his favorite players.

Doomsday occurred for Allen in 1966 when the Braves moved to Atlanta. Allen would choose to stay behind. His emotional attachment with the team now broken, Allen refused to watch an Atlanta Braves game. "It just wasn't right, what they did," said Allen. His long time friend and associate, Hank Aaron, finally convinced him to attend one Atlanta Braves game late in his life. "All I could see was the old Braves; Mathews, Aaron, Logan," he said of the game. The Braves move to Atlanta was just one of the reasons Allen would not represent any current players. He had lost his respect for what Major League baseball had become, along with the players. "Between the owners and idiotic salaries to players, the fan is forgotten," he said. "It's sick. It's all money. I prefer to remember the game the way it used to be," he added.

With the Braves gone, Allen spent 20 years as a sports writer. He also spent some time on the radio and as an official scorer for the American League. In 1984, Allen opened a small advertising agency which later led him to the sports card show frenzy. These shows needed athletes for autographs and Bob Allen knew athletes. "It didn't take long and it started snowballing," Allen said. Bob Allen would soon control 85% of all player representation of athletes at card shows across the nation. Baseball Hall of Fame players like Bob Feller, Eddie Mathews, Bobby Doerr, Stan Musial, Enos Slaughter, Brooks Robinson, Johnny Mize, Duke Snider, Bill Mazeroski, Hank Aaron, and of course his favorite, Warren Spahn, were just some of the players that Bob Allen signed and looked after.

In 1999, after 15 years in the sports agent business, Bob Allen decided to honor baseball and his friend Henry

Aaron with a book he titled, <u>The 500 Home Run Club</u>. These 15 players, led by Aaron, underwent extensive research by Allen and co-writer Bill Gilbert. Over 180 players, umpires, and managers were interviewed. Allen used his long-standing relationships with these players to get a unique perspective on each one of them. "They'll talk to me," he said. Allen often referred to his athletes by the number used during their playing-days. "I talk to '44' regularly," exclaims Allen.

Bob Allen passed away on May 4, 2007 in his home-town of Milwaukee, Wisconsin. He was 75 years young and had spent his last few years working on recording the great living players on videotape and audiotape, explaining what and how they did things as professional baseball players. No doubt about it, Allen was a throwback. He was old-school through and though. He had fallen in love with the game of his youth and protected those memories at every turn. His devotion to the Milwaukee Braves and baseball earned him a ring from the 1957 World Series Championship. Before Allen died, he arranged for the Milwaukee County Museum to display his ring. "I'm just its caretaker," said Allen. "I am lucky enough to wear it until I die." I think he earned it; now where do I sign?

It Was Good To Be a Yankee

Reflexes and instincts, that's what it took to play defense at the hot corner. He was one of the best in the game at third base, no doubt about it. He owned a-cannon for an arm and had the grit to turn that ball loose. He was a mainstay in arguably one of the best infields in baseball history. "It was special," he said, "Pepitone, Bobby, Tony, and me." A great glove, solid bat, and pinstripes, that's what comes to my mind when someone says his name. He was thrilled to be a Yankee and played on five straight American League pennant winners and won two World Series titles from 1960 to 1964. He even set a World Series record with 66 assists at third base. He loved defense and often remarked that he felt like Houdini out there with a baseball glove. "If I had played with anybody else," he said, "The fans wouldn't even know my name." The 1960's was a decade where baseball flourished in America. Several teams, like the Giants, Browns and Dodgers, had already moved across the country. Other teams like the Braves and Senators were in the process of relocating to Atlanta and Minneapolis while brand new teams were created in cities such as Houston, New York, Anaheim, and Seattle. Television in the sixties exposed millions of fans to

America's Pastime. Before 1957, Major League Baseball was played by sixteen teams located in only eight cities, all in the Northeastern part of the United States. In fact, the St. Louis Cardinals and St. Louis Browns were located the farthest West on the United States map and, believe it or not, also the farthest South. It was a city game played downtown in towering concrete and steel parks.

Cletis Leroy "Clete" Boyer was born February 9, 1937, in Cassville, Missouri. As one of fourteen children, seven boys and seven girls, Clete would be surrounded by loved ones. Family would become as important to him as baseball. All his brothers played baseball. Five played professionally and three made it to the Major Leagues. The Boyer's are one of sixteen families to have three or more siblings play Major League baseball. "I knew when I was 17 years old that I was going to play in the big leagues," said Boyer. "Other people didn't know it, but in my heart, I knew it." Cloyd was the oldest and a pitcher for the St. Louis Cardinals during the fifties. Cloyd's career was cut short to five seasons by a rotator cuff injury. Ken was also a third baseman like Clete but played with the Cardinals. Ken was a great player and was elected to seven National League All-Star games while winning five Gold Glove Awards. Brother Ken would also earn the National League MVP Award in 1964, while leading the Cardinals to a World Series title over brother Clete and the New York Yankees. In game seven of that 1964 World Series, Ken and Clete became the first and only pair of brothers to hit a home run in the same World Series game. Their combined total of lifetime homers hit (444) places them fourth for most in history by Major League brothers. Clete always complained that he would have hit more home runs than Ken if he had not had to play half his games in Yankee

Stadium, where the left center field fence stood 457 feet away and center field even further at 461 feet. Clete called it Death Valley, a place where home runs go to die. "I couldn't hit a golf ball that far," laughed Boyer.

Clete began his career in 1955 with the Kansas City Athletics, at the age of 18, but was later traded to the New York Yankees in 1957. After two seasons in the Yankee farm system he would find success in 1959, with the big club. "I hit third in Triple A," said Boyer, "I go to the Yankees and they have Maris, Mantle, Howard, Skowron and Berra. So I had to hit eighth." Hitting in front of the pitcher offered no protection. "You can't hit eighth in front of the pitcher if you have power," Boyer said. "They'll knock you down every time." Clete was considered one of the three best third basemen in Yankee history. Red Rolfe preceded Boyer as a great Yankee third baseman, and Greg Nettles followed him. Most would tell you there was not a bit of difference between the three. Boyer always seemed to be in position to make the tough plays and ranks eighth all-time, with a 2.24 assists per game; and according to Total Baseball, he is second only to Mike Schmidt at saving runs during his career, with 201. During the 1961 World Series, Boyer made two spectacular plays, both with throws to first base from his knees. In the second inning of Game One he moved to his right and backhanded a Gene Freese grounder for a put-out, and then later dived to his left to stop a Dick Gernert ground ball. In 1962, he had 396 assist. In 1965, Boyer started 46 double plays while maintaining a .968 fielding average. If it were not for Brooks Robinson, Boyer may have won six or seven Gold Gloves during his American League career. He was that good but as it was, he won his only Gold Glove Award in the National League with the Atlanta Braves in 1969.

As a hitter, Clete was equally impressive. Boyer's defensive plays in the 1961 World Series victory over the Cincinnati Reds more than made up for his poor batting. In 1962, Boyer hit 18 home runs, and had 68 RBI's while batting .272 in the regular season. In the "62" Series, the Yankees beat the San Francisco Giants as Clete batted .318 with one home run and four RBI's. The 1963 World Series against the Los Angeles Dodgers brought good and bad news for Clete Boyer. It marked the first time that the Yankees as a team have been swept in World Series play, as Boyer shined against pitcher Sandy Koufax. Boyer was the only Yankee regular not to strike out against Koufax. The 1964 season would find the Yankees vs. the Cardinals in a seven-game series that was won by St. Louis. Boyer's ninth inning home run in Game Seven was not enough to beat the Cards, who won 7-5. Clete also hit 18 home runs, with 58 RBI's and a .251 batting average in 1965; but it was not enough to get the Yankees back to the World Series. In World Series play, Boyer always seemed to step it up. At the end of the 1966 season, he was traded by General Manager Lee McPhail to the Atlanta Braves, for Bill Robinson. Interestingly enough, Boyer had his best offensive season in Atlanta. He set career highs for home runs (26) and RBI's (96) in 1967, while batting clean-up behind Hank Aaron. With a line-up that included Boyer, Aaron, Joe Torre and Felipe Alou, the Braves would win their first National League Western Division title, in 1969. Boyer wanted to retire a Yankee, but finished his MLB playing career in 1971 with the Braves. Clete Boyer finished his 16-year career with 162 home runs, 654 RBI's, a .242 batting average and played in 1,725 games. In 1972, Boyer would find himself in Japan playing baseball with the Taiyo Whales. His roommate was none other than the home-run champion of Japan, Sadaharu Oh. After the 1976 season, Clete returned to the States to coach third base for the Braves, Yankees and Oakland Athletes, under his friend, former teammate, and skipper Billy Martin. Boyer's expertise with a glove would help teach and even rejuvenate such great players as Carney Lansford, Wade Boggs and Derek Jeter.

In 2000, Boyer opened a restaurant named, "Clete Boyer's Hamburger Hall of Fame," in Cooperstown, New York. All the sandwiches and burgers were named after many of the Yankee greats. The menu would read something like this: the "Whitey Ford Blue Cheese Burger," "Mickey Mantle Cheeseburger Deluxe," "Reggie Veggie Burger," "Bobby Richardson Cheeseburger," "Yogi's Meatball Sub," and the "Roger Maris Hamburger Deluxe." Although he lived in Atlanta, Georgia, and owned a picture framing business, Boyer loved just hanging out at his restaurant and signing autographs for the fans.

It's funny, with the title of this piece you would expect an article about Ruth, Gehrig, Mantle or maybe DiMaggio, but it was the many unsung heroes that realized how lucky they were to have played for the New York Yankees. Guys like Moose Skowron, Roger Maris, Hank Bauer, Ellie Howard, Billy Martin, Bob Crev, Tom Tresh, and of course Clete Boyer. These were very good, if not great ballplayers who served the purpose of the ball team, to win; and winning may be what they did best. These position players fit in and contributed to the many New York teams that were made up of some of the greatest Hall-of-Fame players of all-time. They made more money than they ever dreamed of, and their World Series shares were icing on the cake. Names like Bobby Richardson, Tony Kubek, Joe Pepitone, Ralph Terry, Gil McDougald, Dale Long, Allie Reynolds,

Bob Turley, Bobby Shantz and the ones I mentioned above will always be remembered because of who they played for, even though some of them had better personal seasons on other teams. Love'em or hate'em, the New York Yankees are baseball, and I can't imagine the game itself being as successful as it is without them. I also know that without players like Clete Boyer, the Yankees would not have won so many pennants.

Clete Boyer threw his last frozen rope to first base on June 4, 2007. He died from complications of a brain hemorrhage in an Atlanta hospital. He was 70 years of age and still very proud to be a Yankee. In fact, Boyer became the first professional athlete to be buried in an Eternal Image branded urn. The Boyer family placed his cremated remains in a New York Yankee urn. Clete was survived by six children and ten grandchildren. It's now time to rest, # 6. Say hi to the "Babe," for me.

The Untouchables

Professional baseball umpire and fellow peer Ron Luciano once wrote, "It's the only profession in the world that expects you to be one hundred percent correct the first time out and get better every day after that." Who would ever want to be an umpire? First, you must love the game of baseball as this fellow did and secondly, have you ever seen a baseball rule book? It's like reading a law book written in hieroglyphics. You've got to love this job to do it well. He was a sandlot catcher who thought nothing of getting down and dirty, playing the game he loved. "Let's just say some of the things he put on weren't always of the finest quality. He had things with holes in them; it didn't bother him," said his son Jerry. Maybe he was just too busy playing baseball to worry about the clothes he wore. As a result, his friends nicknamed him "Shaggy." He was a Philadelphia kid, born in 1917, who would raise a family near the City of Brotherly Love. He not only loved baseball, but also grew up playing football and boxing. He eventually made it into the Philadelphia Phillies Minor League system as a catcher, but he must have been better at calling pitches than hitting them. Thus, he became an umpire and a darn good one.

From 1956 to 1975, National League Umpire, Henry Charles "Shag" Crawford called more than 3,100 games. His childhood nickname had eventually been shortened to "Shag." In the old days, each league had its own umpires. Many of their names are recognizable and some of these "untouchables" are in the Baseball Hall of Fame. Umpires like Al Barlick, Tom Connelly, Bill Klem, Wild Bill Evans, Cal Hubbard, Jocko Conlan, and Bill McGowan have a place in Cooperstown where they will live forever. In my opinion, Shag umpired during the glory years of baseball. Fellow umpires who worked with Shag read like a Who's Who in the record books and most seemed to have their own nicknames. Nestor Chylak, Augie Donatelli, Big Ed Runge, Harry Wendelstedt, and George Honochik were just some of the well-known umpires of Shag's time. As for the names above, only Chylak has been inducted into the Hall of Fame. No doubt, there will be more in the future.

Shag worked the World Series three times and the National League Championship series twice, and was also honored by calling three All-Star contests. During Game Four, he would place his own personal stamp on the 1969 World Series by ejecting Baltimore Orioles Manager Earl Weaver for arguing. Weaver contended that his star player, Frank Robinson, was hit by a pitch. Shag disagreed and Earl escalated the argument with a few choice forbidden words. As a result, Earl Weaver became the first manager to be tossed from a World Series game in 34 years. Shag was also known for "hanging out" right on top of the catcher, from behind home plate. He would place his hands gently on the back of the catcher as he called the game. "He hung on to me when he was calling balls and strikes," exclaimed All-Star catcher, Joe Torre. He liked being in charge as much as he liked the name "Shag." "I think he'd want that on his tombstone as his middle name," said his son Jerry. Both of Shag's sons joined the same profession. Jerry Crawford started his career as a Professional Major League Umpire in 1976, and his brother, Joey, became an official for the National Basketball Association, a year later. "Shag was very proud of what he did," said New York Yankee Manager, Joe Torre. "Evidently his kids were pretty proud of what he did, because they took after him." "When we were young, my brothers and my sister would go watch my dad work," Jerry said. "I'm sure that had something to do with what we did." It appears that the apple never falls very far from the tree.

Shag Crawford, who was one of the founders of the umpire's union, resigned in 1975, after getting into a dispute with Major League Baseball over the rotation of umpires in the World Series. He will always be known for two things, a short fuse and consistency. He would not stand for disrespect and took pride in calling a game as fairly as possible but he would give you the thumb in a heartbeat, if he thought you had gone too far. He thought a good umpire should be untouchable, one who would always respect the game regardless of who were the players. Shag knew that his actions on the field of play mattered. "Otherwise, he was pretty consistent," said Torre. "That's really all you want from an umpire."

It takes a special kind of person to be a baseball umpire. You have no home field; you always have to travel to the next game and regardless of your call, someone will always disagree. I actually went to college with two guys who ended up professional baseball umpires. By knowing them, I feel I have some insight into what it takes to be a good umpire. Joe West and Drew Coble were college buddies, baseball teammates; and we lived in the same dorm. Joe West started in 1977 with the National League and is still calling balls and strikes today. His nickname is "Country Joe," for his love of country music and his ability to sing. Drew Coble became an umpire in the American League in 1983 and worked until 1999, when the merger took place. The umpire's union merged the American and National Leagues together to form one group. The guys I knew back then were fun loving, thick skinned, and loud. Sounds like the perfect combination for an umpire. They also loved the game of baseball and both wanted to be in "The Show." Since neither of them was talented enough to play, umpiring was a way to stay close to the game and make a decent living being a part of something they loved. I imagine that's what Jerry and Joey Crawford experienced by watching their dad as an umpire.

On Wednesday, July 11, 2007, Shag Crawford left the field. He had called his last game in life, at the age of 90. Shag had been staying in an assisted living facility in Philadelphia, Pennsylvania for several years. "For someone who was going to be 91 in August, he was in pretty good health for a long time," said his son Jerry. Shag was buried the following Monday in Havertown, Pennsylvania. He was a credit to the umpire's profession and the game of baseball. Everyone in baseball knew Shag Crawford.

Ten Years Ahead

His system of offense was virtually unstoppable. He was a visionary in terms of learning to move the football using the short passing game, instead of running plays. He drafted and placed athletes in a position to win. He knew exactly what kind of skills these athletes needed to make his new offensive scheme effective. These players he drafted were unconventional for that time. He choose small, quick offensive linemen, mobile quarterbacks, running backs and tight ends, who could catch the ball out of the backfield, and players intelligent enough to learn from a playbook dedicated to a new system. His plays were designed to be effective against what the defense was thinking. Even his own team's defense would have trouble stopping his offense, and they knew the plays. He changed the way teams practiced and the way they trained. He scripted his team's first 15 plays. His positive attitude was contagious and rubbed off on his assistant coaches and players. They believed in him, themselves, and this new offense. Although this new scheme originated in Cincinnati, it was dubbed "The West Coast Offense." This new thinking head coach only needed three years to get his team to the Super Bowl, and while there he would win three titles in 10 years. Along the way, he would make stars out of no-name college athletes like Ken Anderson, Dan Fouts, Ronnie Lott, Charles Haley and Jerry Rice. Many would refer to him as "The Genius."

William Ernest "Bill" Walsh was ten years ahead of the rest of the National Football League. He was born in Los Angeles, California on November 30, 1931. Walsh starred as a running back for Hayward High School. He would attend San Mateo Junior College for two years and then transfer to San Jose State University. His first taste of coaching occurred at Washington High School with the football and swim teams. Walsh would later interview with head football coach Marv Levy, who was coaching at the University of California, Berkeley. "I was very impressed individually, by his knowledge, by his intelligence, and by his personality; and I hired him," Levy said. Walsh would later move on to Stanford as an assistant coach, before joining the pro coaching ranks, in 1966.

Walsh would be groomed under head Coach Sid Gillman with the Oakland Raiders. In 1968, he would find himself with a new expansion team in Cincinnati, known as the Bengal's. Head Coach Paul Brown would turn the offense over to Walsh for seven seasons, while Bill worked his magic with Quarterback Ken Anderson. In 1975, after Paul Brown retired, he left the team with Bill "Tiger" Johnson. A surprised Walsh resigned at the end of that season and joined head Coach Tommy Prothro and the 1976 San Diego Chargers. Walsh's new scheme would help mold Dan Fouts into a Hall of Fame Quarterback. Walsh always blamed Paul Brown for not moving up the coaching ranks to head coach. "He worked against my candidacy to be a head coach anywhere in the league," said Walsh. Walsh would get his first head coaching job at Stanford in 1977, and would stay for two seasons. With players like James Lofton and Steve Dils, he would lead the Cardinals to victories in the Sun Bowl and Bluebonnet Bowl and receive the Pac-8 Coach of the Year Award, in 1977. Then his life would change.

In 1979, the San Francisco 49ers franchise hit the jackpot; they hired Bill Walsh, at the age of 47, as their new head football coach. His first season was nothing to talk about, as the 49ers repeated a 2-14 record, but help was on the way. Walsh had taken a quiet, stooped shouldered Quarterback from Notre Dame, in the third round of the 1979 draft. His name was Joe Montana. In 1980, with Walsh's new system and Montana's strong arm, the 49ers would improve to 6-10 and then go on to win their first Super Bowl in 1981. It had taken Walsh only three years to reach a pinnacle that most lifelong coaches never achieve. It's interesting that in the closing minutes of that 1981 NFC title game against the Dallas Cowboys, Walsh called a series of running plays and moved the ball down the field against a Dallas defense that expected the 49ers to pass. The Niner's came from behind to win, with a remarkable play by Dwight Clark in the end zone that would forever be known as "The Catch." With new players like Ronnie Lott, Charles Haley, Dwight Clark, Roger Craig and Jerry Rice, the 49ers would repeat their Super Bowl win again in 1984 and 1988. Walsh was elected to the NFL Football Hall of Fame in 1993. His 49er record stood at 102-63-1 for a .617 winning percentage. He was dubbed the "Coach of the Eighties," and his team was named the "Team of the Decade." His San Francisco team always played big in the big games, as evidenced by their winning 10 of the 14 postseason games they had played. If that's not good enough for you, listen to this. In seven of his last eight years as head coach with the 49ers, Walsh's teams won 10 or more games during the regular season and appeared in the NFC playoffs. That's called success.

During his ten years in San Francisco, Walsh was able to handpick some of the best coaches in the business. His coaching tree includes many fine NFL head coaches from the past and present. Jim Fassel, Mike Holmgren, George Seifert, Dennis Green, Sam Wyche, and Paul Hackett were all assistant coaches under Walsh. Second-tier coaches included Jeff Fisher, Steve Mariucci, Andy Reid, Brian Billick, Tony Dungy, Jon Gruden, Mike Shanahan, and Mike Tice. The list still continues today with the likes of Jack Del Rio, Lovie Smith, John Fox and Gary Kubiak. All of these fellow coaches continue to run some form of the "West Coast Offense."

At the end of the 1988 season, Walsh left the NFL after Super Bowl XXIII and joined Dick Enberg as part of NBC's lead broadcast team. He would remain there until 1992, when the coaching bug called again and he returned to Stanford as their head football coach for the second time. After a 10-3 season, a Pac-10 co-championship, a # 9 national ranking, and a win over Penn State in the Blockbuster Bowl, Walsh would retire from coaching for good. He authored two books while hitting the motivational speaking tour and taught a few classes in Business, at Stanford. He also served as General Manager and Vice President of the 49ers, on several occasions.

Bill Walsh was told he had leukemia in 2004. By November of 2006, he confirmed that he was receiving treatment for this illness. This was one game his team could not win. At 10:45 A.M. on July 30, 2007, Walsh died at his home in Woodside, California. "The Genius" has left us, but his West Coast Offense remains with us, alive and well. You can see for yourself this Thursday, when the new NFL season begins. He is survived by his wife, Geri, and two children, Craig and Elizabeth. It seems that Bill Walsh's entire life had been scripted just as he had done with his teams. No one in this game has achieved as much success in as short a time span as Walsh. And true to form, in death he had scripted his own funeral. He will be missed but never forgotten.

Wasn't Watching

My father used to describe him like this: "He wasn't as big as a minute." Yes, he was small, five feet five or six inches, weighed maybe a hundred and fifty pounds, soaking wet in a snow suit. But it wasn't how big he was that mattered, it was how big he played, and boy, could this guy play big. From his position of shortstop, his quick release of the baseball overshadowed his poor arm strength. He became a master of the small things that made a difference in the game. He owned the art of bunting for a base hit, hitting behind the runner, and could turn on a dime going to the outfield to catch short fly balls. His outright speed allowed him to compete on equal ground with players much stronger and larger than himself. He was never a flashy player; but stealing bases, perfect slides, and the squeeze play made him a pest against his opponents. His fielding skills were impeccable and he handled a bat like a fishing pole, able to place a ball where ever he wanted, as if he were casting. He may have been fundamentally the best ballplayer of his era. Players of today would describe him this way: "He had skills." In 1952, *Life* Magazine wrote an article about baseball and interviewed the great Ty Cobb. The "Georgia Peach" had very few good things to say about the players of that time. "They don't play baseball anymore," said Cobb. "They don't practice enough or the right way, they don't know the fundamentals, and all they care about is the home run." The article also pictured several prominent players of that day, including Ted Williams, Joe DiMaggio, Stan Musial, Eddie Stanky, Bob Feller, Phil Rizzuto, Ralph Kiner and Jackie Robinson. According to Cobb, only two of those players pictured were good enough to play in his day, Musial and Rizzuto. As for the rest of them, he said, "Throw them a bag of peanuts."

Philip Francis "Scooter" Rizzuto was born, September 25, 1917, in Brooklyn, moved at the age of twelve and entered Richmond Hill High School in Queens, then spent his entire professional baseball and broadcasting career in the Bronx, with the New York Yankees. You could say he was a "New York kind of guy." Phil was one of five children and the son of Rose and Fiore Rizzuto, a streetcar motorman who ran the trolley cars through the streets of Brooklyn. In fact, one of the original Brooklyn team names came from this form of transportation. They were known as the Trolley Dodgers, later to be called the Brooklyn Dodgers, as trolleys became obsolete. Phil's high school baseball coach, Al Kunitz, was the driving force behind his early success. The nickname "Scooter" was born from his size and speed. Heck, even Yogi Berra called him small, but it was actually given to him by another former Major League infielder named Billy Hitchcock. Billy had played in the Minor Leagues with Rizzuto and said, after watching Phil run, "Man, you're not running, you're scootin'." Short legs and quick feet propelled him around the base paths as if he were skating on ice. It was like watching a Chihuahua run.

In 1936, at the age of 19, Rizzuto showed up at Ebbets Field for a try-out with the Dodgers. It was not to be. Skipper Casey Stengel, took one look at him and said, "Yer too small. Go home. Get a shoebox." Rizzuto later said, "I was small. So small, the club house guy thought I was trying to break in to get autographs." So Rizzuto went across town to try-out with the Giants and again was turned away by Manager Bill Terry, for the same reason. Undaunted, Rizzuto was eventually signed by the New York Yankees in 1937, as an amateur free agent.

After a stint in the minors, Scooter finally played his first Major League game on April 14, 1941. The play of veteran shortstop Frank Crosetti was in decline, and the Yanks needed a replacement. Rizzuto's locker would be located between Red Rolfe and Red Ruffing. Rolfe was a tremendous third baseman for the Yankees and Ruffing, a future member of the Hall of Fame, as a pitcher. The year 1941 would be a season of tremendous highs and sad lows in the history of baseball. Rizzuto would witness first-hand DiMaggio hitting safely in 56 games, while helping the Yanks win 101 games. Ted Williams would finish the season with a batting average of over .400. Mel Ott would hit his 400th home run and his 1,500th RBI in the same at-bat. Brooklyn would dominate the National League while winning 100 games and then face the Yanks in the World Series; and the "Iron Horse," Lou Gehrig, would leave us on June 2nd of that same year. The Yankees went on to defeat the Dodgers, as Scooter hit .307 and became a world champion.

Rizzuto loved playing for Joe McCarthy and, in fact, he considered McCarthy his favorite manager. Rizzuto tells this story about McCarthy. "Joe McCarthy was good to me being a rookie and everything. In those years we traveled by train and after a game a bunch of us would play hearts—no poker or anything—no money. He would walk by and watch while remembering that one of us had messed up a hit-and-run play during the game. He would look at us and say, 'you guys can remember every card played in the deck, but you can't remember a hit-and-run sign,' and he kept going. The cards would then be picked up and everybody scattered." During the 1942 season, Rizzuto would play in the first All-Star game of his career. He would play in four more (1950-1953), before his playing days were over. In 1942, the Yanks would end up in the Series again, but this time against the St. Louis Cardinals. The morning after the 1942 World Series ended with a Yankees loss, Rizzuto reported for duty in Norfolk, Virginia. From 1942 until 1945, Phil's career, like many others, would be disrupted by WWII; but even then he would play baseball for the Navy's baseball team, in the South Pacific. Scooter would constantly be compared to other shortstops of his era, like Pee Wee Reese of the Dodgers or Marty Marion of the Cardinals. But to Joe DiMaggio, a teammate for eight years, Rizzuto was the best. Said DiMaggio in later years, "The little guy in front of me, he made my job easy. I didn't have to pick up so many ground balls." McCarthy would be replaced by Bucky Harris while Phil was away.

Rizzuto returned to the Yanks in 1946 and helped the Yankees win eight more pennants by 1956 (under Bucky Harris in 1947, and Casey Stengel from 1949-1953 and 1955-1956). In 1949, after a terrific year, Scooter would be disappointed by finishing second to Ted Williams in the MVP voting for the American League. Rizzuto would not be denied in 1950, and he went on to have the best season of his career. Although he started the season off 0-11, he would end up batting .324 while scoring 125 runs. His fielding percentage that year was .982, and his on-base percentage was recorded at .418. He was moved into the lead-off spot that year and walked 92 times, while leading the American League in singles, with 150. Scooter also handled 238 consecutive chances without an error that season, setting the record for shortstops. Those results would earn him the American League Most Valuable Player Award for 1950. Teammate Jerry Coleman said about Scooter's play, "He had great hands, never made a bad throw, and was always on top of things. He never made a mistake—he was incredible. A couple of times, I thought there were two outs—there was only one. You forget sometimes. He never forgot. He was great, bright and smart. And the best right-handed bunter I've ever seen. Phil could drag the ball with anybody, and beat it out. If he had straightened out half the balls he hit good, he'd have about 57 more home runs than he's got, because he hooked the ball." It sounds to me like Coleman was a Rizzuto fan.

Rizzuto also won the Hickok Belt in 1950, awarded to the top professional athlete of the year. He was voted top Major League shortstop by "The Sporting News" for four consecutive years (1949-1952). He would lead the American League in sacrifice hits for four consecutive seasons and was in the top five in stolen bases, seven times. As for his defense, Rizzuto lead the league in assists once, fielding and put-outs twice, and double plays and chances per game, three times each. In 1951, Phil would also receive the Babe Ruth award. He is still listed in the top ten of several World Series categories, including hits, games, runs, walks and steals. Scooter also set the World Series record of playing in 25 games without an error. "The Thumper" himself (Ted Williams) said it best: "If Rizzuto had been with Boston instead of New York, the Red Sox, not the Yankees, would have won many more pennants."

Although the Yankees had great success under Stengel, Rizzuto was never much of a fan of Casey. Scooter was quoted as saying, "No, I'm not big on him. In the National League, he was considered a clown. He inherited a great team. He was funny and good for baseball, but he didn't get along with the veterans. He wanted young players that he could control." It's interesting now to hear that Casey would never discuss his early wrong call on Rizzuto. Phil recalls, "When Casey became manager of the Yankees in 1949, I reminded him of that, but he pretended he didn't remember. By 1949, I didn't need a shoebox, anyway. The clubhouse boy at the Stadium shined my Yankee spikes every day."

The one play that Rizzuto would become known for was the squeeze play. Very few knew about this play except for his Yankee teammates. Rizzuto developed a unique sign for the squeeze bunt. Anytime Rizzuto would come to bat with a man on third in a tight game, he had the authority to give the runner the sign for the squeeze bunt. Here it is. If the first pitch to Rizzuto was a called strike, while turning to the umpire to argue the location of the pitch, he would grab his bat at both ends at the same time, to put on the sign for the squeeze. When he turned around to get back in the batter's box, he would look at the runner on third; and if the runner tipped his cap, Rizzuto would know the squeeze was on for the next pitch. One of the best examples of this occurred in 1951 against the Cleveland Indians, during a pennant race. It was the bottom of the ninth inning with the score tied at one. Joe DiMaggio was on third with Rizzuto at-bat. The first pitch to Rizzuto was called a strike, and he turned toward the umpire to argue. That gave him time to grab his bat at both ends, signaling the squeeze sign. With a nod of his cap, DiMaggio acknowledged the sign, but broke from third base a bit early on the next pitch. The Cleveland pitcher Bob Lemon threw high and inside, forcing Rizzuto to raise his bat head high in order to put the ball in play. The pitch was bunted and "Joltin' Joe" scored the winning run. Casey Stengel called it, "The greatest play I ever saw."

He has told the story a hundred times of how he was released by the Yankees in 1956. On August 25, after the Yankees had acquired future Hall of Famer, Enos Slaughter, Scooter was asked to come to the front office to discuss the post-season roster. He was asked to look over the roster of players and suggest which player might be released to make room for Slaughter. After a reason was given as to why each player he suggested needed to be kept, he realized that it was "he" who was expendable. Said pal Jerry Coleman, "He was crushed. He really was. They did it badly. Stengel was a great manager, but he was very aloof and had no real warmth to him with his players. That was a tough way to do it. I think Rizzuto got over it—but I'll never forget it. I walked right through the door and he was walking out. I said, 'Where the heck you going? The game is starting,' 'They just released me,' whispered Rizzuto." Scooter was inducted by the Veterans Committee into the Baseball Hall of Fame, in 1994. He had waited 36 years for his moment in the sun. For over 13 seasons, Scooter had played in 1,661 games, batted .273, rapped out 1,588 hits, scored 877 runs, stolen 149 bases, hit 38 homers with 563 RBI's, and recorded a fielding percentage of .968. The 10 American League pennants and 8 World Series Championships he helped the Yankees win didn't hurt his chances either.

"It's the easiest thing, almost like stealing," said Rizzuto about broadcasting. Yankee sponsor, Ballantine Beer, had insisted that the Yankees hire Rizzuto, and General Manager George Weiss was forced to fire Jim Woods to make room for Scooter in the booth. From 1957 to 1996, Scooter would bring his honest, straightforward thoughts to the listener as a game of baseball unfolded before him. He would talk about his wife Cora and wish fans Happy Birthday or Happy Anniversary. He sent get-well wishes to friends, talked about his favorite restaurant, told about his fear of lightning, commented on the style of the umpire's shoes, told what he did last night after the game, and of course described to fans what was happening on the field. His style was a bit quirky, but he did have a great sense of humor. Yes, he would ramble occasionally, but he was a storyteller at heart during the days when broadcasters simply spit out stats. "He didn't try to act like an announcer," Hall of Fame teammate Whitey Ford said. "He just said what he thought. It added fun to the game." Rizzuto admitted to hating to keep score during the game, and maybe that's why he spent so much time on other topics. The scorecard is the broadcaster's bible, a point of reference to be used throughout the game. Once, while announcing a game with pal Joe Garagiola, Joe left the booth to use the restroom. When he returned, he glanced at Rizzuto's scorecard to see what had happened while he was away. It was marked "WW," and Joe asked, "What's this WW?" Rizzuto responded, "Wasn't watching." Scooter would also become known for shouting exclamations during spectacular moments of the game: "Holy cow!" "Unbelievable!" "Way back there!" "Did you see that?" and he also called people a "Huckleberry," when they did something he didn't like. It's true that broadcaster Harry

Caray used "Holy cow," in his broadcast, but Phil claims he had been saying those words his entire life.

Besides Garagiola, Scooter's broadcast partners read like a "Who's Who" in the Ford Frick corner of the Hall of Fame. Red Barber, Mel Allen, and Jerry Coleman top that list, while Tom Seaver, Bobby Murcer, Bill White, Bobby Brown, Tony Kubek, Billy Martin, Jim Kaat, Rick Cerone and Fran Healy were some of the others. Rizzuto never called his teammates or partners in the booth by their first name; it was always "Seaver," "Murcer," "White," or "Coleman." He did create a nickname for one of the Yankees' great pitchers. "Louisiana Lightning" is what Rizzuto called Ron Guidry. Guidry, who was from Lafayette, Louisiana, loved the nickname but hated having to sign his autograph that way. "I told him one day, 'go home tonight, sit down at your desk and sign that darn name about a hundred times and see if you don't get aggravated signing it,'" Guidry said with a grin. Ron would never let Rizzuto forget.

Rizzuto is known for many great calls during his 40 years in the booth. Here are a few you will remember. October 1, 1961 on WCBS radio:

Rizzuto's call, "Here's the windup, fastball, hit deep to right, this could be it! Way back there! Holy cow, he did it! Sixty-one for Maris! And look at the fight for that ball out there! Holy cow, what a shot! Another standing ovation for Maris, and they're still fighting for that ball out there, climbing over each others' backs. One if the greatest sights I've ever seen here at Yankee Stadium." Another memorable call occurred October 14, 1976 on WPIX-TV:

Rizzuto's call, "He hits one deep to right-center! That ball is out of here! The Yankees win the pennant! Holy cow, Chris Chambliss on one swing and the Yankees win the pennant. Unbelievable, what a finish! As dramatic a finish as you'd ever want to see! And this field will never be the same, but the Yankees have won it in the bottom of the 9th, seven to six!" Scooter also called Dave Righetti's no-hitter against the Boston Red Sox on July 4, 1983, and the George Brett "Pine Tar" game on July 24, 1983. Yes, you could say that Phil Rizzuto was a "homer," when it came to calling the Yankees games. One call that will stand out to me was one that Scooter didn't even make. He was scheduled to do the color commentary for a Yankees-Red Sox game on August 15, 1995, the day Mickey Mantle was to be buried in Dallas, Texas. He assumed that he would be there with other teammates, but it was not to be. WPIX refused to let him go. Phil eventually gave in to emotion and left the booth in the middle of the telecast, saying he could not continue. He would announce his retirement shortly after that.

"I guess heaven must have needed a shortstop," Yankees owner George Steinbrenner said in a statement. "He epitomized the Yankee spirit — gritty and hard charging — and he wore the pinstripes proudly." "Everything he did was great," said Yankee roommate Yogi Berra. "He could steal bases, he could bunt, and he was a pretty good hitter." Scooter died in his sleep from pneumonia, August 13, 2007, in a nursing home located in West Orange, New Jersey. At 89, he had been the oldest living member of the Baseball Hall of Fame: now it's Bobby Doerr. "I never thought I deserved to be in the Hall of Fame," Rizzuto once said. "The Hall of Fame is for the big guys, pitchers with 100 mph fastballs and hitters who sock homers and drive in a lot of runs. That's the way it always has been and the way it should be." Rizzuto's #10 had been retired on August 4, 1985; and a plaque was placed in Yankee

Stadium's Monument Park in honor of his two careers, as both a player and an announcer. This year's team now wears his # 10 on their sleeves. In his later years, Rizzuto formed a lasting relationship with current shortstop Derek Jeter. You could often find him talking baseball in the clubhouse with Jeter before the game. "He played with a lot of heart," Jeter said. "I think he exemplifies what it is to be a Yankee." "Scooter, we will miss you," rained down from stadium announcer Bob Sheppard, before game time. Rizzuto's # 10 was painted on the grass in front of both dugouts, and flowers and wreaths were placed in front of his plaque in Monument Park.

I finally met Phil Rizzuto in person and if you know anything about the history of this great game like I do, then you knew his place in baseball. So, let's hear it for the little guy who made big things happen. I think about him as the little engine that could, so to speak. I'm sorry he is gone, but happy to have seen him play and hear him tell us about this great game. Today I miss him. I will end this piece with a typical Rizzuto call that is sure to make you smile. "Uh-oh, deep to left-center, nobody's gonna get that one! Holy cow, somebody got it!" We got it, Phil! We got it! Now it's time to rest.

Can I Borrow Your Helmet?

That was Max, a veteran 34-year-old free spirit, if there ever was one! He had left his own helmet in the locker room. Why bring my helmet, he had thought? After all, he didn't expect to play. The time that he had spent in the end zone with a football that year was zero and, in fact, he had caught only four passes for a measly ninety-one yards. Then there was that other incident where he had broken curfew "again" and spent the night before this game out partying all over the city of Los Angeles. But legends are made in many different ways and this was no ordinary game. It was Sunday, January 15, 1967. Others would call it Super Bowl I.

William Max McGee was born July 16, 1932, in Saxton City, Nevada. His family later moved to East Texas, where he attended White Oak High School. In 1950, he was recruited and signed at Tulane University, located in New Orleans, Louisiana. In 1953, as a running back, he became the nation's top college kick-return specialist. In 1954, he would be drafted in the fifth round, by the Green Bay Packers of the National Football League. Max would join a team with tremendous talent in the backfield, including the likes of future Hall-of-Famers Paul Hornung and Jimmy

Taylor. With so much competition at that position, he would soon be converted to a wide receiver. Max always had good hands, good looks, and found ways to make everyone around him smile. He was colorful and talented. He loved to have a good time, and the fans adored him. He was a good old boy, a cut-up, and a hell-raiser, but no one wanted to win as bad as Max McGee. He was once quoted as saying, "When it's third-and-10, you can take the milk drinkers and I'll take the whiskey drinkers every time." He was also very laid back, uncomplicated, and as calm as a jar of peanut butter. He was always approachable and what he said was what he meant. Nothing seemed to intimidate him including Lombardi. Teammate Jerry Kramer often said, "When everyone was looking at their feet wondering what to do, Max would come up with something."

Max would catch 36 passes his rookie season and score nine touchdowns. Then he received a call from the Air Force, where he became a fighter pilot for the next two years. Despite his service to his country, Max ended his career with 345 receptions for over 6,300 yards in 12 seasons. He would score 306 points on fifty-one touchdowns. His average of 18.4 yards per catch is still the highest in Packer team history. Max was inducted into the Green Bay Packer Hall of Fame in 1975, along with fellow teammates Jerry Kramer, "Fuzzy" Thurston and head coach Vince Lombardi.

There are many stories about the relationship between Max and his legendary coach Vince Lombardi, and the first one goes something like this: Once after playing four games into the season, the Packers had only scored two touchdowns. Lombardi, a tough disciplinarian, was disgusted and gathered the team together before practice. "I must be a lousy teacher," he said. "You guys don't remember a thing." Lombardi then shook his head and continued. "We're going back to the basics, back to fundamentals." He said. Lombardi then reached over and picked up a ball for everyone to see. "Now this gentleman," he said "is a football." Max interrupted. "Hold on, Coach," he said. "You're going too fast." Of course everyone laughed, except Lombardi.

Another favorite was told by offensive guard, Jerry Kramer. It seemed that Hornung and McGee, who were roommates, made a habit out of skipping bed check. One day, as practice was about to end and to their surprise, Lombardi announced that these two would be fined $500 each, for missing curfew the night before. Max and Paul had no idea how Lombardi had found out and proceeded to slip out again the next night. As fate would have it, at the end of that day's practice, Lombardi increased their fine to $1000 each for missing curfew a second night. With that announcement, Lombardi turned and looked directly at Max and Paul and said, "Gentlemen, the next time you miss curfew you will be fined $1,500 each and if you two can find anything in Green Bay, Wisconsin worth $1,500, call me and I will go with you." That brought the house down with laughter.

I never met Max McGee but I have a good friend and business associate named Bill Campbell who lives in the Tampa, Florida area. Bill and Max were best of buddies during Max's Packer days and spent lots of time hanging out together. When he found out that I was going to write a piece about his friend Max McGee, he called to share with me some little-known stories about his buddy Max. "It turns out that about 600 people showed up for his funeral," said Bill. "They spent the entire evening telling jokes and reminding each other about all the fun they had with their

best friend Max McGee." Bill would have dinner every
Friday night with Max unless they were heading to the
West Coast for a game on Sunday. "Max never talked football or even sports during dinner," said Bill. "And I never
saw him with the same woman twice until he met his wife,
Denise." I had also heard that Max McGee was a bit of a
gambler at heart and that he would bet on almost anything.
"Are you kidding me?" hollered Bill. "If two people were
crossing the street, Max would bet on who would arrive at
the curb first. I arrived at a poker game one night just in
time to see him lose his Cadillac," laughed Bill. "He had
thrown his keys in the pot only to lose the hand." "How will
you get home?" asked Bill. "Max shrugged his shoulders
and said, 'I guess I will get a ride home with the winner.'"
That was Max, carefree as can be. There is one final story
that Bill shared with me. In 1963, these two were at dinner
on a Friday night before a big game with the Baltimore
Colts, led by John Unitas. Bart Starr and his back-up Zeke
Bratkowski were both injured, and the odds were stacked
against Green Bay winning without a tenured quarterback.
He asked Max about the outcome of the game and to Bill's
surprise Max said, "Oh, don't worry. We will beat the hell
out of those guys." The score that Sunday was 42-13, in
favor of Green Bay, with a guy named Brock playing quarterback. Bill had always wondered how Max had been so
sure. So one night in a bar several years later, after Max
had retired from football, Bill asked Max about that game.
"Very few people have ever heard this story," said Max.
"Before we left for the Baltimore game, Lombardi came
into our final meeting screaming at the top of his voice,
'Oh no, our savior, Bart Starr is hurt. He can't play and our
back-up savior is also hurt and we can't possibly win this
game. Well, you know what I think? I think we are going

to beat the hell out of these guys because you guys are the greatest bunch of athletes ever assembled for any team, in any sport,'" growled Lombardi. "No one in the room had ever heard such praise from Lombardi and you could feel everyone in the room lifted by his comment. I knew at that moment that we would beat Baltimore," said Max. "That was quite a story," said Bill. I agreed.

Vince Lombardi was hired as coach and general manager of the Packers on February 4, 1959. He was knowledgeable, focused and preached what he called "singleness of purpose." Lombardi simply detested any outside activity of a player that might distract him from concentrating on football. He wanted their best effort each and every time. That's where he and Max differed. At six-three, Max was tall and deceptively fast for his size. Carroll Dale, Boyd Dowler and Max McGee made up the trio of receivers available for Bart Starr. No one was more relaxed than Max on a football field. He was the type of individual who could turn the humor "off" and the concentration "on" at will. He just had a "great sense of timing" and the ability to come up with a great play when it was least expected. That's what made him so unforgettable.

"I'm glad I played when I did," said Max. "I don't even like football anymore because every time a guy gets a hand in on a tackle, he's doing a back-flip or pounding his chest. I played at a great time with some great guys, and even though the money wasn't as close to what it's like today, we had a great time." Max McGee had a great career as a player and joined Jim Irvin in 1979 as the radio play-by-play man for the Packers Radio Network. He brought humor, candor and insight to the broadcast. He retired from radio at the end of the 1998 season. He had been named Wisconsin "Sportscaster of the Year," ten times.

Max also co-founded the Mexican chain restaurant known as "Chi Chi's," during the late seventies. As director of the company, Max owned about 150,000 shares of stock. He would sell his portion of the company in 1998 for millions of dollars. As usual, Max was ahead of the curve. The company folded in 2004. In 1999, McGee founded the Max McGee National Research Center for Juvenile Diabetes at the Children's Hospital of Wisconsin and raised millions on their behalf.

On Saturday, October 20, 2007, Max McGee did as he had always done, which was exactly what he wanted to do. He had told his wife about his intentions of cleaning the leaves off of their home in Deephaven, Minnesota, with a leaf blower. Of course his wife, Denise, who was not home at the time, pleaded with him not to get on the roof. Max fell and lost consciousness. Emergency crews were alerted and on the scene but were unable to revive him. Max McGee died at the age of 75. He will always be thought of as a beloved figure by Green Bay fans everywhere. Paul Hornung said, "I just lost my best friend." It seems that all football fans lost a friend in Max. Max left his wife and four children behind.

So that Sunday, after borrowing a teammate's helmet, Max McGee entered the very first Super Bowl for an injured Boyd Dowler. A few plays later, he would score the very first touchdown with a one-handed catch from Quarterback Bart Starr and run 37 yards to pay dirt. He would finish the day with seven catches for 138 yards and two touchdowns, which helped the Green Bay Packers defeat the Kansas City Chiefs, 35-10. So yes, I have seen the play of Dan Marino, Mickey Mantle, Larry Bird, Tiger Woods, and Michael Jordan. I am also old enough to remember watching Johnny Unitas, Mohammed Ali,

Wilt Chamberlain, Yogi Berra, Arnold Palmer and Max McGee. Max McGee! That's right the whiskey drinker, Max McGee. Some would quip that he wasn't a Hall-of-Fame player, or even considered a great player, but he was the first to score a touchdown in a Super Bowl game and one of the first to become a Super Bowl Champion, twice. It's hard to forget about the guys who were first.

Strength Up The Middle

The program said he stood six-foot two-inches tall, but that may have included him standing on a Chicago phone book. I'm sure he never weighed more than 235 pounds. He was not considered big enough for his chosen profession. What he lacked in height and weight, he made up for with deceptive speed and tenacity. He was also ambitious, dedicated, and likeable, and no one could out-work him. He possessed quickness, technique and smarts, and he would play hurt. From 1954 to 1967, he started 182 straight games during an era when teams only played 12 games during the regular season. He learned how to use his lack of size, to his advantage. If I told you he almost quit a Hall-of-Fame career, you would laugh out loud, but it's true. In 1953, he showed up in Grand Rapids, Minnesota, a little shaken after his college team lost to the University of Alabama, 61-5, in the Orange Bowl. He had thought that his Syracuse team was better than that. At 20 years of age, he had been drafted in the seventh round by the Green Bay Packers, as an offensive center. As he looked around at his competition, he realized that he may be overmatched at that position. He hated the militaristic rules of camp and was homesick to say the least. The truth is, he thought camp was too tough and never thought he had a chance to make the team, because of his size. So he quit, walked out, without saying goodbye. Packers coach Gene Ronzani sent one of his scouts all the way to the East Coast to find him and bring him back. That was not an easy task, as he was told by his family, "You're not welcome at home," he said. "They didn't want a quitter. They said I should at least try." So he returned to the team…and, of course you know the rest of the story. The Green Bay Packers were built around their center, "their strength up the middle." His fellow teammates found out how tough he really was. "Tough as a cowboy boot," someone had said. Not only did he have the quickness to make the cut-off block on the power sweep, but he was also an excellent down-field blocker and a great pass protector. Now you can find his name among the twenty-one players listed on the facade at Lambeau Field. It's located between Packer legends, Willie Woods and Herb Adderley. He played 15 seasons, made the All-NFL Team seven times, played in 10 Pro Bowls, and three NFL Championship Games. He was also chosen for the NFL's All-Decade Team of the 1960's. In 1981, he was inducted into the National Football Hall of Fame as an offensive center.

James Stephen "Jim" Ringo was born November 21, 1931 in Orange, New Jersey. He attended Phillipsberg High School and signed a college scholarship to play center at Syracuse University from 1950 to 1952. Ringo never owned a car while in school but worked at a gas station on Sundays, for extra cash. He would also wash his friends' cars, if they allowed him to use their car. The above-mentioned Orange Bowl appearance against Alabama had been the first bowl game ever for the University. Pat Stark, who had been the quarterback behind Ringo for Syracuse back then, said, "That's the team that started it all for Syracuse." Jim Ringo would become only the fifth football player from the University of Syracuse to be inducted into the Hall of Fame. Former teammate Joe Szombathy was there the day Jim Ringo signed his profession contract. "He got a $5,000 one-year contract and a $500 signing bonus," said Szombathy. Joe and Jim had been high school teammates and decided to attend Syracuse together. Joe also served as Jim's best man when he married his wife, Judy. Jim flourished under Syracuse Head Coach Ben Schwartzwalder's unbalanced offensive line formation, which allowed him to block down on the tackle or to pull and use his speed for the sweep. This formation would go a long way toward preparing Ringo for his days under Lombardi and the feared Green Bay power sweep. When Vince Lombardi arrived in Green Bay as head coach in 1959, Jim Ringo was the only established All-Pro player on the roster. "Here is where I will build my offense," said Lombardi, while pointing at Ringo. Lombardi knew there was strength up the middle.

Under Lombardi's iron fist, the Green Bay Packers would draft and field one of the best teams in pro football history. In his first five seasons, Lombardi's team would post a 50-15-1 record. During that time, they would play in three championship games, winning twice, in 1961 and 1962. The names of players on those teams, along with Ringo, are legendary now. They are Bart Starr, Jim Taylor, Paul Hornung, Forrest Gregg, Ray Nitschke, Willie Davis, Henry Jordon, and the afore-mentioned Willie Woods and Herb Adderley. Many years later, Vince Lombardi was quoted as saying, "Jim epitomized the toughness and determination needed to not only play the center position, but to become one of the game's most dominant offensive linemen of his era." In my opinion, Lombardi owed

Jim Ringo an apology for an incident that occurred after the 1963 season. Forward thinking Jim Ringo was one of the first players to have an agent represent him in contract negotiations. Lombardi's temper and his lack of experience with an intermediary caused Jim to be traded to the Philadelphia Eagles. The story has been added to or changed over the years, but here's how teammate Willie Davis remembers it happened: "Jim came in with an agent to visit with Coach Lombardi about his contract," said Davis. "Lombardi asked, 'Who the hell is this?'" "The agent proceeded to explain to Lombardi how Jim was worth much more than his current salary and that he was a great All-Pro player," said Davis. "Lombardi listened and then excused himself to make a phone call. When he returned, Lombardi said, he agreed with the fact that Jim was a great player and deserved all the money he could get, but that they were talking to the wrong person because, 'Jim Ringo has been traded to the Philadelphia Eagles.'" After eleven great seasons with the Packers, Ringo played four more years with the Philadelphia Eagles, from 1964-1967.

After his playing days, Ringo became an offensive line coach for several teams including the Chicago Bears, Buffalo Bills, New England Patriots and New York Jets. While in Buffalo, he would oversee a great offensive line, including pulling guards, Reggie McKenzie and Joe DeLamielleure. These two, along with tackles Dave Foley, Donnie Green and Paul Seymore at tight end, would lead the way for future Hall-of-Fame running back, O.J. Simpson. They would become known as "The Electric Company." This name was given to them by Simpson who claimed that their expertise in blocking allowed him to turn on the juice, as in O.J. or "Orange Juice," his nickname. O.J. would become the first running back in Pro

Football history to rush for over 2,000 yards in a single season. In 1973, Bills fans everywhere screamed, "The Juice is loose." Buffalo would finish 9-4 for the season and second behind Miami in their conference. They did not make the play-offs, but Simpson was elected to the Pro Bowl. McKenzie ended up in the College Football Hall of Fame and his pal DeLamielleure ended up in Canton. Ringo would find himself Head Coach of the Buffalo Bills in 1976, as Lou Saban stepped down. Ringo would return for the 1977 season, but then was fired after winning only 3 of 14 games. It was during that year that the next Jim Ringo story took place.

"Ringo gave me my start," said University of Baylor linebacker Shane Nelson. Shane and I are not only friends, but after his retirement, we shared a radio booth for 13 years in Corpus Christi, Texas. An un-drafted Nelson had walked on as a rookie, free agent for the Bills and caught the attention of Ringo while running drills. "That guy can help us," said Ringo. I think Jim Ringo saw a bit of himself in Nelson that day and as usual, Ringo was right. In 1977, an undersized Nelson would go on to start every game at the linebacker position while recording 168 tackles, and then was voted to the 1977 NFL All-Rookie Team. It was the start of the feared defense known today as the "Bermuda Triangle." Nelson, joined by fellow inside linebacker Jim Haslett and nose-guard Fred Smerlas, would make up the middle of that 3-4 defensive alignment that spread fear through their opponents and led the Bills to their first division title, in 1980. "Shane and Andy's Insider Sports" radio show aired on 1440 KEYS, and it was there that Shane told this story. Buffalo drafted a defensive back by the name of Dwight Harrison, out of Texas A&M Kingsville, which was then called Texas A&I. Harrison had what was known as a no-cut contract, unheard of in today's game. As camp unfolded under Ringo, Harrison realized that the game and the weather were too tough; and he did everything possible to get released where he would simply receive a paycheck without having to play. "Ringo hated the guy," said Nelson. "Ringo pleaded with owner Ralph Wilson to release him, but to no avail." Nelson went on, "On days when it snowed and we were out on the field doing 6-on-6 drills, you could see the footprints in the snow where everyone was supposed to go when a play was run, except for Harrison. He just stood there in his parka, refusing to practice. This was so far against the work ethic that Ringo believed in, that it ate him up." Nelson continued, "Bobby Chandler was in the sauna before weigh-in day, which was Thursday, and heard Ringo shouting at the top of his voice from the locker room. Ringo was ranting and raving and calling Dwight Harrison every name in the book. Chandler put a towel on and entered the locker room expecting to break up a fight between Ringo and Harrison, only to find Jim Ringo standing in front of Harrison's locker screaming at the top of his voice. Harrison was nowhere to be found. Ringo was cursing, pointing and taking out his frustrations on Harrison's locker, laughed Nelson. "I think Ringo was a better assistant coach than a head coach," later said Nelson.

Ringo would continue to coach offensive linemen after being fired by Buffalo. His next stop would allow him to help great players such as Leon Gray and John Hannah, with the New England Patriots.

According to his wife Judy, Jim had been diagnosed with Alzheimer's in 1996. The last ten years, they had lived in Chesapeake, Virginia, until he was recently moved into a treatment unit in nearby Virginia Beach. While there, he also developed pneumonia. On Monday, November 19,

2007, two days away from his 76th birthday, Jim Ringo left us for a better place. Teammate Willie Davis, who in 1981 entered the Hall of Fame with Ringo, said, "One minute, you're reliving an experience and the next minute, he'd be asking, 'Who's this?'" Davis went on, "What tenacity he had as a center in the NFL. Probably, no one was better." As a kid, I grew up watching two of my favorite football players, Dick Butkus and Jim Ringo. One played defense and the other, offense. They both were great players and were elected to the NFL Hall of Fame and both wore the jersey number 51, which is why I wore the same number when I played football. The news of Ringo's death coupled with the passing of his Packer teammate Max McGee, a few weeks ago, has been sad but somewhat overshadowed by the current team's success. I'm sure both of these great players would approve of another Super Bowl run by the Green Bay Packers.

It has been calculated that in his NFL career, he personally handled the football well over 12,000 times, including 1,000 snapbacks on punts and placekicks. Only a quarterback could match those numbers. To think, he almost quit playing football.

"And Down the Stretch They Come"

He hated being called "Willie," because his closest rival had the same first name. He was competitive to the point of being unfriendly and rude, but that was fine by him. Words like fierce, strong willed, superstar, and smart, were used to describe him. He was simply not the easiest guy to get along with. To say he was small in stature is an understatement. In fact, he most likely needed to run around in the shower just to get wet. His weight was recorded at 111 pounds and was spread out on a 5 foot 4 inch frame. Now that, my friends, is little. He was so thin that if he stuck out his tongue and turned sideways, he would resemble a zipper. The amazing thing about his height was that it predicted his occupation for life. His size would allow him to pursue a career as a jockey in the Thoroughbred Horse Racing industry. Sitting on top of 3,000 pounds of speeding, snorting, muscle and bone for the most exciting two minutes in sports, is not my idea of fun, but he loved it. Being able to control pure galloping thunder in a contest known as "The Sport of Kings," requires tenacity, luck, and a truckload of confidence. It would be an amazing career that would propel him into the Thoroughbred Horse Racing Hall of Fame.

On December 9, 1932, he was born William John Hartack, Jr. and they called him "Bill." Bill was raised on a farm in the Blacklick Township area of Cambria County, Pennsylvania, by a father who worked in the coal mines his entire life. Not only did Bill's family struggle to make ends meet, but the boy lost his mother at the age of eight. Not willing to follow in his father's footsteps, Bill left home at the age of 17. He took a job as a stable boy at Charles Town Race Course in West Virginia. Trainer Junie Corbin would hire and teach Bill how to work out horses, and soon he became an exercise jockey. It didn't take long to see that Bill Hartack was a born jockey, and by 1952, he was riding at West Virginia's Waterford Park. His contract with Corbin had been purchased by trainer T.J. Kelly, who had Bill riding at all the top tracks in Maryland, Illinois and Florida. By the end of 1953, he had ridden his first winner and was well on his way to becoming a star.

During the fifties, Eddie Arcaro, Bill Hartack and Willie Shoemaker would rule the world of horse racing. Hartack was the top money winner in 1956 and 1957, and the leader in victories four times—1955, 1956, 1957 and 1960. In 1955, he entered the winners circle an astounding 417 times. In 1957, he became the first jockey to have purse winnings of more then 3 million dollars in a season. In 1959, Bill Hartack, at the age of 26, would be inducted into Horse Racing Hall of Fame, and he is still the youngest ever elected. Between 1953 and 1974, Bill rode in 21,535 races and recorded 4,272 wins. Known for taking his mounts right to the lead, Bill Hartack would win nearly twenty percent of all the races he entered. He and Arcaro are the only two jockeys to ever win the Kentucky Derby five times each. Hartack also won the Preakness Stakes three times and the Belmont Stakes once. Bill rode in 12 Kentucky Derbys and his Derby winners were: Iron Liege in 1957, Venetian Way in 1960, Decidedly in 1962, Northern Dancer in 1964, and Majestic Prince in 1969. In 1958, Bill had just finished riding Tim Tam to victory in the Florida Derby, two weeks before the Kentucky Derby; but because of a broken leg, Bill had to give up that ride. Yet, Tim Tam would go on to win the Derby. His Preakness winners were: Fabius in 1956, Northern Dancer in 1964, and Majestic Prince in 1969. Sadly, Hartack's bid for the coveted Triple Crown of Horse Racing never matured. His only win at Belmont came in 1960, aboard Celtic Ash. His face graced the cover of *Sports Illustrated* twice; first in 1956 and again in 1964. He was also on the cover of *Time* Magazine, in 1958. It's interesting to note that Hartack's first Derby win would come as a gift from his hated rival, Willie Shoemaker. "Shoe," was aboard Gallant Man in the 1957 Derby and against Hartack, who was riding Iron Liege. Inexplicably, "Shoe" who had the lead down the stretch, misjudged the finish line and stood up in the saddle which enabled Iron Liege to catch Gallant Man at the wire, and win by a nose.

By 1978, Hartack was having problems making the weight required by the standards for horse racing. So, Bill headed to Hong Kong to ride until he retired in 1980. Riders were allowed to ride at heavier weights in Hong Kong than in the United States. He also tried his hand at being a steward for several years. Bill Hartack loved to hunt and fish and often hunted on a friend's property in Freer, Texas. On November 26, 2007, Bill Hartack was found dead inside a cabin in Freer. The chief medical examiner of Webb County announced that 74-year-old Hartack had died of natural causes, from heart disease. Hartack never married and very rarely spoke to his kin. He did have two sisters, Maxine and Florence.

Hall-of-Fame rider Angel Cordero summed it up best when he said, "When I first came to this country and met him, it was like meeting a superstar — he was a jockey everyone had heard about. He was very smart and he was amazing with the whip. He could hit a horse left-handed coming around the turn, and the horse would never go out." When you close your eyes, you can hear the famous announcer Dave Johnson scream into the microphone, "And down the stretch they come in the Kentucky Derby." More than likely he was talking about Bill Hartack.

Famous For Failure

This fellow has a festival, a roller coaster, and a line of action figures named after him. He could be seen in the movies and on television. He was the very definition of "Extreme Sports," before there were extreme sports. He continued to defy death and, at one time or another, has broken over forty bones in his body. He loved to tell outrageous stories to match his incredible feats. As a youngster, he spent more time running from the law than he did at home; eventually, he dropped out of high school. He believed in giving his word and then living up to it. During an interview with the Associated Press in May 2006, he said, "No king or prince has lived a better life; you're looking at a guy who's really done it all. There are some things I wish I had done better; not only for me but for the ones I loved." He has been called crazy, a con man, a daredevil, stuntman, and actor. He served in the Army, ran his own hunting guide service, and owned a Honda dealership, which sold motorcycles. Between the late sixties and early eighties, he would stare death in face from a seat on a Harley-Davidson motorcycle and survive. He may have been the very definition of "thrills and spills." He stills owns a place in four of the top twenty most-watched

ABC Wide World of Sports events. Whatever you do while reading this piece, remember "Please do not try any of this at home."

Robert Craig "Evel" Knievel was born in Butte, Montana, on October 17, 1938, to Robert E. and Ann Kehoe Knievel. After Evel's brother Nic was born, their parents divorced and they were raised by their paternal grandparents. It all started for Evel at the age of eight while attending a Joie Chitwood Auto Daredevil Show. From there, this hard-living man would become famous for jumping Greyhound buses, cars, live sharks, rattle snakes, mountain lions, riding through fire walls, being towed at 200 mph behind a race car, and a failed attempt to jump Idaho's Snake River Canyon on a rocket-powered cycle. On December 31, 1967, his fiery crash at Caesar's Palace in Las Vegas while trying to jump the famous fountains, would be the lead story of every sports broadcast. His successful attempt to jump the fountains was bought by ABC-TV, and after being televised, he became more famous than ever before. He ended up in the hospital with a coma. With his fee now approaching one million dollars for each performance, he found himself pushing the edge of the envelope. He always felt he had to go higher and farther than before. On January 7 and January 8, 1971, Evel set a record by selling over 100,000 tickets each day for a performance at the Houston Astrodome. On February 28 of that same year, he set the record by jumping 19 cars; that broke his old record of 17. On May 10, 1971, he would not be so lucky. His attempt to jump 13 Pepsi Cola trucks left him with a broken collarbone, fractured right arm and two broken legs. After several more jumps and more broken bones, Evel announced that he would jump the Snake River Canyon on September 8, 1972. It was not to be, as Evel was forced to parachute from the sky-cycle due to a mechanical problem. The bike actually made it over the river, but was blown back into the canyon by the wind and landed on the bank of the river, where Evel had also landed. He had escaped the most terrifying jump ever recorded with a few minor scrapes. He had become famous for failure and would be forever known as "America's Legendary Daredevil."

On May 26, 1975, Knievel crashed while trying to jump 13 London buses in front of 90,000 fans at Wembley Stadium, England. A broken pelvis would require surgery. On October 25, 1975, he successfully jumped 14 Greyhound buses at Kings Island, Ohio. This event scored the highest viewer rating ever, on *ABC's Wide World of Sports*. On January 31, 1977, Knievel crashed again while practicing for a jump and broke both arms and his collarbone. In the process a cameraman lost his eye in the accident.

His fame was contagious and his fans were many. Spectators always wanted him to jump one more bus or car than he did on his last jump. They never got enough of Evel and his audacity to defy death. He was a master at marketing his image. Movies, TV shows and interviews occurred each week as Evel traveled the world promoting himself. Toy action figures, pinball machines, books, music videos, and comics were sold at every turn. Actor George Hamilton would star as Evel in the 1971 movie entitled *The Evel Knievel Story*. By 1974, Ideal Toys had created a bendable Knievel action figure and Bally began to promote the Evel Knievel pinball machine as the first fully electronic commercial game. He was seen on the *Tonight Show*, starring Johnny Carson, and *Dinah!* He also played himself in the TV show, *The Bionic Woman*. In 1977, his book Evel Knievel on Tour was released. Evel made only a few jumps after that, with the last one occurring in March of 1981, in Hollywood, Florida. Too many injuries over too many years finally caught up. He would suffer terribly until his death.

At retirement Evel said, "Made $60 million, spent 61…lost $250,000 in blackjack once…had $3 million in the bank, though." He claimed to have been a swindler, a card shark, a safe cracker and a hold-up man. In his last interview before his death, Evel said, "You can't ask a guy like me why I performed. I really wanted to fly through the air. I was a daredevil, a performer. I loved the thrill, the money, the whole macho thing. All those things made me Evel Knievel. Sure, I was scared. You've got to be crazy to not be scared, but I beat the hell out of death." By 1995, Evel had more than likely contracted Hepatitis C as a result of numerous blood transfusions after his many injuries. By 1999, he required a liver transplant, suffered two strokes and had contracted diabetes. He also was inducted into the Motorcycle Hall of Fame. On April 1, 2007, Evel was baptized and accepted Christ on Rev. Robert H. Schuller's *Hour of Power* television program. Evel Knievel died on November 30, 2007, in Clearwater, Florida. He left four children, ten grandchildren and a great-grandchild. His only son Robbie Knievel followed in his father's footsteps as a daredevil.

Superman was, no more.

Building a Story with Words

That's the way he described his style of writing. "It's like building a stone wall without mortar," he once said. "You place the words one at a time, fit them, take them apart and refit them, until they're balanced and solid." He may not have been the best sportswriter of our time, but it surely didn't take long to call roll. "At his best, he's better than any of us," wrote celebrated sportswriter Frank Graham. He was a "pure" sportswriter who believed that the story should be deceptively simple. He was a champion of underwriting, and he wrote as if his job were to simply remind you of what you already knew. "Stay true and straightforward in your writing, and do not go overboard," he'd say. He focused on personalities of athletes and coaches rather than the results of the event. He is considered the link between ancient journalists like Grantland Rice, Jimmy Cannon, John Lardner and Red Smith, to today's writers like David Halberstam, Frank Deford, Tom Wolfe and Gay Talese. All of his stories were written from scores of notes he had taken. He wrote double time, on a portable Remington manual typewriter, given to him in 1932 by his parents. He is best remembered for his writing in the world of sports, but he was not limited in his ability to also write about medicine, civil rights and war. It has been said that he created the "New Journalism" of the 1960's.

Wilfred Charles "Bill" Heinz, otherwise known as W.C. Heinz, was born on January 11, 1915, in Mount Vernon, New York. He was athletic and played hockey in school, but he also liked to read. The shelves in his home were filled with the words of Tennyson, Shakespeare, Twain and Poe. "I so wanted to be a newspaper man," he said during a 2002 interview with The Associated Press. Heinz began his career in journalism as sports editor for the Middlebury College, Vermont school newspaper. He graduated in 1937 with a B.A. degree in political science. For $15 a week, Bill became a copyboy for the *New York Sun*. He covered fires, town meetings and petty crime. In the fall of 1943, the *Sun* sent Bill overseas as a war correspondent to cover allied movements in preparation of the Normandy invasion of D-Day. From a battleship, Bill was able to write the story of the greatest invasion in military history. For millions of Americans, his "you are there" style of writing captured the moment perfectly. After he had returned from Europe in 1945, he was asked to write about sports. His column for the *Sun* became known as "The Sports Scene," which covered boxing, baseball, football, and horse racing. Heinz had found his niche.

One of the many perks of being a sportswriter for a newspaper is that you get to attend major sporting events. In 1948, Heinz attended the 25th reunion of the 1923 Yankees team at Yankee Stadium. It turned out to be Babe Ruth's last public appearance. Ruth died two months later from throat cancer. Heinz enjoyed the game of baseball but would tell you himself that he loved to write about boxing and horse racing. His 1949 column from the *Sun* titled <u>The Death of a Racehorse,</u> is often described as "The Gettysburg Address" of sports writing. It was an article written so well that nothing could be added or taken away, to make it better. This story of a broken-down racehorse is often reprinted. The son of a Kentucky Derby winner was put down after his first race, because of a broken leg. Here is the ending of the story. Read for yourself and see if you are not moved by his words and his description of what took place:

They moved the curious back, the rain falling faster now, and they moved the colt over close to a pile of loose bricks. Gilman had the halter and Catlett had the gun, shaped like a bell with the handle at the top. This bell he placed, the crowd silent, on the colt's forehead, just between the eyes. The colt stood still and then Catlett, with the hammer in his other hand, struck the handle of the bell. There was a short, sharp sound and the colt toppled onto his left side, his eyes staring, his legs straight out, the free legs quivering. "Aw—," someone said. That was all they said. They worked quickly, the two vets removing the broken bones as evidence for the insurance company, the crowd silently watching. Then the heavens opened, the rain pouring down, the lightening flashing, and they rushed for the cover of the stables, leaving alone on his side near the pile of bricks, the rain running off his hide, dead an hour and a quarter after his first start, Air Lift, son of Bold Venture, full brother of Assault.

Heinz would also write a piece for *True* magazine entitled "The Morning They Shot the Spies." This piece, written in 1949 after WWII, described the execution of three German soldiers who had infiltrated American lines.

It has been said that reading this article would make the reader cold and full of fear. Building a story with words can be emotional.

When the *New York Sun* folded in January of 1950, Heinz decided to become a freelance writer. Although he had offers from many other newspapers, he decided to write magazine articles and books. His words would grace the pages of many prestigious magazines such as *Life, the Saturday Evening Post, Esquire, Look* and *Sport* magazine. Written in 1951, what would follow is perhaps his best magazine story. "Brownsville Bum" is the true story of Al "Bummy" Davis, a Brooklyn boxer who died tragically in a shoot-out while he himself was unarmed. In 1952, Heinz wrote a boxing profile entitled "So Long, Rock." The Middleweight title bout in 1947, would find Rocky Graziano standing toe-to-toe in a bloody affair with tough Tony Zale. Winning this bloody fight would earn Graziano the world championship. Articles about Red Grange and Pete Reiser would also fall under his pen.

His first novel, The Professional, was written in 1958. It too was about a boxer and his trainer and drew rave reviews from Ernest Hemingway himself. Run to Daylight, was another bestseller written by Heinz in 1963, would take us through the 1962 NFL season with legendary Green Bay Packer coach, Vince Lombardi. It was later made into a movie and there is no doubt that Lombardi's success on the field, coupled with Heinz's ability to paint his success with words, made Lombardi one of the most well- known football coaches ever. Two more novels would follow that encompassed the medical profession. Their titles were The Surgeon and Emergency. Interestingly, it appears that, in 1968, his most celebrated work actually appeared under the pseudonym, Richard Hooker. Heinz worked with Maine physician H. Richard Hornberger, on a book they titled M*A*S*H. This book helped create the 1971 hit movie and television series known by the same name. In 2001, W. C. Heinz was inducted into the National Sportscasters and Sportswriters Hall of Fame. The year 2004 would find Heinz inducted into the International Boxing Hall of Fame. He was also a five-time winner of the E.P. Dutton Award for the best magazine story of the year. He just always knew what to say to the reader.

Ninety-three-year-old W. C. Heinz put his typewriter away for the last time on February 27, 2008. Since 2002, he had been living in assisted living quarters in Bennington, Vermont. Several recent strokes had taken their toll on his health. Bill's beloved wife Elizabeth "Betty" Heinz died in 2002. They had been married 61 years and lost a daughter, Barbara, to a virulent infection at the age of 16, in 1964. He is survived by a second daughter, Gayl Heinz, of Amesbury, Massachusetts, and a granddaughter. I think it's safe to say that Bill would not approve of the piece I have just written about him. "Too big," he'd say. "Don't go overboard." Writers don't come much bigger than W.C. Heinz.

Spanning the Globe

That voice was crisp, like the wind blowing off of Lake Michigan in winter, and eloquent, like your grandfather telling stories on the back porch. Those eyes were honest and sensitive, and you always believed what he was telling you. If he appeared happy, then so were you; and when he had bad news to report, you felt sad and took it personally. He made you care about who won or lost. He always spoke into the camera, as if he were talking to you and only you. What he may have done better than anyone else was capture the moment. This ability to convey to the viewer, from a reporter's eye, the dramatic world of sports, would require him to travel over 4 ½ million miles and send him on assignment to 40 different countries. From cliff diving to badminton, demolition derby to soap box derby, for forty years he and ABC allowed us to experience sports on a global basis. He took us to places we had never seen before and showed us sports we knew nothing about. He was the first person I ever heard use the word "agony." As a young boy, I didn't know what it meant, but I knew it wasn't good. Before the days of ESPN, he was the heartbeat of sports in this country. Pioneer may be an understatement. Founding father of sports broadcast television is more suitable.

He was born James Kenneth McManus on September 24, 1921. Philadelphia, Pennsylvania would be his birth place, but he would always call Maryland home. Jim attended Loyola Blakefield High School and in 1943, received his bachelor's degree from Loyola College in Maryland. He then served in the U.S. Navy during World War II. After the war, Jim returned home to become a reporter for the Baltimore Sun. In 1947, as luck would have it, the Sun started its own TV station and Jim's voice would be the first ever heard on television in Baltimore. Jim could be heard three hours each weekday on a show dubbed "The Sports Parade." He remained in Baltimore until 1950, and then moved to New York to join CBS TV. With this move came a new show and a new name. Jim McKay would now be the host of a new sports show called *The Real McKay*. By 1961, McKay was at the top of his game and joined ABC to host *ABC's Wide World of Sports*, for the next 40 years. McKay would also cover 12 Olympic Games, many Triple Crown horse races, numerous U.S. and British Opens in golf, and become the long-time voice of the Indianapolis 500. Golf and horse racing were his passions, and he owned and bred many horses on his farm in Monkton, Maryland. I think he liked the history attached to these two sports. McKay was the founder of the Maryland Million Day, a series of twelve races used to promote the horse breeding industry in the state of Maryland. It is now second only to the Preakness.

Jim McKay will always be known for the way he handled the tragic news from the 1972 Munich Olympics. Palestinian terrorists had kidnapped eleven Israeli athletes as hostages, during the games. The horrific results, which ended in their deaths, were described this way by McKay: "When I was a kid my father used to say our greatest hopes and our worst fears are seldom realized. Our worst fears have been realized tonight. They have now said there were eleven hostages; two were killed in their room yesterday morning, nine were killed at the airport tonight. They are all gone." Nothing more needed to be said. I was puzzled when I found out while doing research for this piece that ABC executive Roone Arledge had thought about using the outspoken and controversial Howard Cosell to anchor the hostage coverage. I can't imagine Cosell being better than Jim McKay. It's obvious that Roone made the right choice.

McKay's work spawned many broadcasters that still work today. Bob Costas, Al Michaels, and Jim Nantz are just a few. McKay won numerous awards for his work including two Emmys and the George Polk Award for his coverage of the 1972 Olympics and 12 Emmys overall. In 1988, he was inducted into the U.S. Olympic Hall of Fame. Later, he was inducted into the Television Hall of Fame.

Jim McKay signed off for the last time, June 7, 2008. He left behind his wife Margaret and two children, Sean and Mary. Jim and Margaret met when they were reporters for the Baltimore Sun and would have celebrated their 60th wedding anniversary in October. You know, it's funny. Jim McKay never called a World Series game or a Super Bowl, yet he will be remembered as the greatest broadcast television announcer of them all.

Trapped Between
Mantle and Mattingly

Mickey Mantle enjoyed his last great year in 1964, batting .303 with 35 homers and 111 RBI's. Still, it was all the New York Yankees could do to win the American League pennant and meet the St. Louis Cardinals in the World Series. Mantle and the Yanks would lose that Series in seven games. Very few saw it coming, but now it was painfully obvious after watching them play against the future. The Cardinals were the future; younger, faster, better balanced and blacker. Four starting members of the Cardinals were either African-American or Latin, and man could they hit the ball with power. Not the kind of power that hits a lot of homeruns, but the kind that hits doubles and triples, the kind that keeps the pressure on the other team. Mantle, despite injuries and strikeouts, would hang on a few more years before he finally retired, in 1969. It would be the end of forty-plus years of Yankee domination. Sportswriter Jerry Izanberg may have said it best when he penned,

> "Where is the magic that was Mantle?
> Kubek to Moose, a double play.
> I don't recall getting any older.
> When did they?"

Don Mattingly proved his mettle in the Yankees farm system, while batting .349 in 1979, .358 in 1980, and .316 in 1981. In late 1982, he was called up to the Majors. At the time, he was hitting .315 for the Columbus farm team and the Yankees needed his bat. In 1983, his official rookie season, Don would fill in as a part-time first baseman and outfielder. He played well, hitting .279, but showed little power. 1n 1984, "Donnie Baseball" as he was to be called by Yankee fans, became the fulltime first baseman for the New York Yankees. He hit .343 with 23 homeruns while winning the American League batting title. In 1985, he would win the MVP Award for the AL and the first of his nine Gold Gloves. Don Mattingly would retire at the end of the 1995 season. He is considered the best Yankee player to have never played in a World Series game.

The only Yankee to play with Mickey Mantle and Don Mattingly was Bobby Murcer. In 1964, it was Bobby Murcer who had been signed by Tom Greenwade, the same scout as his hero Mickey Mantle. It was Bobby Murcer who had grown up in Oklahoma and played shortstop, just like his idol, Mantle. It was Bobby Murcer who had excelled in football, basketball and baseball in high school, just like Mantle. In late 1965, it was Bobby Murcer who's first hit in the Major Leagues was a home run, shades of his hero, Mickey Mantle. Some thought Murcer was the second coming of Mantle. You see, the Yankees had always had a star waiting in the wings. From Babe Ruth to Lou Gehrig, then Joe DiMaggio followed by Mickey Mantle, it fell to Bobby Murcer. Fair or not, Yankee success fell to Murcer. On June 1, 1983, Bobby Murcer hit his 100th career homerun at Yankee Stadium, which was the 252nd and final home run of his career. He retired on June 20, 1983, to make room for another future left-handed hitting Yankee star, named Don Mattingly. Murcer played 17 years for three different teams, but primarily for the Yankees. He had recorded a .277 batting average with 1,043 RBI's and played in five All-Star games. Murcer then turned to broadcasting for the next two decades. Bobby Murcer, an excellent baseball player, but a better human being, had been trapped by history between two of the well-loved Yankees to play during the modern era. Nevertheless, Murcer was born to be a Yankee.

Bobby Ray Murcer was born on May 20, 1946, in Oklahoma City, Oklahoma. His athletic ability was incredible, as he made All-State in football and baseball, and All-City in basketball. In 1964, Murcer signed a letter of intent to play football for the Oklahoma Sooners, but later changed his mind when the Yankees offered him a $20,000 bonus contract, in 1965. In 1966, Murcer married his childhood sweetheart, Diana Kay Rhodes. After a brief stint with the Yankees in 1966, Murcer would fulfill his military obligation in 1967 and 1968 and would return to the Yankees in 1969. He would become only the third New York Yankee, behind Joe DiMaggio and Mickey Mantle, to earn over $100,000 per season. He would also become the youngest American League player to accomplish that feat at the young age of 26. Not only could Bobby Murcer hit the long ball, but he excelled at the drag bunt and the delayed steal. His hitting performance against other Hall-of-Fame pitchers was outstanding, and he became feared throughout the American League. Murcer led the Yankees club in home runs six times during the decade of the seventies and all clubs in outfield assists with 119. In the spacious outfield of Yankee Stadium (461 feet deep to the fence in centerfield), fans would often wonder how three guys could cover all that space. Murcer would do his part and more, while playing the centerfield position in the triple-tiered, center of the baseball universe, known as Yankee Stadium, also "The house that Ruth built." Back then, this stadium held 70,000 people.

Murcer started out the 1969 season on fire. Not only did he replace Mantle in centerfield, but he also received "The Mick's" locker after his retirement. On August 10, 1969, Murcer, wearing uniform # 1, became part of the Yankee lore when he and two other teammates hit three consecutive home runs against the Oakland Athletics. Murcer, Thurman Munson and Gene Michaels went back-to-back-to-back. This feat had only happened two other times in Yankee history: In 1947 by Charlie Keller, Joe DiMaggio and Johnny Lindell, followed by Bobby Richardson, Mickey Mantle and Joe Pepitone, in 1966. In 1970, Murcer would tie another sacred Yankee record and American League record by hitting four consecutive home runs himself, in a double header against the Cleveland Indians. Only Lou Gehrig, Johnny Blanchard and Mickey Mantle had accomplished that hitting feat. Other Murcer career hitting feats included hitting three home runs in one game, twice, seven career grand slams; he once scored five runs in one game, and recorded baseball's finest hitting feat, "the cycle," on August 29, 1972. Although he was never considered a Hall-of-Famer, Bobby Murcer was a solid player for 17 years in the big leagues.

Murcer was also outspoken and was once fined $250.00 by Commissioner Bowie Kuhn for comments about pitcher Gaylord Perry and his spitball. Murcer would later apologize to Kuhn but kept a running feud for years with Perry. Once, after hitting a home run off Perry, he was heard hollering," I hit a hanging spitter," while rounding first base. Murcer's fun didn't stop there. He once caught the last out of an inning and spit on the ball before throwing it to Perry; and he was also known for sending Perry a gallon of lard, on occasion. Perry in return, once had a friend coat his hand in grease before shaking hands and saying, "Gaylord says hello."

Murcer also made history by being one of the two $100,000 players to be traded for each other. The 1975 trade of Bobby Mercer for Bobby Bonds (father of Barry Bonds) sent Murcer to the San Francisco Giants. Yankee General Manager Gabe Paul had just told Mercer that he would be playing right field for the Yankees and would never be traded. "Three days later, I was gone," said Murcer. While wearing # 20 for the Giants, he would become the highest paid player for that organization, signing a $175,000 contract. In 1976, he would be voted the Giants MVP. He often made comments about how tough it was to hit home runs in old Candlestick Park. "Patty Hearst could be hiding in the upper deck and nobody would ever find her," he laughed. Murcer found himself on the move again in 1977, and this time he landed in Chicago with the Cubs. Bobby would wear # 7 in honor of his pal Mantle. In 1978, Murcer continued to set hitting records as he joined the first Chicago Cub, Billy Williams, to record eight consecutive hits, in eight straight at-bats. This feat did not occur again until 1989, when Andre Dawson joined these two. Murcer also recorded his first and only five hit game as a Cubbie, that same year.

On June 26, 1979, Bobby became a Yankee again. He would wear uniform # 2 since skipper Billy Martin now wore the # 1. As a pinch-hitter, Murcer would finally reach the World Series against the Los Angeles Dodgers, in 1981. As mentioned above, Murcer's last season was 1983. He would head straight upstairs to the broadcast booth. Bobby would work on broadcast TV, radio WPIX, and the YES Network, for the Yankees. In 1998, when WPIX lost its broadcast rights, Mercer joined WNYW and Tim McCarver, continuing to share play-by-play duties. He would take part in calling David Cone's perfect game in 1999, at the Stadium. In 2001, he moved to the vaunted YES Network owned by George Steinbrenner. As the voice of the Yankees, Murcer won three Emmy Awards for live sports coverage. In November 2007, Murcer was nominated for the Ford C. Frick Award which is presented yearly by the Baseball Hall of Fame to a broadcaster for major contributions to the game of baseball.

Bobby Murcer was involved in many charities and served as chairman of the Baseball Assistance Team, an organization that helped down and out retired players who needed financial support. He also raised millions of dollars to fight cancer.

After noticing sever headaches and a lack of energy, Murcer was diagnosed with a brain tumor on Christmas Eve, 2006. He underwent surgery on the 28th at M.D. Anderson Hospital in Houston, Texas. Murcer, very much a God-fearing man, was surrounded by the love of hundreds of friends and millions of fans. "I can feel the fans. I can feel their thoughts and their prayers, and I want to tell them how much I love them," said Murcer. Bobby Murcer would be on- hand at Yankee Stadium for opening day in 2007. Once everyone realized he was back on the air, the fans gave him a standing ovation and the Yankees came out of their dugout to salute him. Unfortunately it was not to be permanent and Bobby's last broadcast occurred on May 1, 2007. After 18 months of intensive treatment, Murcer suffered a relapse and died at the age of 62 on July 12, 2008. All Yankee fans and kids who grew up in my generation will miss him. You may have heard the old saying that "I said all that, to say this." Well in this case it's true. As good a ballplayer as Murcer was, he was an even better person. He never got down about his misfortune, always handled his battle with cancer with grace and class. Bobby Cox, Manager of the Atlanta Braves, was Mercer's roommate with the Yankees. "He was a great player, quite a hitter," said a saddened Cox. Yankee teammate Lou Piniella said, "It's a sad day. Just a wonderful person, a great teammate and a heck of a baseball player." David Cone talked about having Murcer in the clubhouse during Old-Timers Day games. "He was just a pleasure to have in the clubhouse. The players really loved having him around. Old-Timers Day was always a special day for Bobby," exclaimed Cone. One of the last public statements made by Murcer went like this, "Any time I can walk through these halls and be in this place here, talking about baseball, man, that's right up my alley." It turns out that instead of being just like his idol, Mickey Mantle, Murcer was his opposite. Mantle was a no-doubt Hall-of-Fame baseball player with tremendous skills but at his end, to become a better person, he needed to conquer an alcohol problem and reach out to others he had hurt along the way. Murcer, on the other hand, was a true gentleman and great individual who needed a couple more great years as a player to be considered a Hall-of-Fame player. He was a tough man who never had a bad day. I have a feeling; that Bobby Murcer was completely satisfied with who he was and what he stood for.

Empty Seat

A little part of baseball history died today. He had bushy eyebrows, a big beer belly, lazy eyes and wavy hair; he reminded me of beloved actor Andy Devine. He traveled with suspenders and his ever-ready notepad and pen. He loved to gnaw on cigars and usually spoke out the side of his mouth. He was a gentleman who never smiled, but he always seemed full of good humor and appeared fair in everyway. His passion for writing about baseball was consuming, both for the reader and for the teams he covered. To other writers in the business, he was a walking database for statistics and was considered the godfather of his profession. For over 65 years, he shared America's pastime with millions of fans through the keys of his typewriter. It has been said that no Major League player ever got into the Baseball Hall of Fame without his blessings. As a player, if you weren't interviewed by him then you were nobody. He also wrote or edited more than a dozen books about his game. His articles graced the pages of *The Sporting News* in over 1,000 issues. His most renowned publication was a book written in 1974 and entitled, <u>No Cheering in the Press Box.</u> There is no doubt that he was "The Dean" of American baseball writers. From now on, there will always be an "empty seat" in the press box in Chicago. It belongs to him.

The late Jerome Holtzman was born in Chicago, Illinois, on July 12, 1926. He began his writing career in 1942 as a 17-year-old copy boy with his hometown newspaper, the *Chicago Daily News*. Later, two years would be spent in the Marine Corps during World War II, before he returned to writing in 1946. Holtzman attended both Northwestern University and the University of Chicago. The *News* eventually merged with the *Chicago Sun* to become the *Chicago Sun-Times*. It was here that Holtzman became the newspaper's sports editor and was assigned the baseball beat in 1957. In the early sixties, Holtzman invented what has become known as the "save category" for relief pitchers. The formula he invented evolved into the official statistic in 1966. His idea had evolved from watching pitcher Roy Face record an 18-1 season as a reliever for the Pittsburgh Pirates, in 1959. There is no doubt that relief pitchers like Hoyt Wilhelm, Rollie Fingers, Bruce Sutter, and Dennis Eckersley would not be in the Hall of Fame without his help. He eventually left the *Sun-Times* in 1981 and joined the *Chicago Tribune*. That's where he would stay until he retired in 1999. By the time he had retired, Holtzman had been inducted into the Writer's Wing of Major League's Baseball Hall of Fame in 1989 and was also awarded the 1991 J.G. Spinks Award by the Baseball Writers Association of America. At that point Baseball Commissioner Bud Selig decided to declare Holtzman Major League's Baseball's official historian. It was an honor well deserved. He has been praised as a researcher, writer, columnist, historian, and most importantly a fan. In 2005, he was elected to the International Jewish Sports Hall of Fame. Also, in November of 2007, Holtzman's personal research papers and baseball collection were acquired by the Chicago Baseball Museum. His life of covering the game will now be shared by all. He spent his time writing occasional columns for the mlb.com website and he always wrote the annual recap of the preceding season for <u>The Official Baseball Guide</u>. At reunions, his sports-writing friends kidded him about his age. Membership cards issued by the Baseball Writer's Association of America are numbered in sequence. Holtzman always got a chuckle when others claimed his number was five. Through it all, Holtzman continued to write about baseball. He could be considered the Cal Ripken, Jr. of sports writing.

In Evanston, Illinois, on July 15, 2008, Jerome Holtzman suffered a massive stroke and never recovered. He hung onto life until July, 19, 2008. He had just celebrated his 81st birthday. Major League Baseball Commissioner, Bud Selig said of Holtzman, "As a baseball writer, columnist, and historian for more than 50 years, Jerome Holtzman was a beloved figure and made an incredible impact on the game. He created the "save statistic" which in turn increased the importance of the relief pitcher. He was a giant in his industry." He is survived by his wife of 59 years, Marilyn, and their five children and five grandchildren.

One day at the beginning of a season, he approached a player for an interview and he was told, "I'm not talking to the press today." With that he smiled and slowly lit his big cigar and said, "That's fine, I'll catch you next year, or the next." That was the power of Jerome Holtzman!

Casting Shadows

Gene Upshaw was the first offensive guard ever inducted into the NFL Pro Football Hall of Fame. That speaks to excellence, and anytime you use the word "first" it is so powerful in the world of sports. Upshaw is also the only NFL player to play in a Super Bowl in three different decades with the same team. That hints at longevity, something that most NFL players never achieve because of the violence involved in their sport. The average tenure for a productive NFL player does not exceed seven years. He was also elected to the NFL 75th Anniversary All-Time Team, which shows greatness and respect. Upshaw is one of the few African-Americans to head up a powerful players union like that of the NFL. That speaks to intelligence and influence. So when we lost Gene Upshaw on Thursday, August 20, 2008, to pancreatic cancer, we didn't just lose a 6-foot-5, 275 pound, 16 year, seven-time All-Pro offensive guard, who played in three Super Bowls (1967, 1976, and 1980) while winning two (1976 and 1980), and then was named the executive director of the NFL Players Association for twenty-five years; we lost a significant part of the NFL and a truly great man. The shadow Gene Upshaw cast over America's game will always remain far and wide. Gene Upshaw was a force to be reckoned with, on and off the field.

To his Oakland Raider teammates he was known as "The Governor," but to his opponents and opposing coaches he was referred to as "Highway 63." Playing between two other Hall of Fame players, such as left offensive tackle Art Shell and center Jim Otto, often required Gene to pull out of the offensive line and sprint left, while clearing the way on the sweep play. Picture this gigantic man, wearing a silver and black uniform with the number 63, bearing down on you at full speed, with the ability to blow up everything in his path, just like a stick of dynamite. Known for taping and padding his arms from above his elbow to the tips of his fingers and wearing a white neck collar, nothing could stand in his way. There were no rest stops on Highway 63, you either got out of the way or got run over.

Eugene Thurman Upshaw Jr., was born August 15, 1945, in the sleepy cotton town of Robstown, Texas. He graduated from Robstown High School in 1963, and in 1964 entered Texas A&I University in Kingsville, Texas. Gene had actually enrolled at Texas A&I to play baseball. Legendry South Texas college football coach, Gil Steinke, spotted him on campus and asked him to join his football team. Upshaw would play center, tackle and end, while achieving All-Lone Star Conference status from 1964-66. In 1967, Gene would become the first round choice of the Oakland Raiders in the very first combined AFL-NFL draft. He was the 17th pick overall and moved to offensive guard. The Raiders liked his speed and size against such mammoth defensive tackles as Buck Buchanan of the Kansas City Chiefs and Ernie Ladd of the San Diego Chargers, both teams in the same division as Oakland. Upshaw would return to Texas A&I in the off-season of

1968 to complete his college degree. Gene Upshaw would captain the Raiders for eight seasons while helping establish Oakland's powerful running attack of the Seventies. For 15 seasons, Gene would line up a staggering 307 times in preseason, regular season and post-season games. He only missed one game during the 1981 season and retired in 1982. His intensity and intelligence complimented his speed and size, to propel him to a first-ballot Hall-of-Fame induction in 1987. He was named NFL lineman of the year in both 1973 and 1974. Gene was also honored as a member of the NFL 1970's All-Decade Team. In 1999, *The Sporting News* ranked him number 62 on a list of the 100 greatest NFL players of all time. Upshaw also occupies a place in the Texas Sports Hall of Fame, the Javelina Hall of Fame, and the Lone Star Conference Hall of Honor. Gene mentored his younger brother Marvin Upshaw, who played in the NFL with the Cleveland Browns, Kansas City Chiefs, and St. Louis Cardinals. I had the privilege of meeting Upshaw on one of his return visits to South Texas. He was a stand-up guy who was proud of where he grew up. Not only was he a physically big man, but I noticed how large his hands were when we shook. They looked like shovels.

As good an NFL player as Gene was, he may have been better as the executive director of the National Football League Players Association (NFLPA). He was elected to that position in 1983 by the current players. His tenure (which lasted until his death) was like most executives in high profile jobs, rocky at best. When placed with huge responsibilities, every decision will be turned inside-out, looked at from top to bottom and, of course, will never please everyone. Without a doubt, Upshaw alienated many retired NFL players, who were receiving minimal retirement benefits. Gene's response was, "I don't work for them. They are not union members and they have no vote." In 1987, as Upshaw was being inducted into the NFL Hall of Fame, he also led the second players strike. This short walkout would later be known as "scab football," as replacement players were used and resulted in an embarrassing display of football by the owners. The union would press for a settlement in court in 1989, and by 1993 a new seven-year contract was finally put into place, which would bring a new meaning to the word "free agency" and salary caps. That plan was referred to as "Plan B," and will be Gene Upshaw's legacy. It provided wealth to both union members and owners. The salary cap is currently $116 million per team, and the players share 60% of the 32 teams' total revenue. According to the owners, the players will be paid $4.5 billion this year.

Current Commissioner of the NFL Roger Goodell may have said it best, "Gene Upshaw did everything with great dignity, pride, and conviction. He was the rare individual who earned his place in the Pro Football Hall of Fame both for his accomplishments on the field and for his leadership of the players off the field. He fought hard for the players and always kept his focus on what was best for the game. His leadership played a crucial role in taking the NFL and its players to new heights."

One on One

Here's how it all started, in a small town called Enid, Oklahoma: Under the scorching hot sun, Herman Carr enjoyed playing one-on-one basketball every day against his friend. There was a reason they called this part of the country the "Dust Bowl." The heat could reach well over a hundred degrees and the dirt in the air was so thick that it could choke a horse. Nothing grew very well in this part of the country except jack rabbits and rattlesnakes. Some old timers said it was so flat you could stand in a chair and watch your dog run away for three days. But play they did and Herman wasn't just any old player. He could pass, dribble, play defense, and shoot and score from anywhere on the court. Herman Carr could do whatever he wanted with a basketball, everything except play in college. You see, Herman Carr was African-American and his one-on-one opponent was the one who received all the press. They called Herman's friend the best player in town, All-State, an All-American. He would receive over 100 offers to play basketball in colleges all over the country, while Carr had to join the service to continue playing the game he loved. Carr's pal was none other than Don Haskins, and Don never understood how he could be hailed as such a great player when he couldn't even beat the best player in Enid, Oklahoma, Herman Carr. Don Haskins would end up going to college at Oklahoma A&M, now known as Oklahoma State University, and playing for legendary basketball coach Hank Iba, while Herman Carr played basketball while serving in the United States Army. Although Haskins and Carr would lose touch with each other for a couple of years, that is not by any means the end of their story. So sit down, relax, and read about how this country boy (Haskins) not only played basketball but learned to coach a little bit, along the way. There is no doubt that Haskins' relationship with Carr would have an impact on college basketball that would change the game forever.

Donald Lee Haskins, nicknamed "The Bear," was born on March 14, 1930. After college, he would take a cut in pay to go from coaching high school girls, to a men's college head-coaching job at Texas Western, now known as University of Texas at El Paso, (UTEP). From 1961 to 1999, he took kids no one else wanted, including city kids and African-American kids and compiled a record of 719 victories while losing only 353 games. His teams suffered only five losing seasons in 38 years. Along the trail he won 14 Western Athletic Conference championships, four WAC tournament titles, qualified for 14 NCAA tournament berths, seven trips to the NIT, and of course won the 1966 National Championship against the incredible Kentucky Wildcats, coached by legendary Adolph Rupp. Haskins also led his team to 17 twenty-plus winning seasons and was honored to be the assistant coach of the 1972 USA Men's Olympic Basketball Team. He was enshrined into the Naismith Memorial Basketball Hall of Fame in 1997, as a coach. His entire 1966 championship team would also be inducted into the Hall, on September

7, 2007. The names of Nevil Shed, David Lattin, Willie Cager, Willie Worsley, Harry Flournoy, Bobby Joe Hill, and Orsten Artis will be remembered forever in college basketball history.

When Haskins arrived in El Paso in 1961, he inherited three black players from the previous year. One of those players was Nolan Richardson, who would win a NCAA title as head men's basketball coach at the University of Arkansas. Other well-known black players to play for Haskins included Nate "Tiny" Archibald, Tim Hardaway, Antonio Davis, All-American Jim "Bad News" Barnes, Marlon Maxey, and Greg Foster. Don't misunderstand, there were programs before Texas Western that started black players. UCLA's Jackie Robinson started two years for the Bruins and All-American Don Barksdale played for UCLA in 1947. Wilt Chamberlain led the University of Kansas to greatness in the early fifties. Clem Haskins and Dwight Smith starred for Western Kentucky in the 1963 tournament while Cazzie Russell led the University of Michigan basketball program. In fact, the 1963 NCAA tournament ended with Loyola beating Cincinnati, with seven of the 10 starters for those two teams being African-American. It seemed that a gentleman's agreement had existed in the early years of basketball that prohibited coaches from starting more than three African-American players at one time. But in Cole Field House, on the campus of the University of Maryland, Saturday night, March 19, 1966, that all changed when Don Haskins became the first coach to start five African-American kids and beat "Rupp's Runts" from the University of Kentucky, to win the NCAA Championship. Haskin's team won it with discipline and defense, two things other coaches thought could never happen; and he also won with kids no one else would recruit, just like his friend Herman Carr.

I never met Haskins personally but I do have a book and a basketball, given to me by a friend, which he autographed to me. Interestingly, his wife also signed the book. He loved the movie *"Glory Road,"* but he never insisted the movie be made. In fact, he did not even attend the Hollywood premier. He had rather go fishing. He was disappointed that some of the early scenes with himself and Carr, playing one-on-one, were cut from the movie. He still had some of the hate mail with death threats he received back in the sixties; but the reason for those letters has now turned into a beautiful story. Because of the movie, folks will know that four of the seven black players on that 1966 team earned degrees. The other three became a police officer, a senior buyer for a natural gas company, and an NBA player. This is their story, along with his pal Herman Carr's.

"There was never anyone like him before and there will never be one like him again," said his fishing buddy and fellow coach, Bobby Knight. Don Haskins had been called a lot of things in the world of basketball like giant, pioneer, icon, bigger than life, revered, original, great coach and one of a kind. But really, he was never about ticker-tape parades, neckties and streets named in his honor. Don Haskin was a fifth of whiskey, a fat enchilada, a faded hat and a pair of cowboy boots. He hated the spotlight, crowds, and having to sit down and answer questions about that 1966 team. What others never seem to understand is that he cared for all his teams and all his players the same way he did that championship team. Enough said!

Don Haskins, 78 years old, rode out of El Paso into the sunset for the last time on Sunday, September 9, 2008.

Don left behind his wife Mary, three sons and three grand-sons. He was once asked by Philadelphia Inquirer staff writer, Frank Fitzpatrick, "So how do you like retirement, Coach?" "Love it," Haskins said. "I don't do crap, and I don't start that until noon." That was pure Don Haskins and I'm sure "The Bear" growled while speaking. Haskins had not attended any UTEP home games the previous season. He was too proud to be seen in a wheelchair, a wheelchair he had been forced into because of surgery to remove part of his foot caused by diabetes. He didn't want the attention, hated curtain calls and all the questions that would follow. He had said many times that all he wanted was to win bas-ketball games, so therefore he always started his best five players, even if they happened to be black. Fellow coach Moe Iba once said, "Hell, he'd have played five kids from Mars if they were his best five players." Haskins even wished at times he had never won that 1966 title. "Life would have been a heck of a lot easier for me, my school and my players," he said. No doubt Don Haskins was a Hall-of-Fame coach even if he had never won a national title. Why? Because planned or not, he single-handedly changed the face of college basketball for the better and that made him a national treasure. "He may have been the John Wayne of college basketball," said Nebraska coach Doc Sadler. "Growl!"

Terrific

His locker was next to the great Mickey Mantle's, the person after whom he would later name his only son. He was part of three New York Yankee teams that reached the World Series, but he only won one ring, in 1962. He is one of the few to hit a home run during a World Series game, against two of the best pitchers ever, Sandy Koufax and Bob Gibson; but he never won a batting title. He was a part of one of the best outfields ever assembled for the New York Yankees, but he was the least known of the three. He is only one of seven players and the third Yankee ever to win Major League Baseball's Rookie-of-the-Year honors (1962), while playing for the eventual World Series Champions in the same season; Gil McDougald and Derek Jeter are the other two Yanks. He also won the *Sporting News* Rookie-of-the-Year Award that same year. He was a two-time All-Star, 1962-63 and the son of an All-Star Major League catcher whose only All-Star game (1945) was cancelled due to travel restrictions during World War II. He was a switch-hitting shortstop, who threw right-handed, but earned a Gold Glove as an outfielder, in 1965. He would wear the same number as Yankee teammates Red Ruffing, Tommy Henrich, and Thurman Munson, # 15. I'm sure you have figured out by now about whom I'm writing. He was known as "Tom Terrific" long before Hall-of-Fame pitcher, Tom Seaver came along. Tom Tresh lived his boyhood dream.

Thomas Michael Tresh was not a great player, but don't tell his teammates that. They thought he was terrific. Tresh was born in Detroit, Michigan, on September 20, 1938. From 1938 to 1948, Tom would spend many hours at the ballpark in Chicago watching his dad Mike Tresh play catcher for the White Sox. In 1958, he would attend Central Michigan University and eventually sign an amateur free-agent contract with the New York Yankees, as a shortstop. Tom stood six feet tall, weighed 191 pounds, and could hit home runs with power from both sides of the plate. Does that remind you of anyone? It's a shame that every great player for close to two decades was always compared to Mickey Mantle. It was impossible for most to live up to the standards set by Mantle. Just ask guys like Roger Maris, Bobby Murcer, Hank Bauer, Bob Cerv and Clete Boyer, all great, but underrated players who failed in comparison.

Tom Tresh debuted with the New York Yankees as a fill-in shortstop on September 3, 1961, against the Detroit Tigers, his hometown team. He would begin to stay with the New York club for good, in 1962. Tresh would compete with Phil Linz for the starting shortstop position vacated by Tony Kubek, who was serving time in the Army. Tresh not only won the starting shortstop job but hit .286 with 20 homers, scored 94 runs and recorded 93 RBI's in 157 games. He did split some of his time in left field, flanked by Mantle and Maris. His efforts would earn him the 1962 Rookie-of-the-Year Award and a spot on the 1962 American League All-Star team.

Tom Tresh would be the first one to tell you that dreams do come true. "When you're a 25-year-old kid and your dream has always been to play professional baseball, it's kind of hard to believe," Tresh said. "When you look around and you see all of these great players, it's hard to fathom that you're in the middle of all that and that you're taking a role in that situation. Out of everyone in the country, how come I was the one playing in Yankee Stadium, in a World Series?" Tresh helped the Yanks to a 98-66 win-loss record during that season and secured a date with the San Francisco Giants for the 1962 Championship. It was a classic seven-game Series, with the Yankees winning the Series and Game Seven by the score of 1-0. "You didn't have time to think about things," said Tresh on that exciting seventh game. "Everything happened in a blink of an eye, and just like that the Series was over." All Tresh had done was hit the game-winning homer in Game Five, batted .321 for the Series, and made a terrific backhanded catch on a drive to left-field by Willie Mays in the seventh inning of Game Seven, to keep the Giants from scoring. In three World Series contests, 1962-64, he hit .277, with four home runs and 13 RBI's, in 18 games.

In 1966, he hit a career high 27 homers and led the American League in sacrifice flies. On September 1, 1963, he became only the eighth player in history to homer from each side of the plate in a single game. He also clobbered home runs in the same game, from both sides of the plate, two more times that season. On June 6, 1965, Tom Terrific hit four home runs in a doubleheader against his Dad's old team, the Chicago White Sox. After hurting his knee during spring training in 1967, Tresh began to show signs of slowing down. Two years later, the Yankees traded him to the Detroit Tigers, his hometown team, for outfielder

Ron Woods. On September 29, 1969, Tom Tresh retired after the season with a .245 career average and 153 homers, 530 RBI's in 1,192 games. The Detroit Tigers had told him in advance that he was to be released.

After his playing career, Tresh returned to his alma mater, Central Michigan University and worked as an assistant placement director for many years. He also helped invent the *Slide-Rite,* a training tool to teach the correct way to slide and dive while playing baseball, softball or soccer.

Tom Terrific handled his last fly ball on Wednesday, October 15, 2008, at his home in Venice, Florida. Without a hitch, he had settled under it and caught it with both hands, just as he had been taught by his Dad. He then promptly rolled it towards the pitcher's mound as he ran off the field of play. He was 70 years young, still a boy, and his dream was over. "This is a sad day," said teammate Johnny Blanchard. "He'd played golf the day before and complained about an ache in his back, but I guess he didn't think it was serious. He was just a terrific fellow," Blanchard said. Shortstop Tony Kubek would say about Tresh, "A great shortstop who was a bit unorthodox in his style. He wasn't as fluid or as smooth as some guys, but he was very efficient and very fast with a strong arm. He made all the plays and he was a good clutch hitter." Longtime teammate Joe Pepitone stated, "This hurts. He was my roommate for six years of my life, my hitting instructor and my best friend. He let me be me, but he was also the guy who kept me in at night." Pepitone went on to say, "Tommy was a constant in my life and a calming influence. He was always there for me and stuck up for me. He was like my brother. When I had personal issues, he was always the person on the team I would turn to.

During some rain delays, he would take out his guitar, and we'd sing and dance." "Tommy was a great teammate," Yankees great Yogi Berra said. "He did everything well as a ballplayer and was an easy guy to manage." "Filling in for Tony (Kubek) the way he did in 1962 was so important. We couldn't have won that year without him," said Yankee second baseman, Bobby Richardson. "I always felt badly for him that he was always compared with Mickey."

I understand what Richardson was trying to say, but I'd bet the farm that Tresh loved even being mentioned in the same breath as his hero Mantle. Besides he wasn't called Terrific for nothing.

One-Hit Wonder

As you read further, you may wonder why I have included this next fellow in this book. I met him one summer in Kingsville, Texas, while the University there dedicated their baseball field to Texas legend and Hall-of-Fame Major League pitcher Nolan Ryan. I was playing on a media team from Corpus Christi and the local surrounding area. Ryan's team consisted of other area athletes and celebrities. Even "Dallas" TV star Larry Hageman was present. "Bum" Phillips, coach of the then Houston Oilers, along with defensive tackle Ray Childress, was also there. It was quite a two-day event ending in a softball game played on the newly named "Nolan Ryan Field." Interestingly, my subject was a guest of Ryan's and sat quietly in the dugout during the game. Only my curiosity allowed me to find out who he was and why he was here. He was not a great player by any stretch of the imagination, but by 1989 he had been inducted into the Texas Baseball Hall of Fame. He had pitched in the Major Leagues but only for a cup of coffee. He did have a 1957 Topps Baseball Card (#321), but it was his only one. After baseball, he became a scout for the New York Mets, Montreal Expos, Houston Colt 45's, Atlanta Braves and Chicago Cubs. From 1960 to 1993, he signed over 200 ballplayers to Major League contracts, but he would be most remembered for signing one real superstar, Nolan Ryan. That's why he was there, as a guest of Ryan. He would later be mentioned in Ryan's Hall-of-Fame acceptance speech. As I spoke to this gentleman, I became fascinated with how much he had given to the game of baseball and I had no idea how much more the game would benefit from his tenure. So, was he just a one-hit wonder? Here's the story of just one of the 17,000 baseball players in the history of Major League baseball who have given so much to the game. I think he belongs in this book, but you can decide. By the way, Nolan Ryan thinks so too!

On June 8, 1956, he recorded his one and only Major League hit, off of New York Giants' right-hander Al Worthington. His story reminded me of the famous baseball movie, *Field of Dreams*, where Iowa corn farmer Ray Kinsella not only tears up his cornfield and builds a baseball diamond, but also starts a journey where he ends up in Boston looking for 1960's writer Terrance Mann, and then continues on to Chicago seeking ex-Major League player Archibald "Moonlight" Graham. Graham had played for only one inning of one Major League game in the 1920's, with the New York Giants, and was denied an at-bat. Graham (played by Burt Lancaster in his last movie role before his death) ends up hitch-hiking to Iowa as the young Graham, now played by Frank Whaley. Kinsella played by Kevin Costner, along with Terrance Mann played by James Earl Jones, ends up giving the young Graham a ride to a place where dreams do come true. It's a wonderful story of these three people, along with Kinsella's Dad, who are woven together with each other; and the common thread is baseball.

John Robert "Red" Murff was born on April Fools' Day in 1921. Red would call Burlington, Texas his home. He would grow up loving the game of baseball and, in 1950, eventually joined a Class C Minor League Team from Baton Rouge, Louisiana, known as the "Red Sticks." As a right-handed pitcher, he would post a 17-4 winning record while starting 23 games. In 1951, he would find himself back home in Texas, where he would win 19 games while losing 14, for the Class B Texas City "Texans," of the Gulf Coast League. On June 8 of that year, he pitched a no-hitter against the Harlingen "Capitols" and won by a score of 6-0. Red, who stood 6' 3" and weighed 195 pounds, would start turning the heads of Major League scouts. In 1952, Red would win 23 games for the Tyler "East Texans," before joining the Dallas "Eagles" of the AA Texas League in 1953. He won a total of 54 games in three years with the Eagles and received the 1955 Texas League Pitcher-of-the-Year award. In that same year, Red was also voted the Minor League Pitcher of the Year by the *Sporting News*. At the end of the 1955 season (his best season), Red would be obtained by the New York Giants in a Minor League working agreement. He would immediately be traded to the Milwaukee Braves for Murray Wall.

Murff pitched for the Milwaukee Braves from 1956-1957, while posting a 2-2 record with three saves and a 4.65 ERA in 26 games. He would wear uniform #13 and record his only two wins in 1957 against the Cincinnati Reds and Pittsburg Pirates. Red told this story in his book. "As I sat in the dugout the day before I was to start my first Major League game, I gave myself a pep talk. 'You gotta be all business to be here, Red. It doesn't get any bigger or more serious than this.' The next thing I knew, I looked at Manager Charlie Grimm and his shoelaces were on fire," laughed Murff. Lighting on fire the shoelaces of another player or manager was an old baseball trick designed to break the boredom of sitting in the dugout or the nervousness of your first start. Towards the end of the 1957 season, Red would find himself back down in the Minor League pitching for the Triple A Wichita "Braves" of the American Association. Wichita would continue to be his home during the 1958 season; and he would finish his professional career with the Louisville "Colonels" in 1959 and the Jacksonville "Braves" in 1960. During his eleven years in Minor League baseball, Red Murff won 146 games while losing 95. He recorded a 2.95 ERA with 1,077 strike-outs while pitching 1,934 innings. It is safe to say that Red Murff was a better Minor League pitcher. His love for the game of baseball enticed him to become a big league scout, and he was signed by the New York Mets in 1960. I asked him how someone can see into the future when watching a prospect play baseball. Red just grinned as if his secret would always be safe. Red said to me, "Baseball players don't just show up at Yankee Stadium, Wrigley Field or the Astrodome and begin playing at the Major League level; someone has to go find these kids. That's what I do." He said when he looked at a player; he tried to envision how they would look in a Major League uniform playing his position against today's stars. He did not care how they looked or performed against their current opponents. He watched mechanics, enthusiasm, attitude and work ethic. The rest was just gut instinct. Red Murff signed not only signed Hall-of-Fame pitcher, Nolan Ryan but also Jerry Grote, Jerry Koosman, Kenny Boswell, Mike Stanton and Norm Charlton. Red Murff would be inducted into the Texas Scouts Association Hall of Fame in 1999. He also helped start the baseball program at the

University of Mary Hardin-Baylor in Belton, Texas; and in 1994, their ballpark would be named Red Murff Field.

A few years before meeting Red Murff in person, I met another fellow by the name of Joe Matina. Joe had been a high school coach but more importantly he had worked with Red as a "Birddog," or otherwise known as an associate scout, for the Montreal Expos, from 1969 to 1974. Joe was now in his 70's and he and I would meet for lunch every Wednesday at a local restaurant in Corpus Christi, Texas, and talk baseball. Joe had grown up in New Jersey and, as a kid; he had seen all the great players from the thirties. His favorite player was Joe DiMaggio. I was fascinated to have this fellow as a friend and marveled at the stories. It was Joe Matina's job to keep up with all the high school baseball talent in South Texas and relay his thoughts on each player to Red. Then based on Joe's notes, Red would decide whether the player deserved another look. Before Joe Matina died, he called his pal, Red Murff and asked Red for a signed copy of his new book. Joe gave Red Murff's book entitled The Scout to me for Christmas, along with a hand-written note and his Scouting Pass from the Baltimore Orioles. This pass allowed him into any Major League game.

On November 28, 2008, Red Murff hit his last corner in life. He died in a Tyler nursing home in his beloved state of Texas. He was 87. Red always believed that "good" was the enemy of greatness, and he pushed his prospects to get better every day. Just ask Nolan Ryan. One of my favorite quotations from Red's book went something like this, "Every time I pass by a ballpark, I just have to stop. You never know. The next Nolan Ryan might be there." I just hope there's another Red Murff there watching.

Which Eye?

S ome said his face had character, others said he was just plain ugly; but for 16 years, he was "the face" of the Washington Redskins. He was tall for his day, 6'3" and from small-town Texas, and we all know everything grows big in Texas. He spoke with a Texas drawl that was so bad, you would swear he had a mouth full of gravel; however, he was known for throwing a football, not talking. He was as tough as stale beef jerky, known for chewing tobacco and using salty language, but he would turn into a silent assassin when he trotted onto the football field. He was not the first player to throw a forward pass, but he is considered one of the founding fathers of the modern-day NFL passing game. When he was in college a Texas sportswriter gave him the nickname "Slingin' Sammy," but it was for his baseball skills at third base, not his tailback position in the single-wing offense at Texas Christian University. He signed a professional contract right out of college, but it was with Rogers Hornsby, then a scout of Major League Baseball's St. Louis Cardinals. He set records in three categories of the NFL, some which are still in today's record books. He had his # 33 retired by the Redskins and it's the only number retired by that franchise. He was the first

Coach of the New York Titans (now the Jets), but he would rather have continued playing. In 1963, he became part of the very first Professional Football Hall-of-Fame class, joining other great players like Jim Thorpe, "Red" Grange, George Halas, Don Hutson, "Curly Lambeau, Johnny "Blood" McNally, Ernie Nevers and Bronko Nagurski.

So, in 1937, during his very first practice as a Washington Redskin, he questioned Coach Ray Flaherty about throwing the football. Flaherty said, "They tell me you're quite a passer," and Baugh responded, "I reckon I can throw a little." Flaherty then took him aside and explained that the forward pass was only used as a desperation play, when the team was way behind in points. Coaches believed that when you passed, only three things could happen and two of them were bad. "Passing requires uncanny accuracy," said Flaherty shaking his head. Just then, as Redskin receiver Wayne Millner began to run a buttonhook pattern, Flaherty said, "You must be able to hit that receiver in the eye." Sammy Baugh then raised his arm to throw and asked Flaherty, "Which Eye?" In 1937, he would put the entire league on notice with his very first play from scrimmage, as he dropped back into his own end zone and connected on a 42-yard pass to Cliff Battles. In his first season, he not only led the league in passing, but also led the Redskin franchise to its very first NFL Championship.

If you're my age, late fifties, then you should remember some of the NFL's greatest throwing Quarterbacks. Names like Bob Waterfield, Otto Graham, Sid Luckman, Eddie Lebaron, Y. A. Tittle, and Johnny Unitas. And of course John Elway, Dan Marino, Joe Montana, Dan Fouts, and Steve Young should also be familiar. Present day Quarterbacks Brett Favre and Peyton Manning now stand at the top of this list of names. But who is the best Quarterback of all time? So, where does Sammy Baugh rank on this list? Some would argue that Sammy Baugh is not only the best Quarterback, but *the* best NFL player period. Read on and decide for yourself.

Have you ever seen or heard of tying an old tire or a peach basket to a tree limb with a rope and then swinging it back and forth? Then you try to throw a football through the moving target from different distances. It's not easy; I know I tried it when I was a kid. Sammy Baugh practiced every day for hours, throwing a football through that moving tire. He threw from 10 yards, 20 yards and 30 yards away. He sometimes even practiced by throwing on the run. Yes, he was a perfectionist and he wanted badly to master the art of accurate passing.

Samuel Adrian Baugh was created on March 17, 1914 on a farm near Temple, Texas. The football gods took a long string bean body and attached a slingshot right arm. Then they added that face with character and filled his mouth with cuss words. Add a lot of toughness, a little bit of meanness, the desire to be great, and Sammy Baugh was the finished product. He was the second son of James and Lucy Baugh. At the age of 16, he and his family would move to Sweetwater, Texas where he would start at quarterback for his high school football team. He had always owned a strong arm, as displayed by his throws from the third base position on his high school baseball team, and in fact he had a baseball scholarship offer from Washington State University before he hurt his knee sliding into second base. That injury caused his scholarship to be withdrawn. He was then courted by Texas Christian University, Coach Dutch Meyer. If he would just come to TCU, Meyer promised Sammy he could play all three sports (basketball, football and baseball). Baugh threw 587 passes for 39 touchdowns in his three varsity football seasons. He would be named All-American in 1935 and 1936, and he led TCU to two bowl-game wins, a 3-2 victory over LSU in the 1936 Sugar Bowl and a 16-6 win over Marquette in the very first Cotton Bowl, played in 1937. He was named the very first Cotton Bowl MVP and finished fourth in voting behind winner Larry Kelley of Yale, for the Heisman Trophy in 1936. Baugh would then play for the 1937 College All-Stars who beat the Green Bay Packers 6-0.

He was offered $4,000 dollars to play Pro football by Redskin owner George Preston Marshall, in the spring of his senior season. He did not sign right away with the Redskins, but did sign a contract with the St. Louis Cardinals baseball team. He was sent to their Minor League team in Columbus, Ohio. There, Baugh was converted to shortstop and found himself playing behind Marty Marion and unable to hit a Major League curveball. After it was announced that he had been drafted in the first round of the 1937 NFL draft, Baugh decide to sign a one-year, $8,000 dollar contract with the new Washington Redskins. That amount would make him the highest-paid player on the team. "I didn't know what they were talking about, because frankly, I had never heard of either the draft or the Washington Redskins," laughed Baugh. The Redskins had moved from Boston to Washington at the beginning of the 1937 season, so there was no way for Baugh to know who they were. In 1937, with his leather helmet, and no face mask, Baugh would set his first NFL record by completing 91 passes in 218 attempts, for a league-high of 1,127 yards. He also led the Redskins to their first NFL Championship with a victory over the talented Chicago Bears, by the score of 28-21. All Baugh had done was throw for 335 yards while completing 17 of 33 passes, with touchdown strikes from 55, 78, and 33 yards. That's some start for a rookie. The Redskins and Bears would meet three times in NFL Championship games from 1940-43.

By the mid-1940's, Baugh and the Redskins had introduced the T-formation. In this new formation, the quarterback combined the play calling of the wingback with the passing duties of the tailback. Sammy Baugh now had complete control of the offense and he took full advantage. From 1940 to 1949, Baugh would lead the league in passing five more times giving him a total of six including his rookie season. Only Steve Young has tied that record. From 1937 to 1952, Baugh recorded 1,693 completions out of 2,995 attempts (56.5% average) for 21,886 yards and 187 touchdowns. Sammy Baugh made the forward pass into a quick-strike weapon from anywhere on the field. It was in 1940 that the Bears would record the most lopsided championship victory in NFL history. The Bears demolished the Redskins 73-0. After the Bears had scored their first touchdown in that game, Baugh drove the Redskins downfield and had a touchdown pass dropped in the end zone by his wide receiver, Charlie Malone. When asked if that pass had been caught, would it have changed the outcome of that game? After thinking about it for a minute, Baugh said in that gravelly voice, "Yeah, I suppose it would have made it 73-6."

Sammy Baugh played with the Washington Redskins for 16 years and perfected the forward pass. He led his team to two NFL Championships and five division titles in his first nine years. When he retired, he held every major passing record in the NFL. But that's not all. Baugh was also a spectacular punter and an outstanding safety on defense. His 1940 single-season punting average of

51.4 yards per game is still an NFL record and his career average of 45.1-yards per punt is still second all time. In the 1942 NFL Championship game, the 85-yard surprise quick kick by Baugh kept the Bears pinned at their end of the field which helped seal the win for the Redskins. In 1943, he threw four touchdowns and intercepted four passes in a game against the Detroit Lions. The four interceptions still tie him for the NFL record, for a single game. In 1945, he posted an unbelievable 73.3% completion rate that has only been topped by one other, Kenny Anderson in 1982. In 1947, he threw for 355 yards and six touchdowns against the Chicago Cardinals in a single game. On October 31, 1948, Baugh established the NFL record for yards-per-catch-average at 18.58, against the Boston Patriots. At game's end, he had recorded 446 yards on only 24 catches. Should we go on? Then think about this! He is still the only player to lead the league in passing, punting and defensive interceptions in the same season. Enough said! They should have paid him triple.

Baugh was a five-time All-Star selection, nine-time All-Pro selection, and is in the Redskin Ring of Fame. He was elected to the College Football Hall of Fame in 1951. He is a member of the NFL 1940s All-Decade Team, the NFL's 50th Anniversary Team, the NFL's 75th Anniversary All-Time Team, and also received many more awards from numerous magazines. He has been idolized in movies *Tender Mercies* and TV shows, especially by actor Robert Duvall who patterned his role of Gus McCrae in the television series *Lonesome Dove*. Baugh even dabbled in film with his role of Tom King, a college quarterback who joins the Texas Rangers to avenge his father's death in Republic Pictures' 12-episode serial called, "King of the Texas Rangers."

Sure, the Redskins have had other great quarterbacks: Eddie LeBaron, Sonny Jurgensen, Billy Kilmer, Joe Theisman, and Doug Williams come to mind, but there was no replacement for Sammy Baugh. No one ever forgot Sammy Baugh. Until the day he died, he still received letters every day from someone asking for his autograph. He had signed his name for thousands of fans until he could no longer hold a pen. "He just finally wore out," said his son David. "There's nobody any better in pro football," said his friend and fellow Hall-of-Famer, Don Maynard. "He was amazing," said Eddie LeBaron. "I've seen him throw the ball over arm, side arm, and under arm and complete them." Coach Weeb Ewbanks, then an assistant coach with the Cleveland Browns, said, "Even at the end of his career, Baugh was something. I told our defensive linemen: 'We've got to make Baugh throw out of a well. Get your hands up. Don't let him see his receivers.' They went in there with their arms up, but Baugh threw under their arms. One play, he flipped his wrist underhanded for an 18-yard completion."

As for Sundays, you could still find Sammy in front of a TV set watching the game he loved. "I'll watch it all damn day long. I like the football they play. They got bigger boys and they also got these damn speed merchants that we didn't have in those days. I'd love to be a quarterback this day in time," laughed Baugh. My favorite story about Slingin' Sammy may be the one he told the *San Antonio Express-News*. "One time there was a defensive lineman who was coming down on me with his fists closed," said Baugh. "A couple of plays later, I found a play we could waste and I told our linemen to just let him come through. The guy got about five feet from me, and I hit him right in the forehead with the ball. He turned red and passed out. It scared the hell out of me."

I met Sammy Baugh in 1997. My dad's favorite team has always been the Washington Redskins and I had in my possession a yellow Redskin helmet from the fifties with the logo on the side and a burgundy stripe down the middle. I have spent many years and quite a bit of money trying to have all my favorite Redskins quarterbacks sign that helmet. He didn't say much when he signed and I thanked him. That helmet now has the signature of every great Redskin QB from 1937 to 1985. It sits on a shelf in front of me in my office. I'm looking at it now. I wish my dad was here to see it.

In Rotan, Texas, on December 17, 2008, at the age of 94, Baugh threw his last incomplete pass. May he never throw another! Of course he didn't throw all that many to start with. Sammy was the last of the living players from that first NFL Hall of Fame class. There's one heck of a football team in Heaven.

The Last Teammate

In 1927, he became the first All-American in basketball that Duke University ever had, and he is enshrined in the Duke Athletic Hall of Fame. He played for Coach Eddie Cameron, for whom Cameron Indoor Stadium is named. Even while in college at the age of 19, he signed a contract to play with the 1927 New York Yankees and traveled with them throughout spring training, until the season started. "They never let me in the batting cage," he said. "The '27 Yankees were one of the greatest ball clubs of all time and they didn't have time to fool around with a college kid." In 1930, after graduating from Duke, he would again join the Yankees. His debut in the line-up occurred on July 25 of that same year. He would be sent back down to the Minor Leagues for what was referred to in those days as "seasoning." He would return again to the big club in 1933 as an infielder, to find a Yankee infield crowded with the likes of Lou Gehrig, Tony Lazzeri, Frankie Crosetti and Joe Sewell. After playing in only three games that year, he would be traded to the Boston Red Sox. At the end of the 1936 season, after three good years at third base, he was traded to the Athletics. In 1937 and 1938, he would call Philadelphia home. Cincinnati was his next stop, from 1939 to 1941. On August 26, 1939, he became the first Major League baseball player to be shown at-bat on television, in a game between the visiting Cincinnati Reds and the Brooklyn Dodgers, at Ebbets Field. His last Major League season was spent in New York with the 1942 Giants. The list of teammates and managers this fellow played with and for, reads like a "Who's Who," of Major League baseball. Including the names listed above, he shared the diamond with Casey Stengel, Mel Ott, Jimmie Foxx, Herb Pennock, Connie Mack, Heinie Manush, Lefty Grove, Eddie Joost, Joe McCarthy, Ernie Lombardi, Bucky Harris, Earl Coombs, Joe Cronin, Bill Dickey, and Lefty Gomez; but even better than that, he was the last living teammate of the "Sultan of Swat," "Babe" Ruth. Once more, I said, he was the last person to play with Babe Ruth, there are no others? On June 20, 2008, he turned the ripe old age of 100 and became the oldest living Major League player. He had outlived Rollie Stiles who passed away on July 22, 2007. Stiles had also lived to be 100. Bill Werber had a lot to remember.

William "Bill" Murray Werber was born just outside of Washington, D.C. in Berwyn Heights, Maryland, on June 20, 1908. He grew up playing baseball and basketball while attending the Boy Scouts. He would later become an Eagle Scout. At Duke, Werber would not only become an All-American in basketball but also played varsity baseball at shortstop for three years, batting .400. Werber revealed an interview that in the twenties and thirties, college basketball only used one referee per game. This would lead to rough play with lots of grabbing arms and jerseys. Bill's high school team would become city champions and was selected to play the New York Original Celtics, a professional barnstorming team that played and won over two hundred games a year. Although Bill's team was thoroughly beaten, he learned several tricks that would later help him at Duke. He remained loyal to Duke University and sent his son and two daughters there to be educated.

After graduation in 1930, Bill returned to the New York Yankees. In his first at-bat, Bill recalls being extremely nervous and ended up taking six straight pitches, two strikes and four balls for a walk. The next batter was the "Great Bambino" himself. Ruth promptly hit one of his 49 home runs hit that season, into the right-field bleachers. Bill said, "Babe Ruth hit a home run and I ran around the bases, full speed, because I wanted to show them how fast I could run. So I get into the dugout, and—finally—Babe got into the dugout. He patted me on the head and said, 'Son, You don't have to run like that when "The Babe" hit one.' " Werber also recalls the endless train rides that occurred in the early days of baseball. "I played bridge with Babe on all the train rides," Werber once said. "He had his partner Lou Gehrig. I had as my partner Bill Dickey. Now actually, Bill Dickey and I were a lot smarter than Ruth and Gehrig and we always beat them." Werber continued, "I always preferred the company of Ruth to Gehrig. Ruth was friendly. He loved to play practical jokes and was always playing them on people. He'd go to hospitals to visit and never take a newspaperman or photographer with him. You'll never see a photo of Ruth in a hospital with a kid. He was just a nice fellow at heart. He would take forever to sign things going out of the stadium. Kids would walk all over his white shoes and tan pants, and he wouldn't mind," laughed Werber. "Gehrig didn't want any part of that. He'd leave the stadium and knock kids out of the way. But he was a tremendous player, and you'd better hustle or he'd get on your ass—they both would. They were great competitors although they didn't like each other," said Werber. Bill spent the next two seasons in the Minors before joining the Yanks again in 1933. He was then traded to the Red Sox.

The next stop for Werber was Boston, where he became the starting third baseman. He led the league in stolen bases three times in four years. In 1934, Werber recorded a .321 batting average, including 200 hits, 41 doubles, 10 triples and 11 home runs with 129 runs scored. He loved hitting the ball off of the "Green Monster." But it wasn't enough to get Boston on top of the American League, so the traded him to the Philadelphia Athletics, in 1937. After two mediocre seasons in Philly, Bill was sent packing to the Cincinnati Reds of the National League.

In his second season with the Reds (1939), Werber would hit .289 in 147 games while scoring 115 runs. He was the spark that was needed to get the Reds to the next step, the World Series. They would face the Yankees and be swept from the Series. In 1940, the Reds were at it again with different results. That year, Cincinnati defeated the Detroit Tigers in seven games to become the World Series Champs. Werber had done his part by hitting .370 in the Series and leading his team. He was the proud owner of a World Series ring. Bill Werber still holds one Major League record, as he is still the only player to hit four consecutive doubles in both leagues (Boston Red Sox and Cincinnati Reds.)

Bill would end his career with the New York Giants, in 1942. At 34 years of age, Bill Werber retired. His highest salary playing baseball had been $13,500, still a tidy sum in those days, but laughable by today's standards. In his 11-season career, Werber hit .271 with 78 home runs and 539 RBI's in 1,295 games. He also stole a total of 215 bases. He was inducted into the Cincinnati Reds Hall of Fame, in 1961.

The insurance business would now receive Bill's full attention. Not only did he become successful but made over $100,000 in his first year, in the business. When he finally retired in the early seventies, Bill had become a millionaire and owned a three handicap on the golf course. He would also write three books, <u>Circling the Bases,</u> <u>Hunting is for the Birds,</u> and <u>Memories of a Ballplayer.</u> He admitted that he no longer watched baseball and often wrote and complained to Major League Commissioner, Bud Selig. Werber didn't think women should sing the national anthem; he hated the length of the players' hair and felt the games were too long.

By 1991, diabetes had taken one of Bill's legs. He lived in an assisted living center in Charlotte, North Carolina, where he got around just fine in a motorized chair. As he grew older, Werber obtained a special status with baseball collectors. He continued to receive letters and notes daily, in the mail. Whenever Bill leaned back in his chair to remember another story about baseball's golden era, you would swear that he was going to say, "Those were good times." On January 22, 2009, at the age of 100, the last teammate of Babe Ruth faded away. If I may borrow and adapt a line spoken by General Douglas McArthur, "Old soldiers (and baseball players) never die; they just fade away."

I Don't Know on Third

Bud Abbott and Lou Costello's famous baseball rift entitled "Who's on First," goes something like this. Lou is curious about Bud's new baseball team and proceeds to ask him the names of the players on his team. The conversation that follows is pure baseball magic. "Who's on first, what's on second, I don't know is on third" has been listened to more times than Happy Birthday. It remains a timeless classic like The Wizard of Oz. Abbott and Costello originally used this sketch live in 1937 during a burlesque comedy routine. By 1938, you could hear "Who's on First," on the radio. In 1940, they performed this routine on film and eventually took their act to television, in 1945. In 1999, *Time* magazine declared it the greatest comedy sketch of the 20th Century. It would be interesting to find out if any of you folks reading this article could name all the players in the sketch. If you have read this far, you now know three of the names; here is a hint of a fourth with the ending. A frustrated Lou Costello never understands that "Who" is the last name of the first baseman and ends his portion of the sketch by saying loudly, "I don't give a darn." Bud Abbott's response was, "Oh, that's our shortstop!!!"

What's even more intriguing is the fact that only thirteen third-baseman have been inducted into the Baseball Hall of Fame since they opened the doors of Cooperstown in 1936. Out of nine positions available, it is the position with the least inductees. Indeed, even the most baseball-educated fans may not be able to name all thirteen. So, "I don't know is on third," could apply to a lot of these guys and maybe even this fellow, but I hope not. Naming the Ten Commandants may be easier. If asked about Hall-of-Fame third basemen, most of you would blurt out Wade Boggs (2005), George Brett (1999), and Mike Schmidt (1995). After a bit of thought, Brooks Robinson (1983) and Eddie Mathews (1978) would be added to your list, but by now most of you would run out of guesses. Older fans might remember Pie Traynor (1948) of the Pirates and maybe even Frank "Homerun" Baker (1955) of the Athletics, who got his nickname by hitting just 12 home runs in one season, but that would only add up to a total of seven. Baseball historians would eventually get NY Giant Freddie Lindstrom (1976) and Negro League players Judy Johnson (1975) and Ray Dandridge (1987). You'd still have three more to go. Two of the last three you probably have never heard of, and finding out the answer would require some research. Turn of the Century third sacker, Jimmy Collins (1945) played for the Boston Beaneaters and Negro League inductee, Jud Wilson was added in a special class, in 2006. That leaves only one. I hope you know who was left out. He was inducted in 1983 by the Veterans Committee along with fellow third baseman Brooks Robinson, who was voted in on a first ballot, by the writers. His name was George Kell and from the mid forties to the late fifties, he was considered the best third baseman in the American League. Aren't you glad you weren't asked to name the 81 pitchers in Cooperstown?

George Clyde Kell was born on August 23, 1922, in Swifton, Arkansas and he was the best thing to come out of that State since Paul "Bear" Bryant, Razorbacks and the Dean Brothers. Some believe that if he had not been hit in the face by a screamer off the bat of Joe DiMaggio, he might still be playing. They don't call it the "Hot Corner," for nothing. After his jaw was broken, his confidence as a third baseman was never the same. Kell said that after he had been hit in the face by the line drive, "I got up, made the play at third, and then passed out." This down-home kid walked right out of the hills of Arkansas with a strong sense of family, a pocket full of nothing, and dreams of playing baseball. He had nothing to do and all day to do it. In 1938, at a high school ceremony, he announced that his intention after school was to play baseball. "Everyone laughed," remembered Kell. He was as genuine as apple pie, owned a canyon-deep baritone voice and was as honest as old Abe Lincoln himself.

George Kell would attend Arkansas State University for awhile before finally being signed by the Brooklyn Dodgers as an amateur free agent, in 1940. He reported to their Class B team in North Carolina. "You played wherever that told you to play and for how much they wanted to pay you, or you went home. In those days, you didn't have a choice," said Kell. In 1942, the Dodgers moved Kell to their club in Lancaster, Pennsylvania. His great play would be seen by the legendary owner and manager of the Philadelphia Athletics, Connie Mack. By 1943, Kell was purchased by the A's. For the next fifteen years, Kell would knock'em down and throw'em out from the third sack. Kell just loved to play baseball. Mack would eventually trade

Kell to Detroit on May, 18, 1946. Former Tiger Manager Red Rolfe once said about Kell, "He's a seven-day-a-week ballplayer." On June 3, 1953, Kell was shipped off to the Boston Red Sox and would stay there until May 23, 1954. It was on this date that Kell was again traded, but this time to the Chicago White Sox. Kell's last stop would come in Baltimore, with the Orioles. It was here that Kell with his career winding down would mentor another future Hall-of-Fame third baseman from Arkansas, and his name was Brooks Robinson. Kell was also injured some of the time in 1957 while with Baltimore, and dabbled in broadcasting while receiving some advice from future Hall-of-Fame radio broadcaster, Ernie Harwell. Kell had no idea what he was doing, but he knew baseball and his voice was full of that smooth southern charm. George Kell retired from playing baseball on September 14, 1957.

George Kell was a ten-time All-Star, batted over .300 nine times, topped the American League's third baseman in assists and total chances four times, and in fielding percentage seven times. In 1949, Kell beat the great Ted Williams to win his only batting title. He also holds the record for fewest strike-outs by a batting champion in a season, with 13. Kell batted .306 for his career with 78 home runs, 870 RBI's, 2,054 hits, and a .482 slugging average. He did hit for the cycle on June 2, 1950. Kell was inducted into the Baseball Hall of Fame in 1983 with Brooks Robinson. It was quite a day for the Razorback State. "I grew up idolizing Stan Musial and George Kell," said Robinson. Kell may have thought he was through with baseball, but baseball was certainly not finished with him.

By the end of the 1957 season, CBS Television in New York called Kell and asked if he would consider broadcasting the "Game of the Week." Kell refused until he found out that the games broadcast would only be on Saturdays. He could fly to New York on Friday and then back home after the game. Kell was shocked at the opportunity but said, "Yes." Sure, he talked rather slow and funny, kind of like a guy with a mouth full of hard candy, but so did Bryant and Dean. They all spoke that way in Arkansas. He loved to elongate words. Tuesday became Tooosdee, Arlington became Arrrrlington and Cincinnati became Cincinnnattah. Later, his beloved Tigers were identified as the team from "DE-troit" while great players were said to be "One of the best in aaawll of basebaawl." Of course his favorite call was his home run call, "There's a looong… drive…deeeep…waaaay back…and gone!" At the time, Kell had no way of knowing that he would have a Hall-of-Fame career as a broadcaster after his baseball career was over. Kell was having too much fun to notice.

In 1959, his beloved Tigers called him back into the fold, but this time as an announcer. Kell would be the voice of the Tigers on TV until 1996. Kell worked out a deal with Detroit where he could broadcast 50 games a year on TV and still live in Swifton, Arkansas. The day before the game, Kell would drive to Little Rock and board a private plane to wherever Detroit was playing, and then they would fly him back at the end of the broadcast. "I don't know anybody else who lives 1,000 miles away from their job and gets to commute back and forth," Kell said with a laugh. He would never live anywhere else but Arkansas. Standing in his front yard with a reporter, Kell pointed to the ground and said, "I never wanted to be anywhere other than right here."

Detroit also gave another present to Kell when they let him pick his own broadcast partner; Ernie Harwell would spend the next 42 years calling Detroit Tiger games. In

1975, Kell was joined by another partner in the TV booth and his name was Al Kaline. Hall of Fame outfielder Al Kaline became Kell's color commentator, and there's nothing like having two Hall of Famer's on the air at the same time. There are many stories of how Kell would stand quietly by, as fans from every city they visited would rush to get an autograph from Al Kaline. No one seemed to know George Kell. That's what is meant by "I don't know is on third," remember?

Kell owned a car dealership in Swifton and was also a published author with <u>Hello Everybody, I'm George Kell,</u> an autobiography he wrote with the help of Dan Ewald. The title speaks to how he opened every Tiger baseball broadcast. On Tuesday, March 24, 2009, George Kell died as he had lived, peacefully, in his sleep. He had been injured in a car crash in 2004 but was able to walk with a cane. "I have DirecTV and a wide screen," said Kell in one of his last interviews. "I watch the Tigers every night, and watch all the other games I can," a baseball man until the end.

Here below is a list of the names of the players from Abbott and Costello's baseball routine. Do yourself a favor and watch it again. Now you know who's on third!

First	Who
Second	What
Third	I don't know
Left Field	Why
Center Field	Because
Pitcher	Tomorrow
Catcher	Today
Shortstop	I don't give a darn

Right Field   His name is never mentioned although some think it could be Naturally

This last call by Kell was considered a classic. Here's the way he'd describe a runner rounding third and heading home. "They're gonna wave him home," shouted Kell. You can bet when Kell gets to the gates of Heaven, they will wave him home.

Mr. Inside

Sports fans have always been infatuated with creating nicknames for their favorite players and some sports stars reach a level of fame where only one or two words are needed to conjure up the greatness of that individual. If I were to say "Sugar Ray," "Brown Bomber," or "Smokin' Joe" you would think of Ray Leonard, Joe Louis, and Joe Frazier. If you heard me say the nicknames "Snake," "Sweetness," or "Broadway Joe" would you remember Ken Stabler, Walter Payton, and Joe Namath? Willie Mays, Hank Aaron, and Stan Musial were always referred to as "Say Hey Kid," the "Hammer," and "Stan the Man." "Magic," "Pearl," and the "Big O" would remind you of Ervin Johnson, Earl Monroe, and Oscar Robinson. So, when I titled this piece "Mr. Inside," I hope you thought of "Doc" Blanchard. Heck, even the name Doc was a nickname, as his full name was Felix Anthony Blanchard, I can see why he chose to be called Doc. The rest of the football world would know him as "Mr. Inside." His partner in crime, Glenn Davis, was known as "Mr. Outside," and they teamed up together to create one of college football's most famous backfields and won three College Football National Championships at Army. Their record for three years (1944,'45,'46) stood at 27-0-1, with the tie coming in a 0-0 game against powerful Notre Dame. They would score 97 touchdowns in three years and land on the cover of *Time* magazine, together. In fact, in 1944 after a famous season-ending victory over Navy, General Douglas MacArthur took time out from his World War II duties to send this wire:

"The greatest of all Army teams…We have stopped the war to celebrate your magnificent success."
MacArthur.

In 1945, Doc Blanchard became the first college junior to ever win the Heisman Trophy Award. His pal Davis would win the trophy in 1946.

Mr. Inside was born on December 11, 1924, in Bishopville, South Carolina. His father was a doctor who also played football, at Tulane University and Wake Forest University. His son would be called "Little Doc." Blanchard attended Saint Stanislaus School in Bay Saint Louis, Mississippi; and as a senior in 1941; he led his team to an undefeated season. He was recruited by Notre Dame, Army, and many others. Doc would attend the University of North Carolina; and he tried to enroll in the Navy's V-12 program, which would allow a student to complete their college education for a service commitment. He was denied for two reasons, overweight and vision problems. With his father's help, Doc received an appointment to West Point and he enrolled in 1944. Army athletics' would never be the same. Blanchard was listed as No. 35 and stood six feet tall and weighed 208 pounds. He was without a doubt, a bruising fullback. Army Hall-of-Fame Coach Earl "Red" Blaik united Blanchard and Davis in the famed "T" formation. This Army backfield would produce their first national championship in football. Blanchard would score 38 touchdowns while gaining 1,908 yards, in his three years at Army. He also played linebacker and handled the place-kicking and punting duties for Army. You just can't talk about Army football without talking about Blanchard. Notre Dame Football Coach Ed McKeever was quoted as saying, after the 1944 game with Army, "I've just seen Superman in the flesh. He wears No. 35 and goes by the name of Blanchard." Doc became the very first football player to win the Sullivan Award as best amateur athlete. He was drafted by the Pittsburgh Steelers in 1946 with their third overall pick, but never played professional football.

Instead, Blanchard chose to become a jet fighter pilot for the United States Air Force. He would see duty during the Korean and Vietnam Wars. He retired in 1971 with the rank of Colonel.

His hometown of Bishopville, South Carolina, will unveil a three-statue bronze of Doc in December of this year. It will depict his life as a young boy, as a football hero and as an Air Force fighter pilot. They were hoping he would be present, but of course that will not happen now. They waited too long in my opinion. You see, I lived in Sumter, a town about 16 miles from Bishopville and was responsible for running the local Pizza Hut there. I knew they had a street named after him, but never thought that was enough. Blanchard's sister, Mary Elizabeth Blanchard, still lives in Sumter and calls the project long overdue. I'm still glad they decided to honor him. Very few people have heard of Bishopville, South Carolina, but most have heard of Doc Blanchard.

At 84 years of age, Doc Blanchard was finally stopped at the line of scrimmage, by pneumonia. He was living with his daughter in Bulverde, a small Texas town, until his death on April 19, 2009. His pal Glenn Davis had died four years earlier, in 2005. These two will always be joined in the conversation of who was best. They had played on the biggest stage of college football, before President Harry Truman and 102,000 fans at the 1945 Army-Navy game. Blanchard scored three times. Author Tim Cohane described one of Blanchard's touchdown runs against a Navy defender like this: "Doc ran through him as if he were a paper bag." Both Davis and Blanchard gave their Heisman Trophies to their high schools.

The Real DiMaggio

It was one o'clock in the morning when he passed. He had not been able to sleep, and the Friday night game with his beloved Red Sox was being replayed on TV; a Boston fan until the end.

He loved his family, friends, baseball, and dunking his toast in his coffee in the mornings. Most of his peers would agree that he was not only the best lead-off hitter in the American League and the best defensive outfielder in the game, but also the most under-rated player of his time. His son Paul was quoted as saying, "He was a great player, but a better person." He grew up the youngest of nine, the son of Sicilian immigrants, and his father's favorite. He was smaller than most outfielders and the smallest of his brothers. He also wore glasses, which was quite rare at the time. There were no such things as contacts. His business-like approach to the game of baseball, his use of the English language, and those glasses landed him a nickname by the New York Yankee Hall-of-Fame announcer, Mel Allen: "The Little Professor."

On February 12, 1917, Dominic "Dom" Paul DiMaggio became the fifth and last son born to Giuseppe Paola DiMaggio, a fisherman, and Rosalie Mercurio DiMaggio, in San Francisco, California. There were also four sisters. It was said that Dom got all the brains in the family and indeed his father wanted him to be a lawyer. As a young-ster, Dom delivered newspapers and eventually worked for Simmons Bed Company, making mattresses. Dominic himself wanted to be a chemical engineer, but his athletic talent on the diamond altered his decision. At Galileo High School, Dom played and went to bat ninth in the line-up, but he still hit .400. Swayed by his older brothers, Vince and Joe, Dominic had become a shortstop. Dom attended a try-out with 143 other players and was hands-down the best of the bunch. He signed a contract with the San Francisco Seals of the Pacific Coast League, in 1937. Vince was a rookie with the Boston Braves and Joe was in his second year with the Yankees. Dom always gave credit to Seals manager Lefty O'Doul for not only teaching him how to hit better, but he also suggested moving Dom from shortstop to the outfield. O'Doul felt that a hard ball hit right at Dom could take a bad hop and hit him in the face, therefore breaking his glasses. He also knew that Dom's training as an infielder would benefit him in the outfield, by making him more aggressive in scooping up ground balls. Lefty taught Dom to stand with his left foot forward in the outfield while at a right angle to home plate. This allowed him to get a much better jump on the ball when it was hit. In 1939, Dom hit .360 and won the Most Valuable Player Award for the entire Pacific Coast League. It would be good enough for the Boston Red Sox to pick up his contract.

Dom DiMaggio, Vince and Joe's little brother, debuted with the Boston Red Sox on April 16, 1940. Dom's first roommate, Jimmie Foxx, was in his last year of a Hall-of-Fame career. Foxx was tremendously strong, and it was said even his hair had muscles. Foxx was a positive influence on Dom from the very start. Dom hit .301 as a rookie and found himself in right field. His teammates in the Red Sox outfield included All-Stars, Doc Cramer and Ted Williams. Dom used to tell stories about how Ted Williams could rub his bat handle between his hands so hard he would make it squeak. Opposing pitchers hated that sound. With Dom now in the outfield, Foxx would play 42 games at the catcher's position, along with 95 games at first base, to keep his bat in the line-up. The designated hitter rule had not yet been thought of. By 1941, Dom's play had been so good that Cramer was traded and Dom was moved to centerfield. This would place all three DiMaggio brothers in centerfield for different Major League teams. Joe with the Yankees, Dom with the Red Sox, and older brother Vince would record 21 home runs and score 100 runs for the Pittsburgh Pirates. On July 25, 1941, Dom caught the fly ball in centerfield that sealed the 300th win for another future Hall-of-Famer, Red Sox pitcher, Lefty Grove.

Dom's career would run from 1940 to 1942 and then 1946 to 1953. Like most Major League players during that time, he spent three years in the United States Navy, protecting his country. Dom would make the All-Star team seven of his eleven years in the Majors. He scored 100 or more runs a year, seven times, which totaled 1,046. He also led the league in steals and triples on several occasions. In his career, he recorded 1,680 hits, 308 doubles, 87 home runs and 618 RBI's. Dom batted over .300 four times in his career, pushing his lifetime batting average up to .298. In 1940, the great Ty Cobb said about Dom, "Dom's a throwback to the kind of player we used to have." That was some compliment coming from Cobb.

The only dark cloud on Dominic DiMaggio's career occurred during Game 7 of the 1946 World Series versus the St. Louis Cardinals. Dom came to bat in the top of the eighth inning and promptly doubled home two runs, to tie the score 3-3. Unfortunately, he pulled up lame as he trotted into second base and had to be removed from the game. Leon Culberson replaced him in centerfield in the bottom of the eighth. With two outs, Cardinals' Enos Slaughter was on first base when Harry Walker approached the plate. Walker smashed a double to centerfield, just as Slaughter broke for second base. Culberson was slow getting to the ball and provided a weak throw to shortstop Johnny Pesky. Slaughter; aware that DiMaggio was no longer playing centerfield, never stopped running and headed for home, putting the Cards in the lead 4-3. This score would hold up and the St. Louis Cardinals would be World Series Champions of 1946. Slaughter had scored from first base without a throw. DiMaggio was sick and blamed himself. He always said that if he had been in centerfield, not only would Slaughter not have scored, but he would have thrown him out at third. To his credit, Slaughter was quoted as saying, "If they hadn't taken DiMaggio out of the game, I wouldn't have tried it." Up to that point in this Series, Dom had already thrown out three runners, and Slaughter could have easily been the fourth. Slaughters "Mad Dash" would go down in baseball history.

In 1950, Dom had a tremendous year at the plate and also led the American League in steals and triples. On June 30, that same year, Dom and Joe became only the fourth pair of siblings to hit a homer in the same game, against each other. There is also a story told by Yankee shortstop Phil Rizzuto how Dom hit a screaming line drive at him one day with Red Sox players on first and second.

"As I reached into my glove to turn the double play," said Rizzuto, "I found my glove empty. The ball was hit so hard it went through the webbing." Dominic DiMaggio retired May 9, 1953. He would become a successful plastics manufacturer.

On Friday, May 8, 2009, in Marion, Massachusetts, the "Real" DiMaggio left us behind here on earth. Dominic was 92 years young and had never faced the demons his brother Joe had endured. Dominic lived a clean, spirit free life, where he quietly taught his values with dignity to his family and friends. He handled his stardom with humility and may have been a true hero in every sense of the word, even while living in his brother's shadow. I find myself intrigued how different things would have turned out for these two brothers had they played for one another's team. Because Joe DiMaggio played with the World Series Champion, New York Yankees, and recorded his most famous feat by hitting safely in 56 consecutive games in 1941, it could be said he was the most successful and perhaps even the better baseball player. I contend that Dom was equally as good a baseball player, on a mediocre team, but without a doubt, a better person both publicly and privately. "It's been a struggle all my life," said Dom in a *Boston Globe* interview. "I was always Joe's kid brother." Most casual baseball fans may not know that Dominic DiMaggio had his own hitting streak, in 1949. On August 9th, Dominic's consecutive game hitting streak reached 34 games, before Brother Joe ended the streak by catching a line drive hit to centerfield. "The Joe DiMaggio legend was just too strong," said Dom. Dom may have been just the "other brother," to some fans, but to me he was the better DiMaggio. That 34 consecutive-game hitting streak is still a Red Sox record, and Dominic followed it up with a 27-game streak in 1951. He would be inducted into the Boston Red Sox Hall of Fame in 1995.

Dom left behind his wife Emily, his sons Dominic Jr. and Peter, and a daughter Emily. His Brothers Vince and Joe passed away in 1986 and 1999, respectively.

In 1990, with the help of author Bill Gilbert, Dominic DiMaggio wrote a book entitled, <u>Real Grass, Real Heroes, Baseball's Historic 1941 Season.</u> I purchased two copies of Dom's book with the intentions of having him sign them both. While signing, he was warm and friendly; and I later found out that all the proceeds from his autograph sales went to support retired players who did not earn a pension. Later I tried to get his brother Joe DiMaggio to sign Dom's books and was told Joe did not sign multiple signed items. I mentioned to Joe these books were written by his brother Dom, but to no avail. I wasn't happy at first, but later realized that I already had the real DiMaggio's signature.

Index

Eddie Robinson 4/3/07

Bob Allen 5/4/07

Clete Boyer 6/4/07

Shag Crawford 7/11/07

Bill Walsh 7/30/07

Phil Rizzuto 8/13/07

Max McGee 10/20/07

Jim Ringo 11/19/07

Bill Hartack 11/26/07

Evel Knievel 11/30/07

W. C. Heinz 2/27/08

Jim McKay 6/7/08

Bobby Murcer 7/12/08

Jerome Holtzman 7/19/08

Gene Upshaw 8/20/08

Don Haskins 9/9/08

Tom Tresh 10/15/08

Red Murff 11/28/08

Sammy Baugh 12/17/08

Bill Werber 1/22/09

George Kell 3/24/09

Doc Blanchard 4/19/09

Dom DiMaggio 5/8/09

About the Author, Andy Purvis

Andy Purvis lives in Corpus Christi, Texas, with his wife and two cats. He has four grandchildren ages from 10-22. They are also in his Hall of Fame! He has been in restaurant management for over 30 years and has always had extreme interest in and knowledge of sports. He had a radio talk show about sports with a couple of different partners for 13 years and continues as a guest host on occasion. He maintains contact with sports "greats" and other sports friends.

CPSIA information can be obtained at www.ICGtesting.com
Printed in the USA
LVOW11s0817230415

435773LV00001B/191/P